Just The facts101

Textbook Key Facts

Doing Business and Investing in Saint Lucia Guide

by Cram101

Texbook NOT Included

Table of Contents

Title Page

Copyright

Foundations of Business

Management

Business law

Finance

Human resource management

Information systems

Marketing

Manufacturing

Commerce

Business ethics

Accounting

Index: Answers

Just The Facts101

Exam Prep for

Doing Business and Investing in Saint Lucia Guide

Just The Facts101 Exam Prep is your link from
the textbook and lecture to your exams.

Just The Facts101 Exam Preps are unauthorized and comprehensive reviews of your textbooks.

Textbook publishers and textbook authors do not participate in or contribute to these reviews.

Just The Facts101 Exam Prep

eAIN 444633

Foundations of Business

A business, also known as an enterprise, agency or a firm, is an entity involved in the provision of goods and/or services to consumers. Businesses are prevalent in capitalist economies, where most of them are privately owned and provide goods and services to customers in exchange for other goods, services, or money.

:: Management ::

In business, a _________ is the attribute that allows an organization to outperform its competitors. A _________ may include access to natural resources, such as high-grade ores or a low-cost power source, highly skilled labor, geographic location, high entry barriers, and access to new technology.

Exam Probability: **Medium**

1. *Answer choices:*

(see index for correct answer)

- a. Information excellence
- b. Marketing management
- c. Competitive advantage
- d. Supply network

Guidance: level 1

:: Marketing ::

_________ or stock is the goods and materials that a business holds for the ultimate goal of resale .

Exam Probability: **Medium**

2. *Answer choices:*

(see index for correct answer)

- a. Branding national myths and symbols
- b. Grand cru
- c. Inventory
- d. Cannibalization

Guidance: level 1

:: Marketing ::

A __________ is something that is necessary for an organism to live a healthy life. __________ s are distinguished from wants in that, in the case of a __________ , a deficiency causes a clear adverse outcome: a dysfunction or death. In other words, a __________ is something required for a safe, stable and healthy life while a want is a desire, wish or aspiration. When __________ s or wants are backed by purchasing power, they have the potential to become economic demands.

Exam Probability: **Low**

3. *Answer choices:*

(see index for correct answer)

- a. Product bundling
- b. Content partnership
- c. LIDA
- d. Processing fluency

Guidance: level 1

:: Corporate crime ::

_________ LLP, based in Chicago, was an American holding company. Formerly one of the "Big Five" accounting firms , the firm had provided auditing, tax, and consulting services to large corporations. By 2001, it had become one of the world`s largest multinational companies.

Exam Probability: **Low**

4. *Answer choices:*

(see index for correct answer)

- a. Compass Group
- b. Medco Health Solutions
- c. Holdings of American International Group
- d. Arthur Andersen

Guidance: level 1

:: Goods ::

In most contexts, the concept of _________ denotes the conduct that should be preferred when posed with a choice between possible actions. _________ is generally considered to be the opposite of evil, and is of interest in the study of morality, ethics, religion and philosophy. The specific meaning and etymology of the term and its associated translations among ancient and contemporary languages show substantial variation in its inflection and meaning depending on circumstances of place, history, religious, or philosophical context.

Exam Probability: **Low**

5. *Answer choices:*

(see index for correct answer)

- a. Merit good
- b. Independent goods
- c. Ersatz good
- d. Refined goods

Guidance: level 1

:: Management ::

In organizational studies, _________ is the efficient and effective development of an organization`s resources when they are needed. Such resources may include financial resources, inventory, human skills, production resources, or information technology and natural resources.

Exam Probability: **Low**

6. *Answer choices:*

(see index for correct answer)

- a. Investment control
- b. Advisory board
- c. Resource management
- d. Perth leadership outcome model

Guidance: level 1

:: ::

_________ is the means to see, hear, or become aware of something or someone through our fundamental senses. The term _________ derives from the Latin word perceptio, and is the organization, identification, and interpretation of sensory information in order to represent and understand the presented information, or the environment.

Exam Probability: **Medium**

7. *Answer choices:*

(see index for correct answer)

- a. imperative
- b. information systems assessment

- c. hierarchical perspective
- d. surface-level diversity

Guidance: level 1

:: International trade ::

An _________ is a good brought into a jurisdiction, especially across a national border, from an external source. The party bringing in the good is called an _________ er. An _________ in the receiving country is an export from the sending country. _________ ation and exportation are the defining financial transactions of international trade.

Exam Probability: **Medium**

8. *Answer choices:*

(see index for correct answer)

- a. Trade in Services Agreement
- b. Extraterritorial income exclusion
- c. Westline
- d. Reciprocity

Guidance: level 1

:: Analysis ::

_________ is the process of breaking a complex topic or substance into smaller parts in order to gain a better understanding of it. The technique has been applied in the study of mathematics and logic since before Aristotle , though _________ as a formal concept is a relatively recent development.

Exam Probability: **High**

9. *Answer choices:*

(see index for correct answer)

- a. Hydrogen pinch
- b. Gompertz constant
- c. Water pinch analysis
- d. Analysis

Guidance: level 1

:: Bribery ::

_________ is the act of giving or receiving something of value in exchange for some kind of influence or action in return, that the recipient would otherwise not offer. _________ is defined by Black`s Law Dictionary as the offering, giving, receiving, or soliciting of any item of value to influence the actions of an official or other person in charge of a public or legal duty. Essentially, _________ is offering to do something for someone for the expressed purpose of receiving something in exchange. Gifts of money or other items of value which are otherwise available to everyone on an equivalent basis, and not for dishonest purposes, is not _________ . Offering a discount or a refund to all purchasers is a legal rebate and is not _________ . For example, it is legal for an employee of a Public Utilities Commission involved in electric rate regulation to accept a rebate on electric service that reduces their cost for electricity, when the rebate is available to other residential electric customers. Giving the rebate to influence them to look favorably on the electric utility`s rate increase applications, however, would be considered _________ .

Exam Probability: **High**

10. *Answer choices:*

(see index for correct answer)

- a. Holyland Case
- b. Kickback
- c. English football bribery scandal
- d. Bribery

Guidance: level 1

:: Debt ::

__________ is when something, usually money, is owed by one party, the borrower or __________ or, to a second party, the lender or creditor. __________ is a deferred payment, or series of payments, that is owed in the future, which is what differentiates it from an immediate purchase. The __________ may be owed by sovereign state or country, local government, company, or an individual. Commercial __________ is generally subject to contractual terms regarding the amount and timing of repayments of principal and interest. Loans, bonds, notes, and mortgages are all types of __________ . The term can also be used metaphorically to cover moral obligations and other interactions not based on economic value. For example, in Western cultures, a person who has been helped by a second person is sometimes said to owe a " __________ of gratitude" to the second person.

Exam Probability: **High**

11. *Answer choices:*

(see index for correct answer)

- a. Vulture fund
- b. Debt
- c. Crown debt
- d. Cohort default rate

Guidance: level 1

:: Management accounting ::

_________ s are costs that change as the quantity of the good or service that a business produces changes. _________ s are the sum of marginal costs over all units produced. They can also be considered normal costs. Fixed costs and _________ s make up the two components of total cost. Direct costs are costs that can easily be associated with a particular cost object. However, not all _________ s are direct costs. For example, variable manufacturing overhead costs are _________ s that are indirect costs, not direct costs. _________ s are sometimes called unit-level costs as they vary with the number of units produced.

Exam Probability: **Low**

12. *Answer choices:*

(see index for correct answer)

- a. Activity-based management
- b. Fixed cost
- c. Institute of Cost and Management Accountants of Bangladesh
- d. Institute of Certified Management Accountants

Guidance: level 1

:: Stock market ::

A shareholder is an individual or institution that legally owns one or more shares of stock in a public or private corporation. _________ may be referred to as members of a corporation. Legally, a person is not a shareholder in a corporation until their name and other details are entered in the corporation`s register of _________ or members.

Exam Probability: **Low**

13. *Answer choices:*

(see index for correct answer)

- a. Chi-X Global
- b. S chip
- c. Central securities depository
- d. H share

Guidance: level 1

:: Treaties ::

An __________ is a relationship among people, groups, or states that have joined together for mutual benefit or to achieve some common purpose, whether or not explicit agreement has been worked out among them. Members of an __________ are called allies. __________ s form in many settings, including political __________ s, military __________ s, and business __________ s. When the term is used in the context of war or armed struggle, such associations may also be called allied powers, especially when discussing World War I or World War II.

Exam Probability: **High**

14. *Answer choices:*

(see index for correct answer)

- a. Bilateral treaty
- b. Reservation
- c. Guillotine clause
- d. Subsidiary alliance

Guidance: level 1

:: ::

Competition arises whenever at least two parties strive for a goal which cannot be shared: where one`s gain is the other`s loss .

Exam Probability: **High**

15. *Answer choices:*

(see index for correct answer)

- a. cultural
- b. Competitor
- c. co-culture
- d. Sarbanes-Oxley act of 2002

Guidance: level 1

:: Statistical terminology ::

_________ es can be learned implicitly within cultural contexts. People may develop _________ es toward or against an individual, an ethnic group, a sexual or gender identity, a nation, a religion, a social class, a political party, theoretical paradigms and ideologies within academic domains, or a species. _________ ed means one-sided, lacking a neutral viewpoint, or not having an open mind. _________ can come in many forms and is related to prejudice and intuition.

Exam Probability: **High**

16. *Answer choices:*

(see index for correct answer)

- a. Bias
- b. Inherent zero
- c. Fisher consistency
- d. Geometric standard deviation

Guidance: level 1

:: Management ::

The _________ is a strategy performance management tool – a semi-standard structured report, that can be used by managers to keep track of the execution of activities by the staff within their control and to monitor the consequences arising from these actions.

Exam Probability: **Low**

17. *Answer choices:*

(see index for correct answer)

- a. Project management information system
- b. Balanced scorecard
- c. Libertarian management
- d. Success-oriented management

Guidance: level 1

:: Legal terms ::

An _________ is an action which is inaccurate or incorrect. In some usages, an _________ is synonymous with a mistake. In statistics, " _________ " refers to the difference between the value which has been computed and the correct value. An _________ could result in failure or in a deviation from the intended performance or behaviour.

Exam Probability: **Medium**

18. *Answer choices:*

(see index for correct answer)

- a. Objection
- b. Error
- c. Appearance
- d. Possession proceedings

Guidance: level 1

:: Decision theory ::

Within economics the concept of _________ is used to model worth or value, but its usage has evolved significantly over time. The term was introduced initially as a measure of pleasure or satisfaction within the theory of utilitarianism by moral philosophers such as Jeremy Bentham and John Stuart Mill. But the term has been adapted and reapplied within neoclassical economics, which dominates modern economic theory, as a _________ function that represents a consumer`s preference ordering over a choice set. As such, it is devoid of its original interpretation as a measurement of the pleasure or satisfaction obtained by the consumer from that choice.

Exam Probability: **Low**

19. *Answer choices:*

(see index for correct answer)

- a. Weighted product model
- b. House of Quality
- c. Group decision-making
- d. Clarity test

Guidance: level 1

:: Real estate valuation ::

_________ or OMV is the price at which an asset would trade in a competitive auction setting. _________ is often used interchangeably with open _________ , fair value or fair _________ , although these terms have distinct definitions in different standards, and may or may not differ in some circumstances.

Exam Probability: **High**

20. *Answer choices:*

(see index for correct answer)

- a. Lamudi
- b. International Right of Way Association
- c. Market value
- d. Uniform Standards of Professional Appraisal Practice

Guidance: level 1

:: Monopoly (economics) ::

A _________ is a form of intellectual property that gives its owner the legal right to exclude others from making, using, selling, and importing an invention for a limited period of years, in exchange for publishing an enabling public disclosure of the invention. In most countries _________ rights fall under civil law and the _________ holder needs to sue someone infringing the _________ in order to enforce his or her rights. In some industries _________ s are an essential form of competitive advantage; in others they are irrelevant.

Exam Probability: **Low**

21. *Answer choices:*

(see index for correct answer)

- a. Legal monopoly
- b. Demonopolization
- c. De facto monopoly
- d. Patent

Guidance: level 1

:: Unemployment ::

In economics, a _________ is a business cycle contraction when there is a general decline in economic activity. Macroeconomic indicators such as GDP , investment spending, capacity utilization, household income, business profits, and inflation fall, while bankruptcies and the unemployment rate rise. In the United Kingdom, it is defined as a negative economic growth for two consecutive quarters.

Exam Probability: **Medium**

22. *Answer choices:*

(see index for correct answer)

- a. Hysteresis
- b. Labour Force Survey

- c. Employment protection legislation
- d. Recession

Guidance: level 1

:: Financial statements ::

In financial accounting, a _________ or statement of financial position or statement of financial condition is a summary of the financial balances of an individual or organization, whether it be a sole proprietorship, a business partnership, a corporation, private limited company or other organization such as Government or not-for-profit entity. Assets, liabilities and ownership equity are listed as of a specific date, such as the end of its financial year. A _________ is often described as a "snapshot of a company`s financial condition". Of the four basic financial statements, the _________ is the only statement which applies to a single point in time of a business` calendar year.

Exam Probability: **Low**

23. *Answer choices:*

(see index for correct answer)

- a. Statement on Auditing Standards No. 55
- b. Financial statement
- c. Balance sheet
- d. Statements on auditing standards

Guidance: level 1

:: Stock market ::

__________ is a form of corporate equity ownership, a type of security. The terms voting share and ordinary share are also used frequently in other parts of the world; " __________ " being primarily used in the United States. They are known as Equity shares or Ordinary shares in the UK and other Commonwealth realms. This type of share gives the stockholder the right to share in the profits of the company, and to vote on matters of corporate policy and the composition of the members of the board of directors.

Exam Probability: **Medium**

24. *Answer choices:*

(see index for correct answer)

- a. Bagholder
- b. Selling climax
- c. Blue chip
- d. Common stock

Guidance: level 1

:: Data collection ::

A __________ is an utterance which typically functions as a request for information. __________ s can thus be understood as a kind of illocutionary act in the field of pragmatics or as special kinds of propositions in frameworks of formal semantics such as alternative semantics or inquisitive semantics. The information requested is expected to be provided in the form of an answer. __________ s are often conflated with interrogatives, which are the grammatical forms typically used to achieve them. Rhetorical __________ s, for example, are interrogative in form but may not be considered true __________ s as they are not expected to be answered. Conversely, non-interrogative grammatical structures may be considered __________ s as in the case of the imperative sentence "tell me your name".

Exam Probability: **High**

25. *Answer choices:*

(see index for correct answer)

- a. Natural experiment
- b. BanxQuote
- c. Dye tracing
- d. Public survey

Guidance: level 1

:: Quality management ::

_________ ensures that an organization, product or service is consistent. It has four main components: quality planning, quality assurance, quality control and quality improvement. _________ is focused not only on product and service quality, but also on the means to achieve it. _________, therefore, uses quality assurance and control of processes as well as products to achieve more consistent quality. What a customer wants and is willing to pay for it determines quality. It is written or unwritten commitment to a known or unknown consumer in the market . Thus, quality can be defined as fitness for intended use or, in other words, how well the product performs its intended function

Exam Probability: **Low**

26. *Answer choices:*

(see index for correct answer)

- a. Quality circle
- b. Quality Management Maturity Grid
- c. Institute of Standards and Industrial Research of Iran
- d. Quality management

Guidance: level 1

:: ::

_________ is the study and management of exchange relationships. _________ is the business process of creating relationships with and satisfying customers. With its focus on the customer, _________ is one of the premier components of business management.

Exam Probability: **Low**

27. *Answer choices:*

(see index for correct answer)

- a. levels of analysis
- b. process perspective
- c. Character
- d. Marketing

Guidance: level 1

:: Statistical terminology ::

_________ is the ability to avoid wasting materials, energy, efforts, money, and time in doing something or in producing a desired result. In a more general sense, it is the ability to do things well, successfully, and without waste. In more mathematical or scientific terms, it is a measure of the extent to which input is well used for an intended task or function . It often specifically comprises the capability of a specific application of effort to produce a specific outcome with a minimum amount or quantity of waste, expense, or unnecessary effort. _________ refers to very different inputs and outputs in different fields and industries.

Exam Probability: **Medium**

28. *Answer choices:*

(see index for correct answer)

- a. Inherent zero
- b. Aggregate data
- c. Testimator
- d. Chain linking

Guidance: level 1

:: Credit cards ::

A __________ is a payment card issued to users to enable the cardholder to pay a merchant for goods and services based on the cardholder`s promise to the card issuer to pay them for the amounts plus the other agreed charges. The card issuer creates a revolving account and grants a line of credit to the cardholder, from which the cardholder can borrow money for payment to a merchant or as a cash advance.

Exam Probability: **Medium**

29. *Answer choices:*

(see index for correct answer)

- a. InteliSpend Prepaid Solutions
- b. Credit CARD Act
- c. Wirecard
- d. Credit card

Guidance: level 1

:: Reputation management ::

_________ or image of a social entity is an opinion about that entity, typically as a result of social evaluation on a set of criteria.

Exam Probability: **High**

30. *Answer choices:*

(see index for correct answer)

- a. Meta-moderation system
- b. Conversocial
- c. TrustRank
- d. Advogato

Guidance: level 1

:: Derivatives (finance) ::

_________ is any bodily activity that enhances or maintains physical fitness and overall health and wellness. It is performed for various reasons, to aid growth and improve strength, preventing aging, developing muscles and the cardiovascular system, honing athletic skills, weight loss or maintenance, improving health and also for enjoyment. Many individuals choose to _________ outdoors where they can congregate in groups, socialize, and enhance well-being.

Exam Probability: **High**

31. *Answer choices:*

(see index for correct answer)

- a. Stock market index option
- b. Derivative and Commodity Exchange Nepal Ltd.
- c. Exercise
- d. Basket option

Guidance: level 1

:: Human resource management ::

_________ is the corporate management term for the act of reorganizing the legal, ownership, operational, or other structures of a company for the purpose of making it more profitable, or better organized for its present needs. Other reasons for _________ include a change of ownership or ownership structure, demerger, or a response to a crisis or major change in the business such as bankruptcy, repositioning, or buyout. _________ may also be described as corporate _________, debt _________ and financial _________.

Exam Probability: **Medium**

32. *Answer choices:*

(see index for correct answer)

- a. Adaptive performance

- b. Restructuring
- c. The Giving of Orders
- d. Turnover

Guidance: level 1

:: Logistics ::

_________ is generally the detailed organization and implementation of a complex operation. In a general business sense, _________ is the management of the flow of things between the point of origin and the point of consumption in order to meet requirements of customers or corporations. The resources managed in _________ may include tangible goods such as materials, equipment, and supplies, as well as food and other consumable items. The _________ of physical items usually involves the integration of information flow, materials handling, production, packaging, inventory, transportation, warehousing, and often security.

Exam Probability: **Medium**

33. *Answer choices:*

(see index for correct answer)

- a. TI-HI
- b. Navy lighterage pontoons
- c. Spetstyazhavtotrans
- d. Terminal Operating System

Guidance: level 1

:: ::

__________ is the collection of techniques, skills, methods, and processes used in the production of goods or services or in the accomplishment of objectives, such as scientific investigation. __________ can be the knowledge of techniques, processes, and the like, or it can be embedded in machines to allow for operation without detailed knowledge of their workings. Systems applying __________ by taking an input, changing it according to the system`s use, and then producing an outcome are referred to as __________ systems or technological systems.

Exam Probability: **Low**

34. *Answer choices:*

(see index for correct answer)

- a. levels of analysis
- b. interpersonal communication
- c. Technology
- d. Character

Guidance: level 1

:: Commercial item transport and distribution ::

A __________ is a commitment or expectation to perform some action in general or if certain circumstances arise. A __________ may arise from a system of ethics or morality, especially in an honor culture. Many duties are created by law, sometimes including a codified punishment or liability for non-performance. Performing one`s __________ may require some sacrifice of self-interest.

Exam Probability: **Low**

35. *Answer choices:*

(see index for correct answer)

- a. Automated Export System
- b. Forklift truck
- c. Containerlift
- d. Duty

Guidance: level 1

:: ::

In regulatory jurisdictions that provide for it , __________ is a group of laws and organizations designed to ensure the rights of consumers as well as fair trade, competition and accurate information in the marketplace. The laws are designed to prevent the businesses that engage in fraud or specified unfair practices from gaining an advantage over competitors. They may also provides additional protection for those most vulnerable in society. __________ laws are a form of government regulation that aim to protect the rights of consumers. For example, a government may require businesses to disclose detailed information about products—particularly in areas where safety or public health is an issue, such as food.

Exam Probability: **Medium**

36. *Answer choices:*

(see index for correct answer)

- a. hierarchical
- b. imperative
- c. Sarbanes-Oxley act of 2002
- d. Consumer Protection

Guidance: level 1

:: Management accounting ::

In economics, _________ s, indirect costs or overheads are business expenses that are not dependent on the level of goods or services produced by the business. They tend to be time-related, such as interest or rents being paid per month, and are often referred to as overhead costs. This is in contrast to variable costs, which are volume-related and unknown at the beginning of the accounting year. For a simple example, such as a bakery, the monthly rent for the baking facilities, and the monthly payments for the security system and basic phone line are _________ s, as they do not change according to how much bread the bakery produces and sells. On the other hand, the wage costs of the bakery are variable, as the bakery will have to hire more workers if the production of bread increases. Economists reckon _________ as a entry barrier for new entrepreneurs.

Exam Probability: **Medium**

37. *Answer choices:*

(see index for correct answer)

- a. Direct material total variance
- b. Environmental full-cost accounting
- c. Institute of Certified Management Accountants
- d. Fixed cost

Guidance: level 1

:: Production economics ::

In microeconomics, _________ are the cost advantages that enterprises obtain due to their scale of operation , with cost per unit of output decreasing with increasing scale.

Exam Probability: **Medium**

38. *Answer choices:*

(see index for correct answer)

- a. Economies of scale
- b. Ramp up
- c. Sharing
- d. Division of work

Guidance: level 1

:: Fraud ::

In law, _________ is intentional deception to secure unfair or unlawful gain, or to deprive a victim of a legal right. _________ can violate civil law , a criminal law , or it may cause no loss of money, property or legal right but still be an element of another civil or criminal wrong. The purpose of _________ may be monetary gain or other benefits, for example by obtaining a passport, travel document, or driver`s license, or mortgage _________ , where the perpetrator may attempt to qualify for a mortgage by way of false statements.

Exam Probability: **Medium**

39. *Answer choices:*

(see index for correct answer)

- a. Overbilling
- b. Fraud
- c. Transcript fraud
- d. Telephone numbers in the Dominican Republic

Guidance: level 1

:: ::

_________ refers to a business or organization attempting to acquire goods or services to accomplish its goals. Although there are several organizations that attempt to set standards in the _________ process, processes can vary greatly between organizations. Typically the word " _________ " is not used interchangeably with the word "procurement", since procurement typically includes expediting, supplier quality, and transportation and logistics in addition to _________ .

Exam Probability: **Low**

40. *Answer choices:*

(see index for correct answer)

- a. imperative
- b. cultural
- c. personal values

- d. Purchasing

Guidance: level 1

:: Human resource management ::

_________ encompasses values and behaviors that contribute to the unique social and psychological environment of a business. The _________ influences the way people interact, the context within which knowledge is created, the resistance they will have towards certain changes, and ultimately the way they share knowledge. _________ represents the collective values, beliefs and principles of organizational members and is a product of factors such as history, product, market, technology, strategy, type of employees, management style, and national culture; culture includes the organization`s vision, values, norms, systems, symbols, language, assumptions, environment, location, beliefs and habits.

Exam Probability: **High**

41. *Answer choices:*

(see index for correct answer)

- a. Randstad Holding
- b. Job knowledge
- c. Co-determination
- d. Organizational culture

Guidance: level 1

:: Production economics ::

__________ is the joint use of a resource or space. It is also the process of dividing and distributing. In its narrow sense, it refers to joint or alternating use of inherently finite goods, such as a common pasture or a shared residence. Still more loosely, " __________ " can actually mean giving something as an outright gift: for example, to "share" one's food really means to give some of it as a gift. __________ is a basic component of human interaction, and is responsible for strengthening social ties and ensuring a person's well-being.

Exam Probability: **High**

42. *Answer choices:*

(see index for correct answer)

- a. Productivity world
- b. Diseconomies of scale
- c. Split-off point
- d. Sharing

Guidance: level 1

:: Infographics ::

A _________ is a symbolic representation of information according to visualization technique. _________ s have been used since ancient times, but became more prevalent during the Enlightenment. Sometimes, the technique uses a three-dimensional visualization which is then projected onto a two-dimensional surface. The word graph is sometimes used as a synonym for _________ .

Exam Probability: **High**

43. *Answer choices:*

(see index for correct answer)

- a. News Illustrated
- b. Chartjunk
- c. DataViva
- d. Diagram

Guidance: level 1

:: Auditing ::

_________ , as defined by accounting and auditing, is a process for assuring of an organization`s objectives in operational effectiveness and efficiency, reliable financial reporting, and compliance with laws, regulations and policies. A broad concept, _________ involves everything that controls risks to an organization.

Exam Probability: **Low**

44. *Answer choices:*

(see index for correct answer)

- a. External audit
- b. Audit plan
- c. Mitigating control
- d. Auditor independence

Guidance: level 1

:: Statistical terminology ::

_________ is the magnitude or dimensions of a thing. _________ can be measured as length, width, height, diameter, perimeter, area, volume, or mass.

Exam Probability: **High**

45. *Answer choices:*

(see index for correct answer)

- a. Empirical probability
- b. Contrast
- c. Geometric standard deviation
- d. Pooled variance

Guidance: level 1

:: Evaluation ::

A __________ is an evaluation of a publication, service, or company such as a movie , video game , musical composition , book ; a piece of hardware like a car, home appliance, or computer; or an event or performance, such as a live music concert, play, musical theater show, dance show, or art exhibition. In addition to a critical evaluation, the __________ 's author may assign the work a rating to indicate its relative merit. More loosely, an author may __________ current events, trends, or items in the news. A compilation of __________ s may itself be called a __________ . The New York __________ of Books, for instance, is a collection of essays on literature, culture, and current affairs. National __________ , founded by William F. Buckley, Jr., is an influential conservative magazine, and Monthly __________ is a long-running socialist periodical.

Exam Probability: **High**

46. *Answer choices:*

(see index for correct answer)

- a. Continuous assessment
- b. Server Efficiency Rating Tool
- c. Review
- d. Evaluation approaches

Guidance: level 1

:: Information systems ::

__________ are formal, sociotechnical, organizational systems designed to collect, process, store, and distribute information. In a sociotechnical perspective, __________ are composed by four components: task, people, structure , and technology.

Exam Probability: **High**

47. *Answer choices:*

(see index for correct answer)

- a. Business informatics
- b. Question Manager
- c. Information systems
- d. Data flow diagram

Guidance: level 1

:: Materials ::

A __________ , also known as a feedstock, unprocessed material, or primary commodity, is a basic material that is used to produce goods, finished products, energy, or intermediate materials which are feedstock for future finished products. As feedstock, the term connotes these materials are bottleneck assets and are highly important with regard to producing other products. An example of this is crude oil, which is a __________ and a feedstock used in the production of industrial chemicals, fuels, plastics, and pharmaceutical goods; lumber is a __________ used to produce a variety of products including all types of furniture. The term " __________ " denotes materials in minimally processed or unprocessed in states; e.g., raw latex, crude oil, cotton, coal, raw biomass, iron ore, air, logs, or water i.e. "...any product of agriculture, forestry, fishing and any other mineral that is in its natural form or which has undergone the transformation required to prepare it for internationally marketing in substantial volumes."

Exam Probability: **Medium**

48. *Answer choices:*

(see index for correct answer)

- a. Ice substitute
- b. Raw material
- c. Latex
- d. Exotic material

Guidance: level 1

:: Accounting terminology ::

__________ is a legally enforceable claim for payment held by a business for goods supplied and/or services rendered that customers/clients have ordered but not paid for. These are generally in the form of invoices raised by a business and delivered to the customer for payment within an agreed time frame. __________ is shown in a balance sheet as an asset. It is one of a series of accounting transactions dealing with the billing of a customer for goods and services that the customer has ordered. These may be distinguished from notes receivable, which are debts created through formal legal instruments called promissory notes.

Exam Probability: **Medium**

49. *Answer choices:*

(see index for correct answer)

- a. Chart of accounts
- b. Checkoff
- c. Accounts receivable
- d. profit and loss statement

Guidance: level 1

:: Generally Accepted Accounting Principles ::

In accounting, __________ is the income that a business have from its normal business activities, usually from the sale of goods and services to customers. __________ is also referred to as sales or turnover.Some companies receive __________ from interest, royalties, or other fees. __________ may refer to business income in general, or it may refer to the amount, in a monetary unit, earned during a period of time, as in "Last year, Company X had __________ of $42 million". Profits or net income generally imply total __________ minus total expenses in a given period. In accounting, in the balance statement it is a subsection of the Equity section and __________ increases equity, it is often referred to as the "top line" due to its position on the income statement at the very top. This is to be contrasted with the "bottom line" which denotes net income .

Exam Probability: **Medium**

50. *Answer choices:*

(see index for correct answer)

- a. Profit
- b. Revenue
- c. Expense
- d. Operating income

Guidance: level 1

:: Graphic design ::

An __________ is an artifact that depicts visual perception, such as a photograph or other two-dimensional picture, that resembles a subject—usually a physical object—and thus provides a depiction of it. In the context of signal processing, an __________ is a distributed amplitude of color.

Exam Probability: **High**

51. *Answer choices:*

(see index for correct answer)

- a. Prepress
- b. Plazm
- c. Image
- d. Rubylith

Guidance: level 1

:: Market research ::

__________ is an organized effort to gather information about target markets or customers. It is a very important component of business strategy. The term is commonly interchanged with marketing research; however, expert practitioners may wish to draw a distinction, in that marketing research is concerned specifically about marketing processes, while __________ is concerned specifically with markets.

Exam Probability: **High**

52. *Answer choices:*

(see index for correct answer)

- a. Charles Coolidge Parlin
- b. Frugging
- c. Market research
- d. Online panel

Guidance: level 1

:: Information technology ::

__________ is the use of computers to store, retrieve, transmit, and manipulate data, or information, often in the context of a business or other enterprise. IT is considered to be a subset of information and communications technology . An __________ system is generally an information system, a communications system or, more specifically speaking, a computer system – including all hardware, software and peripheral equipment – operated by a limited group of users.

Exam Probability: **Medium**

53. *Answer choices:*

(see index for correct answer)

- a. Information revolution
- b. Open collaboration
- c. Information technology

- d. CIO-plus

Guidance: level 1

:: Mathematical finance ::

In economics and finance, _________ , also known as present discounted value, is the value of an expected income stream determined as of the date of valuation. The _________ is always less than or equal to the future value because money has interest-earning potential, a characteristic referred to as the time value of money, except during times of negative interest rates, when the _________ will be more than the future value. Time value can be described with the simplified phrase, "A dollar today is worth more than a dollar tomorrow". Here, `worth more` means that its value is greater. A dollar today is worth more than a dollar tomorrow because the dollar can be invested and earn a day`s worth of interest, making the total accumulate to a value more than a dollar by tomorrow. Interest can be compared to rent. Just as rent is paid to a landlord by a tenant without the ownership of the asset being transferred, interest is paid to a lender by a borrower who gains access to the money for a time before paying it back. By letting the borrower have access to the money, the lender has sacrificed the exchange value of this money, and is compensated for it in the form of interest. The initial amount of the borrowed funds is less than the total amount of money paid to the lender.

Exam Probability: **High**

54. *Answer choices:*

(see index for correct answer)

- a. Consumption-based capital asset pricing model
- b. Realized variance

- c. Negative probability
- d. Present value

Guidance: level 1

:: Generally Accepted Accounting Principles ::

An _________ or profit and loss account is one of the financial statements of a company and shows the company's revenues and expenses during a particular period.

Exam Probability: **Medium**

55. *Answer choices:*

(see index for correct answer)

- a. Insurance asset management
- b. Earnings before interest, taxes, depreciation, and amortization
- c. Chinese accounting standards
- d. Gross income

Guidance: level 1

:: Macroeconomics ::

A foreign _________ is an investment in the form of a controlling ownership in a business in one country by an entity based in another country. It is thus distinguished from a foreign portfolio investment by a notion of direct control.

Exam Probability: **High**

56. *Answer choices:*

(see index for correct answer)

- a. Turnpike theory
- b. Crisis theory
- c. Ordoliberalism
- d. European System of Accounts

Guidance: level 1

:: Macroeconomics ::

_________ is the increase in the inflation-adjusted market value of the goods and services produced by an economy over time. It is conventionally measured as the percent rate of increase in real gross domestic product, or real GDP.

Exam Probability: **Low**

57. *Answer choices:*

(see index for correct answer)

- a. Economic growth
- b. Ordoliberalism
- c. Austerity
- d. Country attractiveness

Guidance: level 1

:: Office administration ::

An _________ is generally a room or other area where an organization`s employees perform administrative work in order to support and realize objects and goals of the organization. The word " _________ " may also denote a position within an organization with specific duties attached to it ; the latter is in fact an earlier usage, _________ as place originally referring to the location of one`s duty. When used as an adjective, the term " _________ " may refer to business-related tasks. In law, a company or organization has _________ s in any place where it has an official presence, even if that presence consists of a storage silo rather than an establishment with desk-and-chair. An _________ is also an architectural and design phenomenon: ranging from a small _________ such as a bench in the corner of a small business of extremely small size , through entire floors of buildings, up to and including massive buildings dedicated entirely to one company. In modern terms an _________ is usually the location where white-collar workers carry out their functions. As per James Stephenson, " _________ is that part of business enterprise which is devoted to the direction and co-ordination of its various activities."

Exam Probability: **Medium**

58. *Answer choices:*

(see index for correct answer)

- a. Fish! Philosophy
- b. Activity management
- c. Inter departmental communication
- d. Office

Guidance: level 1

:: Evaluation ::

_________ is the practice of being honest and showing a consistent and uncompromising adherence to strong moral and ethical principles and values.In ethics, _________ is regarded as the honesty and truthfulness or accuracy of one`s actions. _________ can stand in opposition to hypocrisy, in that judging with the standards of _________ involves regarding internal consistency as a virtue, and suggests that parties holding within themselves apparently conflicting values should account for the discrepancy or alter their beliefs. The word _________ evolved from the Latin adjective integer, meaning whole or complete. In this context, _________ is the inner sense of "wholeness" deriving from qualities such as honesty and consistency of character. As such, one may judge that others "have _________ " to the extent that they act according to the values, beliefs and principles they claim to hold.

Exam Probability: **High**

59. *Answer choices:*

(see index for correct answer)

- a. Princeton Application Repository for Shared-Memory Computers
- b. Joint Committee on Standards for Educational Evaluation
- c. Defence Evaluation and Research Agency
- d. Evaluation Assurance Level

Guidance: level 1

Management

Management is the administration of an organization, whether it is a business, a not-for-profit organization, or government body. Management includes the activities of setting the strategy of an organization and coordinating the efforts of its employees (or of volunteers) to accomplish its objectives through the application of available resources, such as financial, natural, technological, and human resources.

:: Psychometrics ::

_________ is a dynamic, structured, interactive process where a neutral third party assists disputing parties in resolving conflict through the use of specialized communication and negotiation techniques. All participants in _________ are encouraged to actively participate in the process. _________ is a "party-centered" process in that it is focused primarily upon the needs, rights, and interests of the parties. The mediator uses a wide variety of techniques to guide the process in a constructive direction and to help the parties find their optimal solution. A mediator is facilitative in that she/he manages the interaction between parties and facilitates open communication. _________ is also evaluative in that the mediator analyzes issues and relevant norms , while refraining from providing prescriptive advice to the parties .

Exam Probability: **Low**

1. *Answer choices:*

(see index for correct answer)

- a. Person-fit analysis
- b. Correction for attenuation
- c. Mediation
- d. Vineland Adaptive Behavior Scale

Guidance: level 1

:: ::

__________ is both a research area and a practical skill encompassing the ability of an individual or organization to "lead" or guide other individuals, teams, or entire organizations. Specialist literature debates various viewpoints, contrasting Eastern and Western approaches to __________ , and also United States versus European approaches. U.S. academic environments define __________ as "a process of social influence in which a person can enlist the aid and support of others in the accomplishment of a common task".

Exam Probability: **Low**

2. *Answer choices:*

(see index for correct answer)

- a. open system
- b. Sarbanes-Oxley act of 2002
- c. process perspective
- d. cultural

Guidance: level 1

:: Business ::

The seller, or the provider of the goods or services, completes a sale in response to an acquisition, appropriation, requisition or a direct interaction with the buyer at the point of sale. There is a passing of title of the item, and the settlement of a price, in which agreement is reached on a price for which transfer of ownership of the item will occur. The seller, not the purchaser typically executes the sale and it may be completed prior to the obligation of payment. In the case of indirect interaction, a person who sells goods or service on behalf of the owner is known as a _________ man or _________ woman or _________ person, but this often refers to someone selling goods in a store/shop, in which case other terms are also common, including _________ clerk, shop assistant, and retail clerk.

Exam Probability: **Low**

3. *Answer choices:*

(see index for correct answer)

- a. American Environmental Assessment and Solutions Inc.
- b. Ian McLeod
- c. Professional services
- d. Sales

Guidance: level 1

:: ::

_________ refers to the overall process of attracting, shortlisting, selecting and appointing suitable candidates for jobs within an organization. _________ can also refer to processes involved in choosing individuals for unpaid roles. Managers, human resource generalists and _________ specialists may be tasked with carrying out _________, but in some cases public-sector employment agencies, commercial _________ agencies, or specialist search consultancies are used to undertake parts of the process. Internet-based technologies which support all aspects of _________ have become widespread.

Exam Probability: **Low**

4. *Answer choices:*

(see index for correct answer)

- a. interpersonal communication
- b. hierarchical
- c. functional perspective
- d. Recruitment

Guidance: level 1

:: Internet privacy ::

An __________ is a private network accessible only to an organization`s staff. Often, a wide range of information and services are available on an organization`s internal __________ that are unavailable to the public, unlike the Internet. A company-wide __________ can constitute an important focal point of internal communication and collaboration, and provide a single starting point to access internal and external resources. In its simplest form, an __________ is established with the technologies for local area networks and wide area networks . Many modern __________ s have search engines, user profiles, blogs, mobile apps with notifications, and events planning within their infrastructure.

Exam Probability: **Low**

5. *Answer choices:*

(see index for correct answer)

- a. Intranet
- b. Secure messaging
- c. Right to be forgotten
- d. Email encryption

Guidance: level 1

:: ::

A __________ or sample __________ is a single measure of some attribute of a sample . It is calculated by applying a function to the values of the items of the sample, which are known together as a set of data.

Exam Probability: **Medium**

6. *Answer choices:*

(see index for correct answer)

- a. personal values
- b. Sarbanes-Oxley act of 2002
- c. Statistic
- d. co-culture

Guidance: level 1

:: Information systems ::

_________ is the process of creating, sharing, using and managing the knowledge and information of an organisation. It refers to a multidisciplinary approach to achieving organisational objectives by making the best use of knowledge.

Exam Probability: **High**

7. *Answer choices:*

(see index for correct answer)

- a. Knowledge management
- b. Payroll automation
- c. Virtual information services

- d. Event stream processing

Guidance: level 1

:: Business terms ::

Centralisation or __________ is the process by which the activities of an organization, particularly those regarding planning and decision-making, framing strategy and policies become concentrated within a particular geographical location group. This moves the important decision-making and planning powers within the center of the organisation.

Exam Probability: **High**

8. *Answer choices:*

(see index for correct answer)

- a. front office
- b. back office
- c. Centralization
- d. organizational capital

Guidance: level 1

:: Organizational theory ::

A __________ is an organizational theory that claims that there is no best way to organize a corporation, to lead a company, or to make decisions. Instead, the optimal course of action is contingent upon the internal and external situation. A contingent leader effectively applies their own style of leadership to the right situation.

Exam Probability: **Medium**

9. *Answer choices:*

(see index for correct answer)

- a. Conflict
- b. Participatory management
- c. Smart city
- d. Contingency theory

Guidance: level 1

:: Corporate governance ::

An __________ is generally a person responsible for running an organization, although the exact nature of the role varies depending on the organization. In many militaries, an __________, or "XO," is the second-in-command, reporting to the commanding officer. The XO is typically responsible for the management of day-to-day activities, freeing the commander to concentrate on strategy and planning the unit`s next move.

Exam Probability: **Low**

10. *Answer choices:*

(see index for correct answer)

- a. Executive officer
- b. Independent director
- c. Proxy firm
- d. Chief brand officer

Guidance: level 1

:: Human resource management ::

__________ is a core function of human resource management and it is related to the specification of contents, methods and relationship of jobs in order to satisfy technological and organizational requirements as well as the social and personal requirements of the job holder or the employee. Its principles are geared towards how the nature of a person`s job affects their attitudes and behavior at work, particularly relating to characteristics such as skill variety and autonomy. The aim of a __________ is to improve job satisfaction, to improve through-put, to improve quality and to reduce employee problems .

Exam Probability: **High**

11. *Answer choices:*

(see index for correct answer)

- a. Diversity Icebreaker
- b. Mechanical aptitude

- c. Job design
- d. Human resources

Guidance: level 1

:: Leadership ::

_________ Theory, or the _________ Model, is a model created by Paul Hersey and Ken Blanchard, developed while working on Management of Organizational Behavior. The theory was first introduced in 1969 as "life cycle theory of leadership". During the mid-1970s, life cycle theory of leadership was renamed " _________ Theory."

Exam Probability: **Low**

12. *Answer choices:*

(see index for correct answer)

- a. Trait leadership
- b. Situational leadership
- c. The Intangibles of Leadership
- d. Authentic leadership

Guidance: level 1

:: Management ::

_________ is the practice of initiating, planning, executing, controlling, and closing the work of a team to achieve specific goals and meet specific success criteria at the specified time.

Exam Probability: **Low**

13. *Answer choices:*

(see index for correct answer)

- a. Decentralized decision-making
- b. Scenario planning
- c. Project management
- d. Pomodoro Technique

Guidance: level 1

:: Labour relations ::

_________ is a field of study that can have different meanings depending on the context in which it is used. In an international context, it is a subfield of labor history that studies the human relations with regard to work – in its broadest sense – and how this connects to questions of social inequality. It explicitly encompasses unregulated, historical, and non-Western forms of labor. Here, _________ define "for or with whom one works and under what rules. These rules determine the type of work, type and amount of remuneration, working hours, degrees of physical and psychological strain, as well as the degree of freedom and autonomy associated with the work."

Exam Probability: **Medium**

14. *Answer choices:*

(see index for correct answer)

- a. Big labor
- b. Work Order Act
- c. Labor relations
- d. Minnesota Nurses Association

Guidance: level 1

:: Systems theory ::

A __________ is a set of policies, processes and procedures used by an organization to ensure that it can fulfill the tasks required to achieve its objectives. These objectives cover many aspects of the organization`s operations . For instance, an environmental __________ enables organizations to improve their environmental performance and an occupational health and safety __________ enables an organization to control its occupational health and safety risks, etc.

Exam Probability: **Medium**

15. *Answer choices:*

(see index for correct answer)

- a. Management system

- b. co-design
- c. decentralized system
- d. equifinality

Guidance: level 1

:: Industrial Revolution ::

The _________ , now also known as the First _________ , was the transition to new manufacturing processes in Europe and the US, in the period from about 1760 to sometime between 1820 and 1840. This transition included going from hand production methods to machines, new chemical manufacturing and iron production processes, the increasing use of steam power and water power, the development of machine tools and the rise of the mechanized factory system. The _________ also led to an unprecedented rise in the rate of population growth.

Exam Probability: **High**

16. *Answer choices:*

(see index for correct answer)

- a. American Woolen Company
- b. Roberts Loom
- c. Cotton-spinning machinery
- d. Industrial Revolution

Guidance: level 1

:: ::

_________ comprises all of the processes of governing – whether undertaken by the government of a state, by a market or by a network – over a social system and whether through the laws, norms, power or language of an organized society. It relates to "the processes of interaction and decision-making among the actors involved in a collective problem that lead to the creation, reinforcement, or reproduction of social norms and institutions".In lay terms, it could be described as the political processes that exist in and between formal institutions.

Exam Probability: **Low**

17. *Answer choices:*

(see index for correct answer)

- a. process perspective
- b. surface-level diversity
- c. Governance
- d. Sarbanes-Oxley act of 2002

Guidance: level 1

:: Management ::

A _________ is an idea of the future or desired result that a person or a group of people envisions, plans and commits to achieve. People endeavor to reach _________ s within a finite time by setting deadlines.

Exam Probability: **High**

18. *Answer choices:*

(see index for correct answer)

- a. Failure demand
- b. Preparation
- c. Modes of leadership
- d. Community of practice

Guidance: level 1

:: Human resource management ::

An organizational chart is a diagram that shows the structure of an organization and the relationships and relative ranks of its parts and positions/jobs. The term is also used for similar diagrams, for example ones showing the different elements of a field of knowledge or a group of languages.

Exam Probability: **Low**

19. *Answer choices:*

(see index for correct answer)

- a. Organization chart
- b. Senior management
- c. Skill mix

- d. Job analysis

Guidance: level 1

:: Project management ::

_________ and Theory Y are theories of human work motivation and management. They were created by Douglas McGregor while he was working at the MIT Sloan School of Management in the 1950s, and developed further in the 1960s. McGregor`s work was rooted in motivation theory alongside the works of Abraham Maslow, who created the hierarchy of needs. The two theories proposed by McGregor describe contrasting models of workforce motivation applied by managers in human resource management, organizational behavior, organizational communication and organizational development. _________ explains the importance of heightened supervision, external rewards, and penalties, while Theory Y highlights the motivating role of job satisfaction and encourages workers to approach tasks without direct supervision. Management use of _________ and Theory Y can affect employee motivation and productivity in different ways, and managers may choose to implement strategies from both theories into their practices.

Exam Probability: **High**

20. *Answer choices:*

(see index for correct answer)

- a. Deployment Plan
- b. Theory X
- c. Cone of Uncertainty
- d. Graphical Evaluation and Review Technique

Guidance: level 1

:: ::

__________ is the assignment of any responsibility or authority to another person to carry out specific activities. It is one of the core concepts of management leadership. However, the person who delegated the work remains accountable for the outcome of the delegated work. __________ empowers a subordinate to make decisions, i.e. it is a shifting of decision-making authority from one organizational level to a lower one. __________, if properly done, is not fabrication. The opposite of effective __________ is micromanagement, where a manager provides too much input, direction, and review of delegated work. In general, __________ is good and can save money and time, help in building skills, and motivate people. On the other hand, poor __________ might cause frustration and confusion to all the involved parties. Some agents, however, do not favour a __________ and consider the power of making a decision rather burdensome.

Exam Probability: **Low**

21. *Answer choices:*

(see index for correct answer)

- a. Character
- b. Delegation
- c. Sarbanes-Oxley act of 2002
- d. hierarchical

Guidance: level 1

:: Monopoly (economics) ::

A __________ is a form of intellectual property that gives its owner the legal right to exclude others from making, using, selling, and importing an invention for a limited period of years, in exchange for publishing an enabling public disclosure of the invention. In most countries __________ rights fall under civil law and the __________ holder needs to sue someone infringing the __________ in order to enforce his or her rights. In some industries __________ s are an essential form of competitive advantage; in others they are irrelevant.

Exam Probability: **Low**

22. *Answer choices:*

(see index for correct answer)

- a. Patent
- b. Eisenkammer Pirna
- c. Privatization
- d. Patent portfolio

Guidance: level 1

:: Customs duties ::

A __________ is a tax on imports or exports between sovereign states. It is a form of regulation of foreign trade and a policy that taxes foreign products to encourage or safeguard domestic industry. __________ s are the simplest and oldest instrument of trade policy. Traditionally, states have used them as a source of income. Now, they are among the most widely used instruments of protection, along with import and export quotas.

Exam Probability: **Low**

23. *Answer choices:*

(see index for correct answer)

- a. Tariff
- b. Malaysian motor vehicle import duties
- c. Canadian import duties
- d. Customs area

Guidance: level 1

:: Social psychology ::

In social psychology, __________ is the phenomenon of a person exerting less effort to achieve a goal when he or she works in a group than when working alone. This is seen as one of the main reasons groups are sometimes less productive than the combined performance of their members working as individuals, but should be distinguished from the accidental coordination problems that groups sometimes experience.

Exam Probability: **Low**

24. *Answer choices:*

(see index for correct answer)

- a. Social loafing
- b. thought control
- c. indoctrination
- d. brainwriting

Guidance: level 1

:: Critical thinking ::

An __________ is someone who has a prolonged or intense experience through practice and education in a particular field. Informally, an __________ is someone widely recognized as a reliable source of technique or skill whose faculty for judging or deciding rightly, justly, or wisely is accorded authority and status by peers or the public in a specific well-distinguished domain. An __________, more generally, is a person with extensive knowledge or ability based on research, experience, or occupation and in a particular area of study. __________ s are called in for advice on their respective subject, but they do not always agree on the particulars of a field of study. An __________ can be believed, by virtue of credential, training, education, profession, publication or experience, to have special knowledge of a subject beyond that of the average person, sufficient that others may officially rely upon the individual's opinion. Historically, an __________ was referred to as a sage . The individual was usually a profound thinker distinguished for wisdom and sound judgment.

Exam Probability: **Medium**

25. *Answer choices:*

(see index for correct answer)

- a. Interpretive discussion
- b. Attacking Faulty Reasoning
- c. Socratic questioning
- d. Inquiry: Critical Thinking Across the Disciplines

Guidance: level 1

:: Marketing ::

_________ or stock is the goods and materials that a business holds for the ultimate goal of resale .

Exam Probability: **High**

26. *Answer choices:*

(see index for correct answer)

- a. Jonathan Grado
- b. Product
- c. Inbound marketing
- d. customer-perceived value

Guidance: level 1

:: Telecommuting ::

__________ , also called telework, teleworking, working from home, mobile work, remote work, and flexible workplace, is a work arrangement in which employees do not commute or travel to a central place of work, such as an office building, warehouse, or store. Teleworkers in the 21st century often use mobile telecommunications technology such as Wi-Fi-equipped laptop or tablet computers and smartphones to work from coffee shops; others may use a desktop computer and a landline phone at their home. According to a Reuters poll, approximately "one in five workers around the globe, particularly employees in the Middle East, Latin America and Asia, telecommute frequently and nearly 10 percent work from home every day." In the 2000s, annual leave or vacation in some organizations was seen as absence from the workplace rather than ceasing work, and some office employees used telework to continue to check work e-mails while on vacation.

Exam Probability: **Low**

27. *Answer choices:*

(see index for correct answer)

- a. Telecommuting
- b. E-professional
- c. Canadian Telework Association
- d. Planet Soho

Guidance: level 1

:: ::

_________ is the reason for people`s actions, willingness and goals. _________ is derived from the word motive in the English language which is defined as a need that requires satisfaction. These needs could also be wants or desires that are acquired through influence of culture, society, lifestyle, etc. or generally innate. _________ is one`s direction to behaviour, or what causes a person to want to repeat a behaviour, a set of force that acts behind the motives. An individual`s _________ may be inspired by others or events or it may come from within the individual . _________ has been considered as one of the most important reasons that inspires a person to move forward in life. _________ results from the interaction of both conscious and unconscious factors. Mastering _________ to allow sustained and deliberate practice is central to high levels of achievement e.g. in the worlds of elite sport, medicine or music.

Exam Probability: **High**

28. *Answer choices:*

(see index for correct answer)

- a. functional perspective
- b. corporate values
- c. Motivation
- d. empathy

Guidance: level 1

:: Evaluation ::

_________ is a way of preventing mistakes and defects in manufactured products and avoiding problems when delivering products or services to customers; which ISO 9000 defines as "part of quality management focused on providing confidence that quality requirements will be fulfilled". This defect prevention in _________ differs subtly from defect detection and rejection in quality control and has been referred to as a shift left since it focuses on quality earlier in the process .

Exam Probability: **Low**

29. *Answer choices:*

(see index for correct answer)

- a. Common Criteria Testing Laboratory
- b. Expression
- c. Joint Committee on Standards for Educational Evaluation
- d. Quality assurance

Guidance: level 1

:: ::

An _________ is, most an organized examination or formal evaluation exercise. In engineering activities _________ involves the measurements, tests, and gauges applied to certain characteristics in regard to an object or activity. The results are usually compared to specified requirements and standards for determining whether the item or activity is in line with these targets, often with a Standard _________ Procedure in place to ensure consistent checking. _________s are usually non-destructive.

Exam Probability: **High**

30. *Answer choices:*

(see index for correct answer)

- a. Character
- b. corporate values
- c. functional perspective
- d. information systems assessment

Guidance: level 1

:: ::

A _________ is a problem offering two possibilities, neither of which is unambiguously acceptable or preferable. The possibilities are termed the horns of the _________, a clichéd usage, but distinguishing the _________ from other kinds of predicament as a matter of usage.

Exam Probability: **Low**

31. *Answer choices:*

(see index for correct answer)

- a. corporate values
- b. similarity-attraction theory
- c. functional perspective

- d. Dilemma

Guidance: level 1

:: ::

The _________ officer or just _________ , is the most senior corporate, executive, or administrative officer in charge of managing an organization especially an independent legal entity such as a company or nonprofit institution. CEOs lead a range of organizations, including public and private corporations, non-profit organizations and even some government organizations . The CEO of a corporation or company typically reports to the board of directors and is charged with maximizing the value of the entity, which may include maximizing the share price, market share, revenues or another element. In the non-profit and government sector, CEOs typically aim at achieving outcomes related to the organization`s mission, such as reducing poverty, increasing literacy, etc.

Exam Probability: **Medium**

32. *Answer choices:*

(see index for correct answer)

- a. imperative
- b. Character
- c. personal values
- d. hierarchical

Guidance: level 1

:: Poker strategy ::

_________ is any measure taken to guard a thing against damage caused by outside forces. _________ can be provided to physical objects, including organisms, to systems, and to intangible things like civil and political rights. Although the mechanisms for providing _________ vary widely, the basic meaning of the term remains the same. This is illustrated by an explanation found in a manual on electrical wiring.

Exam Probability: **Medium**

33. *Answer choices:*

(see index for correct answer)

- a. Fold equity
- b. Bluff
- c. M-ratio
- d. Position

Guidance: level 1

:: Human resource management ::

Frederick Herzberg, an American psychologist, originally developed the concept of ` _________ ` in 1968, in an article that he published on pioneering studies at A T&T. The concept stemmed from Herzberg`s motivator-hygiene theory, which is based on the premise that job attitude is a construct of two independent factors, namely job satisfaction and job dissatisfaction. Job satisfaction encompasses intrinsic factors that arise from the work itself, including achievement and advancement; whilst job dissatisfaction stems from factors external to the actual work, including company policy and the quality of supervision.

Exam Probability: **Medium**

34. *Answer choices:*

(see index for correct answer)

- a. Attendance management
- b. Lego Serious Play
- c. Talent supply chain management
- d. Job enrichment

Guidance: level 1

:: ::

A _________ is a research instrument consisting of a series of questions for the purpose of gathering information from respondents. The _________ was invented by the Statistical Society of London in 1838.

Exam Probability: **High**

35. *Answer choices:*

(see index for correct answer)

- a. cultural
- b. hierarchical perspective
- c. Questionnaire
- d. open system

Guidance: level 1

:: Management ::

A _________ is a formal written document containing business goals, the methods on how these goals can be attained, and the time frame within which these goals need to be achieved. It also describes the nature of the business, background information on the organization, the organization`s financial projections, and the strategies it intends to implement to achieve the stated targets. In its entirety, this document serves as a road map that provides direction to the business.

Exam Probability: **Medium**

36. *Answer choices:*

(see index for correct answer)

- a. Management cockpit

- b. Business plan
- c. Critical path method
- d. middle manager

Guidance: level 1

:: Project management ::

In economics, _________ is the assignment of available resources to various uses. In the context of an entire economy, resources can be allocated by various means, such as markets or central planning.

Exam Probability: **High**

37. *Answer choices:*

(see index for correct answer)

- a. Cash flow diagram
- b. Rolling Wave planning
- c. Master of Science in Project Management
- d. Cost-benefit

Guidance: level 1

:: ::

_________ is the moral stance, political philosophy, ideology, or social outlook that emphasizes the moral worth of the individual. Individualists promote the exercise of one`s goals and desires and so value independence and self-reliance and advocate that interests of the individual should achieve precedence over the state or a social group, while opposing external interference upon one`s own interests by society or institutions such as the government. _________ is often defined in contrast to totalitarianism, collectivism, and more corporate social forms.

Exam Probability: **Medium**

38. *Answer choices:*

(see index for correct answer)

- a. similarity-attraction theory
- b. Individualism
- c. corporate values
- d. Character

Guidance: level 1

:: Leadership ::

_________ /Management is a part of a style of leadership that focuses on supervision, organization, and performance; it is an integral part of the Full Range Leadership Model. _________ is a style of leadership in which leaders promote compliance by followers through both rewards and punishments. Through a rewards and punishments system, transactional leaders are able to keep followers motivated for the short-term. Unlike transformational leaders, those using the transactional approach are not looking to change the future, they look to keep things the same. Leaders using _________ as a model pay attention to followers` work in order to find faults and deviations.

Exam Probability: **Low**

39. *Answer choices:*

(see index for correct answer)

- a. Spirit of Enniskillen Trust
- b. Consideration and Initiating Structure
- c. Transactional leadership
- d. Moral example

Guidance: level 1

:: Leadership ::

_________ is a theory of leadership where a leader works with teams to identify needed change, creating a vision to guide the change through inspiration, and executing the change in tandem with committed members of a group; it is an integral part of the Full Range Leadership Model. _________ serves to enhance the motivation, morale, and job performance of followers through a variety of mechanisms; these include connecting the follower`s sense of identity and self to a project and to the collective identity of the organization; being a role model for followers in order to inspire them and to raise their interest in the project; challenging followers to take greater ownership for their work, and understanding the strengths and weaknesses of followers, allowing the leader to align followers with tasks that enhance their performance.

Exam Probability: **Low**

40. *Answer choices:*

(see index for correct answer)

- a. Transformational leadership
- b. Strategic leadership
- c. Consideration and Initiating Structure
- d. The Saint, the Surfer, and the CEO

Guidance: level 1

:: Discrimination ::

In social psychology, a _________ is an over-generalized belief about a particular category of people. _________ s are generalized because one assumes that the _________ is true for each individual person in the category. While such generalizations may be useful when making quick decisions, they may be erroneous when applied to particular individuals. _________ s encourage prejudice and may arise for a number of reasons.

Exam Probability: **High**

41. *Answer choices:*

(see index for correct answer)

- a. Elitism
- b. Anti-Americanism
- c. Stereotype

Guidance: level 1

:: Free trade agreements ::

A _________ is a wide-ranging taxes, tariff and trade treaty that often includes investment guarantees. It exists when two or more countries agree on terms that helps them trade with each other. The most common _________ s are of the preferential and free trade types are concluded in order to reduce tariffs, quotas and other trade restrictions on items traded between the signatories.

Exam Probability: **High**

42. *Answer choices:*

(see index for correct answer)

- a. Trade agreement
- b. Central Asian Union
- c. New West Partnership
- d. South Asian Free Trade Area

Guidance: level 1

:: Project management ::

A __________ is a professional in the field of project management. __________ s have the responsibility of the planning, procurement and execution of a project, in any undertaking that has a defined scope, defined start and a defined finish; regardless of industry. __________ s are first point of contact for any issues or discrepancies arising from within the heads of various departments in an organization before the problem escalates to higher authorities. Project management is the responsibility of a __________ . This individual seldom participates directly in the activities that produce the end result, but rather strives to maintain the progress, mutual interaction and tasks of various parties in such a way that reduces the risk of overall failure, maximizes benefits, and minimizes costs.

Exam Probability: **Medium**

43. *Answer choices:*

(see index for correct answer)

- a. American Society of Professional Estimators
- b. Project manager
- c. Graphical Evaluation and Review Technique
- d. Indian Institute of Project Management

Guidance: level 1

:: Management ::

_________ is an area of management concerned with designing and controlling the process of production and redesigning business operations in the production of goods or services. It involves the responsibility of ensuring that business operations are efficient in terms of using as few resources as needed and effective in terms of meeting customer requirements. _________ is primarily concerned with planning, organizing and supervising in the contexts of production, manufacturing or the provision of services.

Exam Probability: **High**

44. *Answer choices:*

(see index for correct answer)

- a. Organizational hologram
- b. Corporate transparency
- c. Work breakdown structure
- d. Operations management

Guidance: level 1

:: ::

_________ is the collection of mechanisms, processes and relations by which corporations are controlled and operated. Governance structures and principles identify the distribution of rights and responsibilities among different participants in the corporation and include the rules and procedures for making decisions in corporate affairs. _________ is necessary because of the possibility of conflicts of interests between stakeholders, primarily between shareholders and upper management or among shareholders.

Exam Probability: **Medium**

45. *Answer choices:*

(see index for correct answer)

- a. Corporate governance
- b. empathy
- c. open system
- d. imperative

Guidance: level 1

:: Information science ::

__________ is the resolution of uncertainty; it is that which answers the question of "what an entity is" and thus defines both its essence and nature of its characteristics. __________ relates to both data and knowledge, as data is meaningful __________ representing values attributed to parameters, and knowledge signifies understanding of a concept. __________ is uncoupled from an observer, which is an entity that can access __________ and thus discern what it specifies; __________ exists beyond an event horizon for example. In the case of knowledge, the __________ itself requires a cognitive observer to be obtained.

Exam Probability: **High**

46. *Answer choices:*

(see index for correct answer)

- a. Informative modelling
- b. Library and Information Science Abstracts
- c. Journal of the Association for Information Science and Technology
- d. Mental model

Guidance: level 1

:: Business models ::

A __________ is "an autonomous association of persons united voluntarily to meet their common economic, social, and cultural needs and aspirations through a jointly-owned and democratically-controlled enterprise". __________ s may include.

Exam Probability: **Low**

47. *Answer choices:*

(see index for correct answer)

- a. Cooperative
- b. Lemonade stand
- c. Gratis
- d. Market game

Guidance: level 1

:: Project management ::

A __________ is a team whose members usually belong to different groups, functions and are assigned to activities for the same project. A team can be divided into sub-teams according to need. Usually __________ s are only used for a defined period of time. They are disbanded after the project is deemed complete. Due to the nature of the specific formation and disbandment, __________ s are usually in organizations.

Exam Probability: **High**

48. *Answer choices:*

(see index for correct answer)

- a. Project team
- b. Bid manager

- c. Hammock activity
- d. Lean project management

Guidance: level 1

:: Manufacturing ::

A _________ is a building for storing goods. _________ s are used by manufacturers, importers, exporters, wholesalers, transport businesses, customs, etc. They are usually large plain buildings in industrial parks on the outskirts of cities, towns or villages.

Exam Probability: **Low**

49. *Answer choices:*

(see index for correct answer)

- a. Motoman
- b. Warehouse
- c. Production Systems Engineering
- d. ANSI/ISA-95

Guidance: level 1

:: ::

__________ is the process of two or more people or organizations working together to complete a task or achieve a goal. __________ is similar to cooperation. Most __________ requires leadership, although the form of leadership can be social within a decentralized and egalitarian group. Teams that work collaboratively often access greater resources, recognition and rewards when facing competition for finite resources.

Exam Probability: **Low**

50. *Answer choices:*

(see index for correct answer)

- a. corporate values
- b. empathy
- c. cultural
- d. hierarchical perspective

Guidance: level 1

:: Project management ::

A __________ is a source or supply from which a benefit is produced and it has some utility. __________ s can broadly be classified upon their availability—they are classified into renewable and non-renewable __________ s.Examples of non renewable __________ s are coal ,crude oil natural gas nuclear energy etc. Examples of renewable __________ s are air,water,wind,solar energy etc. They can also be classified as actual and potential on the basis of level of development and use, on the basis of origin they can be classified as biotic and abiotic, and on the basis of their distribution, as ubiquitous and localized . An item becomes a __________ with time and developing technology. Typically, __________ s are materials, energy, services, staff, knowledge, or other assets that are transformed to produce benefit and in the process may be consumed or made unavailable. Benefits of __________ utilization may include increased wealth, proper functioning of a system, or enhanced well-being. From a human perspective a natural __________ is anything obtained from the environment to satisfy human needs and wants. From a broader biological or ecological perspective a __________ satisfies the needs of a living organism .

Exam Probability: **High**

51. *Answer choices:*

(see index for correct answer)

- a. Commissioning management systems
- b. Task
- c. Responsibility assignment matrix
- d. Resource

Guidance: level 1

:: Lean manufacturing ::

__________ is the Sino-Japanese word for "improvement". In business, __________ refers to activities that continuously improve all functions and involve all employees from the CEO to the assembly line workers. It also applies to processes, such as purchasing and logistics, that cross organizational boundaries into the supply chain. It has been applied in healthcare, psychotherapy, life-coaching, government, and banking.

Exam Probability: **Low**

52. *Answer choices:*

(see index for correct answer)

- a. Kaizen
- b. Continuous improvement
- c. Fixed Repeating Schedule
- d. Supply chain responsiveness matrix

Guidance: level 1

:: Human resource management ::

__________ expands the capacity of individuals to perform in leadership roles within organizations. Leadership roles are those that facilitate execution of a company's strategy through building alignment, winning mindshare and growing the capabilities of others. Leadership roles may be formal, with the corresponding authority to make decisions and take responsibility, or they may be informal roles with little official authority .

Exam Probability: **Low**

53. *Answer choices:*

(see index for correct answer)

- a. Leadership development
- b. Illness rate
- c. Training and development
- d. At-will employment

Guidance: level 1

:: Information technology management ::

__________ is a collective term for all approaches to prepare , support and help individuals, teams, and organizations in making organizational change. The most common change drivers include: technological evolution, process reviews, crisis, and consumer habit changes; pressure from new business entrants, acquisitions, mergers, and organizational restructuring. It includes methods that redirect or redefine the use of resources, business process, budget allocations, or other modes of operation that significantly change a company or organization. Organizational __________ considers the full organization and what needs to change, while __________ may be used solely to refer to how people and teams are affected by such organizational transition. It deals with many different disciplines, from behavioral and social sciences to information technology and business solutions.

Exam Probability: **Low**

54. *Answer choices:*

(see index for correct answer)

- a. IT risk
- b. Change management
- c. Croquet Project
- d. E-Booking

Guidance: level 1

:: Data analysis ::

In statistics, the _________ is a measure that is used to quantify the amount of variation or dispersion of a set of data values. A low _________ indicates that the data points tend to be close to the mean of the set, while a high _________ indicates that the data points are spread out over a wider range of values.

Exam Probability: **Medium**

55. *Answer choices:*

(see index for correct answer)

- a. Multiscale geometric analysis
- b. Ratio estimator
- c. Standard deviation
- d. Boolean analysis

Guidance: level 1

:: ::

_________ is the practice of protecting the natural environment by individuals, organizations and governments. Its objectives are to conserve natural resources and the existing natural environment and, where possible, to repair damage and reverse trends.

Exam Probability: **Low**

56. *Answer choices:*

(see index for correct answer)

- a. open system
- b. information systems assessment
- c. similarity-attraction theory
- d. process perspective

Guidance: level 1

:: Autonomy ::

In developmental psychology and moral, political, and bioethical philosophy, _________ is the capacity to make an informed, uncoerced decision. Autonomous organizations or institutions are independent or self-governing. _________ can also be defined from a human resources perspective, where it denotes a level of discretion granted to an employee in his or her work. In such cases, _________ is known to generally increase job satisfaction. _________ is a term that is also widely used in the field of medicine — personal _________ is greatly recognized and valued in health care.

Exam Probability: **Medium**

57. *Answer choices:*

(see index for correct answer)

- a. Autonomy
- b. Self-ownership
- c. Equality of autonomy
- d. European Charter of Local Self-Government

Guidance: level 1

:: Business ::

_________ is a trade policy that does not restrict imports or exports; it can also be understood as the free market idea applied to international trade. In government, _________ is predominantly advocated by political parties that hold liberal economic positions while economically left-wing and nationalist political parties generally support protectionism, the opposite of _________ .

Exam Probability: **Low**

58. *Answer choices:*

(see index for correct answer)

- a. Professional services
- b. Free trade
- c. Business interoperability interface
- d. Signed number

Guidance: level 1

:: ::

_________ Corporation was an American energy, commodities, and services company based in Houston, Texas. It was founded in 1985 as a merger between Houston Natural Gas and InterNorth, both relatively small regional companies. Before its bankruptcy on December 3, 2001, _________ employed approximately 29,000 staff and was a major electricity, natural gas, communications and pulp and paper company, with claimed revenues of nearly $101 billion during 2000. Fortune named _________ "America`s Most Innovative Company" for six consecutive years.

Exam Probability: **High**

59. *Answer choices:*

(see index for correct answer)

- a. imperative
- b. levels of analysis
- c. interpersonal communication
- d. Enron

Guidance: level 1

Business law

Corporate law (also known as business law) is the body of law governing the rights, relations, and conduct of persons, companies, organizations and businesses. It refers to the legal practice relating to, or the theory of corporations. Corporate law often describes the law relating to matters which derive directly from the life-cycle of a corporation. It thus encompasses the formation, funding, governance, and death of a corporation.

:: Latin legal terms ::

In law and government, _________ describes practices that are legally recognised, regardless whether the practice exists in reality. In contrast, de facto describes situations that exist in reality, even if not legally recognised. The terms are often used to contrast different scenarios: for a colloquial example, "I know that, _________ , this is supposed to be a parking lot, but now that the flood has left four feet of water here, it`s a de facto swimming pool". To further explain, even if the signs around the flooded parking lot say "Parking Lot" it is "in fact" a swimming pool .

Exam Probability: **Medium**

1. *Answer choices:*

(see index for correct answer)

- a. De jure
- b. pari delicto
- c. Quid pro quo
- d. Nolo contendere

Guidance: level 1

:: Real property law ::

_________ is the judicial process whereby a will is "proved" in a court of law and accepted as a valid public document that is the true last testament of the deceased, or whereby the estate is settled according to the laws of intestacy in the state of residence [or real property] of the deceased at time of death in the absence of a legal will.

Exam Probability: **Medium**

2. *Answer choices:*

(see index for correct answer)

- a. Probate
- b. Urbarium
- c. Deed
- d. Statute of Uses

Guidance: level 1

:: ::

_________ is the administration of an organization, whether it is a business, a not-for-profit organization, or government body. _________ includes the activities of setting the strategy of an organization and coordinating the efforts of its employees to accomplish its objectives through the application of available resources, such as financial, natural, technological, and human resources. The term " _________ " may also refer to those people who manage an organization.

Exam Probability: **High**

3. *Answer choices:*

(see index for correct answer)

- a. personal values
- b. Management
- c. surface-level diversity
- d. functional perspective

Guidance: level 1

:: Generally Accepted Accounting Principles ::

In accounting, _________ is the income that a business have from its normal business activities, usually from the sale of goods and services to customers. _________ is also referred to as sales or turnover.Some companies receive _________ from interest, royalties, or other fees. _________ may refer to business income in general, or it may refer to the amount, in a monetary unit, earned during a period of time, as in "Last year, Company X had _________ of $42 million". Profits or net income generally imply total _________ minus total expenses in a given period. In accounting, in the balance statement it is a subsection of the Equity section and _________ increases equity, it is often referred to as the "top line" due to its position on the income statement at the very top. This is to be contrasted with the "bottom line" which denotes net income .

Exam Probability: **High**

4. *Answer choices:*

(see index for correct answer)

- a. Completed-contract method
- b. Gross profit
- c. deferred revenue
- d. Indian Accounting Standards

Guidance: level 1

:: ::

_________ is a legal term which, in its broadest sense, is a synonym for anyone in a position of trust and so can refer to any person who holds property, authority, or a position of trust or responsibility for the benefit of another. A _________ can also refer to a person who is allowed to do certain tasks but not able to gain income. Although in the strictest sense of the term a _________ is the holder of property on behalf of a beneficiary, the more expansive sense encompasses persons who serve, for example, on the board of _________s of an institution that operates for a charity, for the benefit of the general public, or a person in the local government.

Exam Probability: **Low**

5. *Answer choices:*

(see index for correct answer)

- a. Trustee
- b. hierarchical
- c. Sarbanes-Oxley act of 2002
- d. process perspective

Guidance: level 1

:: Legal terms ::

__________ is the set of laws that governs how members of a society are to behave. It is contrasted with procedural law, which is the set of procedures for making, administering, and enforcing __________ . __________ defines rights and responsibilities in civil law, and crimes and punishments in criminal law. It may be codified in statutes or exist through precedent in common law.

Exam Probability: **Medium**

6. *Answer choices:*

(see index for correct answer)

- a. Substantive law
- b. Querulant
- c. Charging order
- d. Nonjoinder of party

Guidance: level 1

:: ::

The __________ is the highest court within the hierarchy of courts in many legal jurisdictions. Other descriptions for such courts include court of last resort, apex court, and high court of appeal. Broadly speaking, the decisions of a __________ are not subject to further review by any other court. __________s typically function primarily as appellate courts, hearing appeals from decisions of lower trial courts, or from intermediate-level appellate courts.

Exam Probability: **Medium**

7. *Answer choices:*

(see index for correct answer)

- a. levels of analysis
- b. similarity-attraction theory
- c. Character
- d. Supreme Court

Guidance: level 1

:: Business law ::

A _________ is a contractual arrangement calling for the lessee to pay the lessor for use of an asset. Property, buildings and vehicles are common assets that are _________ d. Industrial or business equipment is also _________ d.

Exam Probability: **Low**

8. *Answer choices:*

(see index for correct answer)

- a. Economic torts
- b. Business courts
- c. Forward-looking statement
- d. Refusal to deal

Guidance: level 1

:: ::

Credit is the trust which allows one party to provide money or resources to another party wherein the second party does not reimburse the first party immediately , but promises either to repay or return those resources at a later date. In other words, credit is a method of making reciprocity formal, legally enforceable, and extensible to a large group of unrelated people.

Exam Probability: **Low**

9. *Answer choices:*

(see index for correct answer)

- a. hierarchical
- b. Character
- c. functional perspective
- d. open system

Guidance: level 1

:: Criminal procedure ::

_________ is the adjudication process of the criminal law. While _________ differs dramatically by jurisdiction, the process generally begins with a formal criminal charge with the person on trial either being free on bail or incarcerated, and results in the conviction or acquittal of the defendant. _________ can be either in form of inquisitorial or adversarial _________.

Exam Probability: **Medium**

10. *Answer choices:*

(see index for correct answer)

- a. Exoneration
- b. Criminal procedure

Guidance: level 1

:: ::

An _________ is a contingent motivator. Traditional _________ s are extrinsic motivators which reward actions to yield a desired outcome. The effectiveness of traditional _________ s has changed as the needs of Western society have evolved. While the traditional _________ model is effective when there is a defined procedure and goal for a task, Western society started to require a higher volume of critical thinkers, so the traditional model became less effective. Institutions are now following a trend in implementing strategies that rely on intrinsic motivations rather than the extrinsic motivations that the traditional _________ s foster.

Exam Probability: **Low**

11. *Answer choices:*

(see index for correct answer)

- a. Incentive
- b. empathy
- c. imperative
- d. corporate values

Guidance: level 1

:: ::

In general, _________ is a form of dishonesty or criminal activity undertaken by a person or organization entrusted with a position of authority, often to acquire illicit benefit. _________ may include many activities including bribery and embezzlement, though it may also involve practices that are legal in many countries. Political _________ occurs when an office-holder or other governmental employee acts in an official capacity for personal gain. _________ is most commonplace in kleptocracies, oligarchies, narco-states and mafia states.

Exam Probability: **Medium**

12. *Answer choices:*

(see index for correct answer)

- a. personal values
- b. information systems assessment

- c. hierarchical
- d. Corruption

Guidance: level 1

:: Business ::

__________ is a trade policy that does not restrict imports or exports; it can also be understood as the free market idea applied to international trade. In government, __________ is predominantly advocated by political parties that hold liberal economic positions while economically left-wing and nationalist political parties generally support protectionism, the opposite of __________ .

Exam Probability: **Low**

13. *Answer choices:*

(see index for correct answer)

- a. Free trade
- b. Architecture of Interoperable Information Systems
- c. Disadvantaged business enterprise
- d. Qualifying event

Guidance: level 1

:: Majority–minority relations ::

__________ , also known as reservation in India and Nepal, positive discrimination / action in the United Kingdom, and employment equity in Canada and South Africa, is the policy of promoting the education and employment of members of groups that are known to have previously suffered from discrimination. Historically and internationally, support for __________ has sought to achieve goals such as bridging inequalities in employment and pay, increasing access to education, promoting diversity, and redressing apparent past wrongs, harms, or hindrances.

Exam Probability: **Low**

14. *Answer choices:*

(see index for correct answer)

- a. cultural dissonance
- b. cultural Relativism
- c. Affirmative action

Guidance: level 1

:: Euthenics ::

_________ is an ethical framework and suggests that an entity, be it an organization or individual, has an obligation to act for the benefit of society at large. _________ is a duty every individual has to perform so as to maintain a balance between the economy and the ecosystems. A trade-off may exist between economic development, in the material sense, and the welfare of the society and environment, though this has been challenged by many reports over the past decade. _________ means sustaining the equilibrium between the two. It pertains not only to business organizations but also to everyone whose any action impacts the environment. This responsibility can be passive, by avoiding engaging in socially harmful acts, or active, by performing activities that directly advance social goals. _________ must be intergenerational since the actions of one generation have consequences on those following.

Exam Probability: **Low**

15. *Answer choices:*

(see index for correct answer)

- a. Social responsibility
- b. Home economics
- c. Minnie Cumnock Blodgett
- d. Family and consumer science

Guidance: level 1

:: ::

The __________ to the United States Constitution prevents the government from making laws which respect an establishment of religion, prohibit the free exercise of religion, or abridge the freedom of speech, the freedom of the press, the right to peaceably assemble, or the right to petition the government for redress of grievances. It was adopted on December 15, 1791, as one of the ten amendments that constitute the Bill of Rights.

Exam Probability: **Medium**

16. *Answer choices:*

(see index for correct answer)

- a. deep-level diversity
- b. First Amendment
- c. imperative
- d. process perspective

Guidance: level 1

:: ::

A __________ is the party who initiates a lawsuit before a court. By doing so, the __________ seeks a legal remedy; if this search is successful, the court will issue judgment in favor of the __________ and make the appropriate court order . " __________ " is the term used in civil cases in most English-speaking jurisdictions, the notable exception being England and Wales, where a __________ has, since the introduction of the Civil Procedure Rules in 1999, been known as a "claimant", but that term also has other meanings. In criminal cases, the prosecutor brings the case against the defendant, but the key complaining party is often called the "complainant".

Exam Probability: **High**

17. *Answer choices:*

(see index for correct answer)

- a. Plaintiff
- b. Sarbanes-Oxley act of 2002
- c. co-culture
- d. levels of analysis

Guidance: level 1

:: Business law ::

_________ is where a person's financial liability is limited to a fixed sum, most commonly the value of a person's investment in a company or partnership. If a company with _________ is sued, then the claimants are suing the company, not its owners or investors. A shareholder in a limited company is not personally liable for any of the debts of the company, other than for the amount already invested in the company and for any unpaid amount on the shares in the company, if any. The same is true for the members of a _________ partnership and the limited partners in a limited partnership. By contrast, sole proprietors and partners in general partnerships are each liable for all the debts of the business .

Exam Probability: **Low**

18. *Answer choices:*

(see index for correct answer)

- a. Complex structured finance transactions
- b. Limited liability
- c. Forged endorsement
- d. Bulk sale

Guidance: level 1

:: Contract Clause case law ::

The _________ appears in the United States Constitution, Article I, section 10, clause 1. The clause prohibits a State from passing any law that "impairs the obligation of contracts" or "makes any thing but gold and silver coin a tender in payment of debts". It states.

Exam Probability: **Medium**

19. *Answer choices:*

(see index for correct answer)

- a. Contract Clause
- b. Charles River Bridge v. Warren Bridge
- c. Smyth v. Ames

Guidance: level 1

:: Contract law ::

A _________, unlike a void contract, is a valid contract which may be either affirmed or rejected at the option of one of the parties. At most, one party to the contract is bound. The unbound party may repudiate the contract, at which time the contract becomes void.

Exam Probability: **High**

20. *Answer choices:*

(see index for correct answer)

- a. Tertius
- b. Rescission
- c. Non est factum
- d. Voidable contract

Guidance: level 1

:: ::

A _________ is a formal presentation of a matter such as a complaint, indictment or bill of exchange. In early-medieval England, juries of _________ would hear inquests in order to establish whether someone should be presented for a crime.

Exam Probability: **Low**

21. *Answer choices:*

(see index for correct answer)

- a. Presentment
- b. corporate values
- c. surface-level diversity
- d. co-culture

Guidance: level 1

:: Contract law ::

_________ is a legal process for collecting a monetary judgment on behalf of a plaintiff from a defendant. _________ allows the plaintiff to take the money or property of the debtor from the person or institution that holds that property . A similar legal mechanism called execution allows the seizure of money or property held directly by the debtor.

Exam Probability: **Medium**

22. *Answer choices:*

(see index for correct answer)

- a. Formal contract
- b. Garnishment
- c. Executory contract
- d. Collateral assurance

Guidance: level 1

:: Legal terms ::

An _________ is a legal and equitable remedy in the form of a special court order that compels a party to do or refrain from specific acts. "When a court employs the extraordinary remedy of _________ , it directs the conduct of a party, and does so with the backing of its full coercive powers." A party that fails to comply with an _________ faces criminal or civil penalties, including possible monetary sanctions and even imprisonment. They can also be charged with contempt of court. Counter _________ s are _________ s that stop or reverse the enforcement of another _________ .

Exam Probability: **Low**

23. *Answer choices:*

(see index for correct answer)

- a. Argumentative
- b. Harmless error
- c. Offer of proof
- d. Judicial estoppel

Guidance: level 1

:: ::

The _________ of 1977 is a United States federal law known primarily for two of its main provisions: one that addresses accounting transparency requirements under the Securities Exchange Act of 1934 and another concerning bribery of foreign officials. The Act was amended in 1988 and in 1998, and has been subject to continued congressional concerns, namely whether its enforcement discourages U.S. companies from investing abroad.

Exam Probability: **Medium**

24. *Answer choices:*

(see index for correct answer)

- a. deep-level diversity
- b. process perspective

- c. corporate values
- d. open system

Guidance: level 1

:: Business law ::

A __________ is a form of partnership similar to a general partnership except that while a general partnership must have at least two general partners , a __________ must have at least one GP and at least one limited partner.

Exam Probability: **Low**

25. *Answer choices:*

(see index for correct answer)

- a. Limited partnership
- b. Lessor
- c. Contract A
- d. Family and Medical Leave Act of 1993

Guidance: level 1

:: ::

__________ is a marketing communication that employs an openly sponsored, non-personal message to promote or sell a product, service or idea. Sponsors of __________ are typically businesses wishing to promote their products or services. __________ is differentiated from public relations in that an advertiser pays for and has control over the message. It differs from personal selling in that the message is non-personal, i.e., not directed to a particular individual. __________ is communicated through various mass media, including traditional media such as newspapers, magazines, television, radio, outdoor __________ or direct mail; and new media such as search results, blogs, social media, websites or text messages. The actual presentation of the message in a medium is referred to as an advertisement, or "ad" or advert for short.

Exam Probability: **Low**

26. *Answer choices:*

(see index for correct answer)

- a. open system
- b. Sarbanes-Oxley act of 2002
- c. corporate values
- d. Advertising

Guidance: level 1

:: ::

__________, in law, is a transaction or action that is valid but may be annulled by one of the parties to the transaction. __________ is usually used in distinction to void ab initio and unenforceable.

Exam Probability: **High**

27. *Answer choices:*

(see index for correct answer)

- a. hierarchical perspective
- b. levels of analysis
- c. Voidable
- d. co-culture

Guidance: level 1

:: Insurance terms ::

_________ is the assumption by a third party of another party`s legal right to collect a debt or damages. It is a legal doctrine whereby one person is entitled to enforce the subsisting or revived rights of another for one`s own benefit. A right of _________ typically arises by operation of law, but can also arise by statute or by agreement. _________ is an equitable remedy, having first developed in the English Court of Chancery. It is a familiar feature of common law systems. Analogous doctrines exist in civil law jurisdictions.

Exam Probability: **High**

28. *Answer choices:*

(see index for correct answer)

- a. Death spiral
- b. Wheel calculator
- c. Copayment
- d. Adjustment clause

Guidance: level 1

:: ::

The _________ Act of 1890 was a United States antitrust law that regulates competition among enterprises, which was passed by Congress under the presidency of Benjamin Harrison.

Exam Probability: **Medium**

29. *Answer choices:*

(see index for correct answer)

- a. Sherman Antitrust
- b. co-culture
- c. Sarbanes-Oxley act of 2002
- d. corporate values

Guidance: level 1

:: ::

A __________ is a formal written enactment of a legislative authority that governs the legal entities of a city, state, or country by way of consent. Typically, __________s command or prohibit something, or declare policy. __________s are rules made by legislative bodies; they are distinguished from case law or precedent, which is decided by courts, and regulations issued by government agencies.

Exam Probability: **High**

30. *Answer choices:*

(see index for correct answer)

- a. levels of analysis
- b. process perspective
- c. co-culture
- d. similarity-attraction theory

Guidance: level 1

:: ::

A __________ is a law passed by a legislative body in a common law system to set the maximum time after an event within which legal proceedings may be initiated.

Exam Probability: **Low**

31. *Answer choices:*

(see index for correct answer)

- a. Statute of limitations
- b. cultural
- c. information systems assessment
- d. Sarbanes-Oxley act of 2002

Guidance: level 1

:: ::

_________ is a concept of English common law and is a necessity for simple contracts but not for special contracts . The concept has been adopted by other common law jurisdictions, including the US.

Exam Probability: **High**

32. *Answer choices:*

(see index for correct answer)

- a. corporate values
- b. deep-level diversity
- c. similarity-attraction theory
- d. Consideration

Guidance: level 1

:: Generally Accepted Accounting Principles ::

Expenditure is an outflow of money to another person or group to pay for an item or service, or for a category of costs. For a tenant, rent is an _________ . For students or parents, tuition is an _________ . Buying food, clothing, furniture or an automobile is often referred to as an _________ . An _________ is a cost that is "paid" or "remitted", usually in exchange for something of value. Something that seems to cost a great deal is "expensive". Something that seems to cost little is "inexpensive". " _________ s of the table" are _________ s of dining, refreshments, a feast, etc.

Exam Probability: **High**

33. *Answer choices:*

(see index for correct answer)

- a. Reserve
- b. Expense
- c. Paid in capital
- d. Net income

Guidance: level 1

:: Business law ::

The ________ , first published in 1952, is one of a number of Uniform Acts that have been established as law with the goal of harmonizing the laws of sales and other commercial transactions across the United States of America through UCC adoption by all 50 states, the District of Columbia, and the Territories of the United States.

Exam Probability: **High**

34. *Answer choices:*

(see index for correct answer)

- a. Oppression remedy
- b. Apparent authority
- c. Uniform Commercial Code
- d. Holder

Guidance: level 1

:: Business ethics ::

________ is a type of harassment technique that relates to a sexual nature and the unwelcome or inappropriate promise of rewards in exchange for sexual favors. ________ includes a range of actions from mild transgressions to sexual abuse or assault. Harassment can occur in many different social settings such as the workplace, the home, school, churches, etc. Harassers or victims may be of any gender.

Exam Probability: **Low**

35. *Answer choices:*

(see index for correct answer)

- a. Conflict-of-interest editing on Wikipedia
- b. TG Soft
- c. Philosophy of business
- d. Equator Principles

Guidance: level 1

:: ::

_________ , or auditory perception, is the ability to perceive sounds by detecting vibrations, changes in the pressure of the surrounding medium through time, through an organ such as the ear. The academic field concerned with _________ is auditory science.

Exam Probability: **High**

36. *Answer choices:*

(see index for correct answer)

- a. Hearing
- b. interpersonal communication
- c. levels of analysis
- d. deep-level diversity

Guidance: level 1

:: Decision theory ::

Within economics the concept of _________ is used to model worth or value, but its usage has evolved significantly over time. The term was introduced initially as a measure of pleasure or satisfaction within the theory of utilitarianism by moral philosophers such as Jeremy Bentham and John Stuart Mill. But the term has been adapted and reapplied within neoclassical economics, which dominates modern economic theory, as a _________ function that represents a consumer`s preference ordering over a choice set. As such, it is devoid of its original interpretation as a measurement of the pleasure or satisfaction obtained by the consumer from that choice.

Exam Probability: **Medium**

37. *Answer choices:*

(see index for correct answer)

- a. Outcome primacy
- b. Rational planning model
- c. Feasible region
- d. Utility

Guidance: level 1

:: Equity (law) ::

An assignment is a legal term used in the context of the law of contract and of property. In both instances, assignment is the process whereby a person, the assignor, transfers rights or benefits to another, the _________ . An assignment may not transfer a duty, burden or detriment without the express agreement of the _________ . The right or benefit being assigned may be a gift or it may be paid for with a contractual consideration such as money.

Exam Probability: **Low**

38. *Answer choices:*

(see index for correct answer)

- a. Assignee
- b. assignor

Guidance: level 1

:: Legal doctrines and principles ::

In law, a _________ is an event sufficiently related to an injury that the courts deem the event to be the cause of that injury. There are two types of causation in the law: cause-in-fact, and proximate cause. Cause-in-fact is determined by the "but for" test: But for the action, the result would not have happened. The action is a necessary condition, but may not be a sufficient condition, for the resulting injury. A few circumstances exist where the but for test is ineffective . Since but-for causation is very easy to show , a second test is used to determine if an action is close enough to a harm in a "chain of events" to be legally valid. This test is called _________ . _________ is a key principle of Insurance and is concerned with how the loss or damage actually occurred. There are several competing theories of _________ . For an act to be deemed to cause a harm, both tests must be met; _________ is a legal limitation on cause-in-fact.

Exam Probability: **High**

39. *Answer choices:*

(see index for correct answer)

- a. Duty to rescue
- b. negligence
- c. Mutual assent
- d. Proximate cause

Guidance: level 1

:: United States federal public corruption crime ::

Mail fraud and __________ are federal crimes in the United States that involve mailing or electronically transmitting something associated with fraud. Jurisdiction is claimed by the federal government if the illegal activity crosses interstate or international borders.

Exam Probability: **High**

40. *Answer choices:*

(see index for correct answer)

- a. Wire fraud
- b. RICO Act

Guidance: level 1

:: ::

A contract is a legally-binding agreement which recognises and governs the rights and duties of the parties to the agreement. A contract is legally enforceable because it meets the requirements and approval of the law. An agreement typically involves the exchange of goods, services, money, or promises of any of those. In the event of breach of contract, the law awards the injured party access to legal remedies such as damages and cancellation.

Exam Probability: **Low**

41. *Answer choices:*

(see index for correct answer)

- a. surface-level diversity
- b. deep-level diversity
- c. hierarchical
- d. empathy

Guidance: level 1

:: Anti-competitive behaviour ::

Restraints of trade is a common law doctrine relating to the enforceability of contractual restrictions on freedom to conduct business. It is a precursor of modern competition law. In an old leading case of Mitchel v Reynolds Lord Smith LC said,

Exam Probability: **Medium**

42. *Answer choices:*

(see index for correct answer)

- a. History of United States antitrust law
- b. Net Book Agreement
- c. Restraint of trade
- d. Horizontal territorial allocation

Guidance: level 1

:: Contract law ::

Offer and acceptance analysis is a traditional approach in contract law. The offer and acceptance formula, developed in the 19th century, identifies a moment of formation when the parties are of one mind. This classical approach to contract formation has been modified by developments in the law of estoppel, misleading conduct, misrepresentation and unjust enrichment.

Exam Probability: **High**

43. *Answer choices:*

(see index for correct answer)

- a. Sweetheart deal
- b. Handshake deal
- c. Co-signing
- d. French contract law

Guidance: level 1

:: ::

An __________, for United States federal income tax, is a closely held corporation that makes a valid election to be taxed under Subchapter S of Chapter 1 of the Internal Revenue Code. In general, __________ s do not pay any income taxes. Instead, the corporation's income or losses are divided among and passed through to its shareholders. The shareholders must then report the income or loss on their own individual income tax returns.

Exam Probability: **Medium**

44. *Answer choices:*

(see index for correct answer)

- a. levels of analysis
- b. functional perspective
- c. cultural
- d. imperative

Guidance: level 1

:: International trade ::

A __________ is a document issued by a carrier to acknowledge receipt of cargo for shipment. Although the term historically related only to carriage by sea, a __________ may today be used for any type of carriage of goods.

Exam Probability: **Medium**

45. *Answer choices:*

(see index for correct answer)

- a. Currency substitution
- b. Westline
- c. Swiss Formula
- d. Bill of lading

Guidance: level 1

:: Services management and marketing ::

A __________ or servicemark is a trademark used in the United States and several other countries to identify a service rather than a product.

Exam Probability: **Low**

46. *Answer choices:*

(see index for correct answer)

- a. Service mark
- b. Business service provider
- c. Service climate
- d. Industrialization of services business model

Guidance: level 1

:: Meetings ::

A __________ is a body of one or more persons that is subordinate to a deliberative assembly. Usually, the assembly sends matters into a __________ as a way to explore them more fully than would be possible if the assembly itself were considering them. __________ s may have different functions and their type of work differ depending on the type of the organization and its needs.

Exam Probability: **High**

47. *Answer choices:*

(see index for correct answer)

- a. Extraordinary general meeting
- b. Speed geeking
- c. Committee
- d. Audience

Guidance: level 1

:: Contract law ::

In common law jurisdictions, an _________ is a contract law term for certain assurances that are presumed to be made in the sale of products or real property, due to the circumstances of the sale. These assurances are characterized as warranties irrespective of whether the seller has expressly promised them orally or in writing. They include an _________ of fitness for a particular purpose, an _________ of merchantability for products, _________ of workmanlike quality for services, and an _________ of habitability for a home.

Exam Probability: **High**

48. *Answer choices:*

(see index for correct answer)

- a. Terms of service
- b. Implied warranty
- c. Ticket cases
- d. Firm commitment

Guidance: level 1

:: ::

_________ is the act or practice of forbidding something by law; more particularly the term refers to the banning of the manufacture, storage , transportation, sale, possession, and consumption of alcoholic beverages. The word is also used to refer to a period of time during which such bans are enforced.

Exam Probability: **High**

49. *Answer choices:*

(see index for correct answer)

- a. personal values
- b. Prohibition
- c. Character
- d. functional perspective

Guidance: level 1

:: ::

__________ , in United States trademark law, is a statutory cause of action that permits a party to petition the Trademark Trial and Appeal Board of the Patent and Trademark Office to cancel a trademark registration that "may disparage or falsely suggest a connection with persons, living or dead, institutions, beliefs, or national symbols, or bring them into contempt or disrepute." Unlike claims regarding the validity of the mark, a __________ claim can be brought "at any time," subject to equitable defenses such as laches.

Exam Probability: **Low**

50. *Answer choices:*

(see index for correct answer)

- a. corporate values
- b. cultural
- c. Character
- d. Sarbanes-Oxley act of 2002

Guidance: level 1

:: Contract law ::

An __________ —or acceleration covenant— in the law of contracts, is a term that fully matures the performance due from a party upon a breach of the contract. Such clauses are most prevalent in mortgages and similar contracts to purchase real estate in installments.

Exam Probability: **Low**

51. *Answer choices:*

(see index for correct answer)

- a. Domicilium citandi et executandi
- b. Acceleration clause
- c. Firm commitment
- d. Formal contract

Guidance: level 1

:: Statutory law ::

_________ or statute law is written law set down by a body of legislature or by a singular legislator . This is as opposed to oral or customary law; or regulatory law promulgated by the executive or common law of the judiciary. Statutes may originate with national, state legislatures or local municipalities.

Exam Probability: **Medium**

52. *Answer choices:*

(see index for correct answer)

- a. Statutory Law
- b. statute law
- c. incorporation by reference
- d. Statute of repose

Guidance: level 1

:: ::

In regulatory jurisdictions that provide for it , __________ is a group of laws and organizations designed to ensure the rights of consumers as well as fair trade, competition and accurate information in the marketplace. The laws are designed to prevent the businesses that engage in fraud or specified unfair practices from gaining an advantage over competitors. They may also provides additional protection for those most vulnerable in society. __________ laws are a form of government regulation that aim to protect the rights of consumers. For example, a government may require businesses to disclose detailed information about products—particularly in areas where safety or public health is an issue, such as food.

Exam Probability: **Medium**

53. *Answer choices:*

(see index for correct answer)

- a. similarity-attraction theory
- b. Character
- c. deep-level diversity
- d. imperative

Guidance: level 1

:: ::

__________, also referred to as orthostasis, is a human position in which the body is held in an upright position and supported only by the feet.

Exam Probability: **High**

54. *Answer choices:*

(see index for correct answer)

- a. personal values
- b. similarity-attraction theory
- c. functional perspective
- d. imperative

Guidance: level 1

:: Marketing ::

A _________ is an overall experience of a customer that distinguishes an organization or product from its rivals in the eyes of the customer. _________ s are used in business, marketing, and advertising. Name _________ s are sometimes distinguished from generic or store _________ s.

Exam Probability: **Medium**

55. *Answer choices:*

(see index for correct answer)

- a. Corporate capabilities package
- b. Personalized marketing
- c. Performance-based advertising

- d. Consumer culture theory

Guidance: level 1

:: ::

In legal terminology, a _________ is any formal legal document that sets out the facts and legal reasons that the filing party or parties believes are sufficient to support a claim against the party or parties against whom the claim is brought that entitles the plaintiff to a remedy . For example, the Federal Rules of Civil Procedure that govern civil litigation in United States courts provide that a civil action is commenced with the filing or service of a pleading called a _________ . Civil court rules in states that have incorporated the Federal Rules of Civil Procedure use the same term for the same pleading.

Exam Probability: **High**

56. *Answer choices:*

(see index for correct answer)

- a. imperative
- b. Character
- c. Complaint
- d. functional perspective

Guidance: level 1

:: Legal procedure ::

An __________ is generally the first occasion that the trier of fact has to hear from a lawyer in a trial, aside possibly from questioning during voir dire. The __________ is generally constructed to serve as a "road map" for the fact-finder. This is especially essential, in many jury trials, since jurors know nothing at all about the case before the trial, . Though such statements may be dramatic and vivid, they must be limited to the evidence reasonably expected to be presented during the trial. Attorneys generally conclude __________s with a reminder that at the conclusion of evidence, the attorney will return to ask the fact-finder to find in his or her client`s favor.

Exam Probability: **Low**

57. *Answer choices:*

(see index for correct answer)

- a. appellate
- b. Closing argument
- c. civil procedure
- d. Procedural law

Guidance: level 1

:: ::

Advertising is a marketing communication that employs an openly sponsored, non-personal message to promote or sell a product, service or idea. Sponsors of advertising are typically businesses wishing to promote their products or services. Advertising is differentiated from public relations in that an advertiser pays for and has control over the message. It differs from personal selling in that the message is non-personal, i.e., not directed to a particular individual.Advertising is communicated through various mass media, including traditional media such as newspapers, magazines, television, radio, outdoor advertising or direct mail; and new media such as search results, blogs, social media, websites or text messages. The actual presentation of the message in a medium is referred to as an _________, or "ad" or advert for short.

Exam Probability: **High**

58. *Answer choices:*

(see index for correct answer)

- a. corporate values
- b. Advertisement
- c. cultural
- d. open system

Guidance: level 1

:: ::

An __________ is a criminal accusation that a person has committed a crime. In jurisdictions that use the concept of felonies, the most serious criminal offence is a felony; jurisdictions that do not use the felonies concept often use that of an indictable offence, an offence that requires an __________ .

Exam Probability: **Low**

59. *Answer choices:*

(see index for correct answer)

- a. similarity-attraction theory
- b. Sarbanes-Oxley act of 2002
- c. co-culture
- d. interpersonal communication

Guidance: level 1

Finance

Finance is a field that is concerned with the allocation (investment) of assets and liabilities over space and time, often under conditions of risk or uncertainty. Finance can also be defined as the science of money management. Participants in the market aim to price assets based on their risk level, fundamental value, and their expected rate of return. Finance can be split into three sub-categories: public finance, corporate finance and personal finance.

:: Generally Accepted Accounting Principles ::

An __________ or profit and loss account is one of the financial statements of a company and shows the company's revenues and expenses during a particular period.

Exam Probability: **Medium**

1. *Answer choices:*

(see index for correct answer)

- a. Earnings before interest, taxes and depreciation
- b. Write-off
- c. Access to finance
- d. AICPA Statements of Position

Guidance: level 1

:: ::

_________ is the production of products for use or sale using labour and machines, tools, chemical and biological processing, or formulation. The term may refer to a range of human activity, from handicraft to high tech, but is most commonly applied to industrial design, in which raw materials are transformed into finished goods on a large scale. Such finished goods may be sold to other manufacturers for the production of other, more complex products, such as aircraft, household appliances, furniture, sports equipment or automobiles, or sold to wholesalers, who in turn sell them to retailers, who then sell them to end users and consumers.

Exam Probability: **Medium**

2. *Answer choices:*

(see index for correct answer)

- a. Manufacturing
- b. interpersonal communication
- c. functional perspective
- d. empathy

Guidance: level 1

:: International trade ::

In finance, an _________ is the rate at which one currency will be exchanged for another. It is also regarded as the value of one country's currency in relation to another currency. For example, an interbank _________ of 114 Japanese yen to the United States dollar means that ¥114 will be exchanged for each US$1 or that US$1 will be exchanged for each ¥114. In this case it is said that the price of a dollar in relation to yen is ¥114, or equivalently that the price of a yen in relation to dollars is $1/114.

Exam Probability: **Low**

3. *Answer choices:*

(see index for correct answer)

- a. Team Canada Mission
- b. Swiss Formula
- c. Organisation for Economic Co-operation and Development
- d. Volga trade route

Guidance: level 1

:: ::

__________ or accountancy is the measurement, processing, and communication of financial information about economic entities such as businesses and corporations. The modern field was established by the Italian mathematician Luca Pacioli in 1494. __________, which has been called the "language of business", measures the results of an organization`s economic activities and conveys this information to a variety of users, including investors, creditors, management, and regulators. Practitioners of __________ are known as accountants. The terms " __________ " and "financial reporting" are often used as synonyms.

Exam Probability: **High**

4. *Answer choices:*

(see index for correct answer)

- a. hierarchical
- b. Accounting
- c. open system
- d. similarity-attraction theory

Guidance: level 1

:: Manufacturing ::

_________ s are goods that have completed the manufacturing process but have not yet been sold or distributed to the end user.

Exam Probability: **Low**

5. *Answer choices:*

(see index for correct answer)

- a. Tanning
- b. Manufacture of Cheddar cheese
- c. IEC 61511
- d. Manufacturing bill of materials

Guidance: level 1

:: Margin policy ::

In finance, a _________ is a standardized forward contract, a legal agreement to buy or sell something at a predetermined price at a specified time in the future, between parties not known to each other. The asset transacted is usually a commodity or financial instrument. The predetermined price the parties agree to buy and sell the asset for is known as the forward price. The specified time in the future—which is when delivery and payment occur—is known as the delivery date. Because it is a function of an underlying asset, a _________ is a derivative product.

Exam Probability: **Low**

6. *Answer choices:*

(see index for correct answer)

- a. Regulation T
- b. Futures contract

Guidance: level 1

:: Materials ::

A __________ , also known as a feedstock, unprocessed material, or primary commodity, is a basic material that is used to produce goods, finished products, energy, or intermediate materials which are feedstock for future finished products. As feedstock, the term connotes these materials are bottleneck assets and are highly important with regard to producing other products. An example of this is crude oil, which is a __________ and a feedstock used in the production of industrial chemicals, fuels, plastics, and pharmaceutical goods; lumber is a __________ used to produce a variety of products including all types of furniture. The term " __________ " denotes materials in minimally processed or unprocessed in states; e.g., raw latex, crude oil, cotton, coal, raw biomass, iron ore, air, logs, or water i.e. "...any product of agriculture, forestry, fishing and any other mineral that is in its natural form or which has undergone the transformation required to prepare it for internationally marketing in substantial volumes."

Exam Probability: **High**

7. *Answer choices:*

(see index for correct answer)

- a. Technora
- b. Coal tar
- c. Radiant barrier
- d. Raw material

Guidance: level 1

:: Basic financial concepts ::

_________ is a sustained increase in the general price level of goods and services in an economy over a period of time. When the general price level rises, each unit of currency buys fewer goods and services; consequently, _________ reflects a reduction in the purchasing power per unit of money a loss of real value in the medium of exchange and unit of account within the economy. The measure of _________ is the _________ rate, the annualized percentage change in a general price index, usually the consumer price index, over time. The opposite of _________ is deflation.

Exam Probability: **Low**

8. *Answer choices:*

(see index for correct answer)

- a. Present value of costs
- b. Inflation
- c. Eurodollar
- d. Lodgement

Guidance: level 1

:: Decision theory ::

A _________ is a deliberate system of principles to guide decisions and achieve rational outcomes. A _________ is a statement of intent, and is implemented as a procedure or protocol. Policies are generally adopted by a governance body within an organization. Policies can assist in both subjective and objective decision making. Policies to assist in subjective decision making usually assist senior management with decisions that must be based on the relative merits of a number of factors, and as a result are often hard to test objectively, e.g. work-life balance _________ . In contrast policies to assist in objective decision making are usually operational in nature and can be objectively tested, e.g. password _________ .

Exam Probability: **Low**

9. *Answer choices:*

(see index for correct answer)

- a. Cognitive bias
- b. Policy
- c. New Approach to Appraisal
- d. Inference engine

Guidance: level 1

:: Fixed income market ::

The _________ is a financial market where participants can issue new debt, known as the primary market, or buy and sell debt securities, known as the secondary market. This is usually in the form of bonds, but it may include notes, bills, and so on.

Exam Probability: **High**

10. *Answer choices:*

(see index for correct answer)

- a. Pool factor
- b. Yield curve
- c. Fixed-income attribution
- d. Bond market

Guidance: level 1

:: Fixed income market ::

In finance, the _________ is a curve showing several yields or interest rates across different contract lengths for a similar debt contract. The curve shows the relation between the interest rate and the time to maturity, known as the "term", of the debt for a given borrower in a given currency. For example, the U.S. dollar interest rates paid on U.S. Treasury securities for various maturities are closely watched by many traders, and are commonly plotted on a graph such as the one on the right which is informally called "the _________ ". More formal mathematical descriptions of this relation are often called the term structure of interest rates.

Exam Probability: **Low**

11. *Answer choices:*

(see index for correct answer)

- a. Yield curve
- b. Fixed income
- c. Bond market
- d. Fixed-income attribution

Guidance: level 1

:: Costs ::

In economics, _________ is the total economic cost of production and is made up of variable cost, which varies according to the quantity of a good produced and includes inputs such as labour and raw materials, plus fixed cost, which is independent of the quantity of a good produced and includes inputs that cannot be varied in the short term: fixed costs such as buildings and machinery, including sunk costs if any. Since cost is measured per unit of time, it is a flow variable.

Exam Probability: **Low**

12. *Answer choices:*

(see index for correct answer)

- a. Total cost

- b. Khozraschyot
- c. Implicit cost
- d. Direct materials cost

Guidance: level 1

:: Stock market ::

A __________, securities exchange or bourse, is a facility where stock brokers and traders can buy and sell securities, such as shares of stock and bonds and other financial instruments. __________s may also provide for facilities the issue and redemption of such securities and instruments and capital events including the payment of income and dividends. Securities traded on a __________ include stock issued by listed companies, unit trusts, derivatives, pooled investment products and bonds. __________s often function as "continuous auction" markets with buyers and sellers consummating transactions via open outcry at a central location such as the floor of the exchange or by using an electronic trading platform.

Exam Probability: **Medium**

13. *Answer choices:*

(see index for correct answer)

- a. Super-majority amendment
- b. Rogue trader
- c. Relative valuation
- d. Stock exchange

Guidance: level 1

:: Debt ::

__________ is when something, usually money, is owed by one party, the borrower or __________ or, to a second party, the lender or creditor. __________ is a deferred payment, or series of payments, that is owed in the future, which is what differentiates it from an immediate purchase. The __________ may be owed by sovereign state or country, local government, company, or an individual. Commercial __________ is generally subject to contractual terms regarding the amount and timing of repayments of principal and interest. Loans, bonds, notes, and mortgages are all types of __________. The term can also be used metaphorically to cover moral obligations and other interactions not based on economic value. For example, in Western cultures, a person who has been helped by a second person is sometimes said to owe a " __________ of gratitude" to the second person.

Exam Probability: **High**

14. *Answer choices:*

(see index for correct answer)

- a. Medical debt
- b. Tax benefits of debt
- c. Cessio bonorum
- d. Bailout

Guidance: level 1

:: Hazard analysis ::

Broadly speaking, a _________ is the combined effort of 1. identifying and analyzing potential events that may negatively impact individuals, assets, and/or the environment ; and 2. making judgments "on the tolerability of the risk on the basis of a risk analysis" while considering influencing factors . Put in simpler terms, a _________ analyzes what can go wrong, how likely it is to happen, what the potential consequences are, and how tolerable the identified risk is. As part of this process, the resulting determination of risk may be expressed in a quantitative or qualitative fashion. The _________ is an inherent part of an overall risk management strategy, which attempts to, after a _________ , "introduce control measures to eliminate or reduce" any potential risk-related consequences.

Exam Probability: **Low**

15. *Answer choices:*

(see index for correct answer)

- a. Hazard identification
- b. Hazardous Materials Identification System
- c. Swiss cheese model

Guidance: level 1

:: Financial ratios ::

The __________ is a financial ratio indicating the relative proportion of shareholders` equity and debt used to finance a company`s assets. Closely related to leveraging, the ratio is also known as risk, gearing or leverage. The two components are often taken from the firm`s balance sheet or statement of financial position , but the ratio may also be calculated using market values for both, if the company`s debt and equity are publicly traded, or using a combination of book value for debt and market value for equity financially.

Exam Probability: **Low**

16. *Answer choices:*

(see index for correct answer)

- a. Debt service ratio
- b. Debt-to-equity ratio
- c. Loan-to-value ratio
- d. Debtor collection period

Guidance: level 1

:: Free accounting software ::

A __________ is the principal book or computer file for recording and totaling economic transactions measured in terms of a monetary unit of account by account type, with debits and credits in separate columns and a beginning monetary balance and ending monetary balance for each account.

Exam Probability: **Low**

17. *Answer choices:*

(see index for correct answer)

- a. LedgerSMB
- b. Ofuz
- c. SQL-Ledger
- d. TurboCASH

Guidance: level 1

:: Social security ::

_________ is "any government system that provides monetary assistance to people with an inadequate or no income." In the United States, this is usually called welfare or a social safety net, especially when talking about Canada and European countries.

Exam Probability: **Low**

18. *Answer choices:*

(see index for correct answer)

- a. Social Security Board
- b. Shidu
- c. SNILS
- d. Social security

Guidance: level 1

:: Global systemically important banks ::

_________ Inc. or Citi is an American multinational investment bank and financial services corporation headquartered in New York City. The company was formed by the merger of banking giant Citicorp and financial conglomerate Travelers Group in 1998; Travelers was subsequently spun off from the company in 2002. _________ owns Citicorp, the holding company for Citibank, as well as several international subsidiaries.

Exam Probability: **Medium**

19. *Answer choices:*

(see index for correct answer)

- a. Sumitomo Mitsui Banking Corporation
- b. UniCredit
- c. The Bank of New York Mellon
- d. Citigroup

Guidance: level 1

:: Stock market ::

A share price is the price of a single share of a number of saleable stocks of a company, derivative or other financial asset.In layman`s terms, the _________ is the highest amount someone is willing to pay for the stock, or the lowest amount that it can be bought for.

Exam Probability: **High**

20. *Answer choices:*

(see index for correct answer)

- a. End of day
- b. Red herring prospectus
- c. Stock price
- d. Bear raid

Guidance: level 1

:: Accounting terminology ::

In management accounting or _________, managers use the provisions of accounting information in order to better inform themselves before they decide matters within their organizations, which aids their management and performance of control functions.

Exam Probability: **Low**

21. *Answer choices:*

(see index for correct answer)

- a. double-entry bookkeeping
- b. Accounts receivable
- c. Managerial accounting
- d. Cash flow management

Guidance: level 1

:: ::

_________ , often abbreviated as B/E in finance, is the point of balance making neither a profit nor a loss. The term originates in finance but the concept has been applied in other fields.

Exam Probability: **Medium**

22. *Answer choices:*

(see index for correct answer)

- a. process perspective
- b. information systems assessment
- c. cultural
- d. Break-even

Guidance: level 1

:: Legal terms ::

_________ s may be governments, corporations or investment trusts. _________ s are legally responsible for the obligations of the issue and for reporting financial conditions, material developments and any other operational activities as required by the regulations of their jurisdictions.

Exam Probability: **Medium**

23. *Answer choices:*

(see index for correct answer)

- a. Letter rogatory
- b. Fair comment
- c. Per curiam decision
- d. Issuer

Guidance: level 1

:: Economics terminology ::

A corporation`s share capital or _________ is the portion of a corporation`s equity that has been obtained by the issue of shares in the corporation to a shareholder, usually for cash. "Share capital" may also denote the number and types of shares that compose a corporation`s share structure.

Exam Probability: **High**

24. *Answer choices:*

(see index for correct answer)

- a. Physical capital
- b. Currency trading
- c. Normal profit
- d. capital accumulation

Guidance: level 1

:: ::

In marketing, a _________ is a ticket or document that can be redeemed for a financial discount or rebate when purchasing a product.

Exam Probability: **Medium**

25. *Answer choices:*

(see index for correct answer)

- a. Character
- b. surface-level diversity
- c. co-culture
- d. interpersonal communication

Guidance: level 1

:: Financial risk ::

The __________ on a financial investment is the expected value of its return . It is a measure of the center of the distribution of the random variable that is the return.

Exam Probability: **Low**

26. *Answer choices:*

(see index for correct answer)

- a. Expected return
- b. Deviation risk measure
- c. Global Association of Risk Professionals
- d. Operational risk management

Guidance: level 1

:: Generally Accepted Accounting Principles ::

In accounting, __________ , gross margin, sales profit, or credit sales is the difference between revenue and the cost of making a product or providing a service, before deducting overheads, payroll, taxation, and interest payments. This is different from operating profit . Gross margin is the term normally used in the U.S., while __________ is the more common usage in the UK and Australia.

Exam Probability: **Low**

27. *Answer choices:*

(see index for correct answer)

- a. Gross profit
- b. Generally Accepted Accounting Practice
- c. Construction in progress
- d. Petty cash

Guidance: level 1

:: Finance ::

_________ , in finance and accounting, means stated value or face value. From this come the expressions at par , over par and under par .

Exam Probability: **Medium**

28. *Answer choices:*

(see index for correct answer)

- a. Par value
- b. Cell Captive
- c. Financial econometrics
- d. Electronic communication network

Guidance: level 1

:: Financial ratios ::

The _________ or dividend-price ratio of a share is the dividend per share, divided by the price per share. It is also a company`s total annual dividend payments divided by its market capitalization, assuming the number of shares is constant. It is often expressed as a percentage.

Exam Probability: **Low**

29. *Answer choices:*

(see index for correct answer)

- a. Dividend yield
- b. Loss ratio
- c. Days sales outstanding
- d. Price-to-book ratio

Guidance: level 1

:: Fundamental analysis ::

_________ is the monetary value of earnings per outstanding share of common stock for a company.

Exam Probability: **Low**

30. *Answer choices:*

(see index for correct answer)

- a. Earnings per share
- b. Goldman Sachs asset management factor model
- c. Continuing value
- d. Restricted stock

Guidance: level 1

:: ::

An _________ is a contingent motivator. Traditional _________ s are extrinsic motivators which reward actions to yield a desired outcome. The effectiveness of traditional _________ s has changed as the needs of Western society have evolved. While the traditional _________ model is effective when there is a defined procedure and goal for a task, Western society started to require a higher volume of critical thinkers, so the traditional model became less effective. Institutions are now following a trend in implementing strategies that rely on intrinsic motivations rather than the extrinsic motivations that the traditional _________ s foster.

Exam Probability: **High**

31. *Answer choices:*

(see index for correct answer)

- a. open system
- b. Incentive
- c. deep-level diversity
- d. Sarbanes-Oxley act of 2002

Guidance: level 1

:: Loans ::

In corporate finance, a __________ is a medium- to long-term debt instrument used by large companies to borrow money, at a fixed rate of interest. The legal term " __________ " originally referred to a document that either creates a debt or acknowledges it, but in some countries the term is now used interchangeably with bond, loan stock or note. A __________ is thus like a certificate of loan or a loan bond evidencing the fact that the company is liable to pay a specified amount with interest and although the money raised by the __________ s becomes a part of the company`s capital structure, it does not become share capital. Senior __________ s get paid before subordinate __________ s, and there are varying rates of risk and payoff for these categories.

Exam Probability: **Medium**

32. *Answer choices:*

(see index for correct answer)

- a. Collateralized loan obligation
- b. Debenture
- c. Logbook loan
- d. Mortgage Assumption Value

Guidance: level 1

:: ::

__________ focuses on ratios, equities and debts. It is useful for portfolio management,distribution of dividend,capital raising,hedging and looking after fluctuations in foreign currency and product cycles.Financial managers are the people who will do research and based on the research, decide what sort of capital to obtain in order to fund the company`s assets as well as maximizing the value of the firm for all the stakeholders. It also refers to the efficient and effective management of money in such a manner as to accomplish the objectives of the organization. It is the specialized function directly associated with the top management. The significance of this function is not seen in the `Line` but also in the capacity of the `Staff` in overall of a company. It has been defined differently by different experts in the field.

Exam Probability: **High**

33. *Answer choices:*

(see index for correct answer)

- a. personal values
- b. hierarchical perspective
- c. open system
- d. Financial management

Guidance: level 1

:: Bonds (finance) ::

A _________ is a fund established by an economic entity by setting aside revenue over a period of time to fund a future capital expense, or repayment of a long-term debt.

Exam Probability: **Medium**

34. *Answer choices:*

(see index for correct answer)

- a. Securities Industry and Financial Markets Association
- b. Bond option
- c. Nominal yield
- d. Bond exchange offer

Guidance: level 1

:: Mutualism (movement) ::

A _________ is a professionally managed investment fund that pools money from many investors to purchase securities. These investors may be retail or institutional in nature.

Exam Probability: **High**

35. *Answer choices:*

(see index for correct answer)

- a. United States Federation of Worker Cooperatives
- b. Communal work
- c. Mutualism
- d. Mutual fund

Guidance: level 1

:: Business economics ::

In finance, _________ is the risk of losses caused by interest rate changes. The prices of most financial instruments, such as stocks and bonds move inversely with interest rates, so investors are subject to capital loss when rates rise.

Exam Probability: **Low**

36. *Answer choices:*

(see index for correct answer)

- a. Risk-seeking
- b. Risk pool
- c. Market area
- d. Round-tripping

Guidance: level 1

:: Basel II ::

All businesses take risks based on two factors: the probability an adverse circumstance will come about and the cost of such adverse circumstance.Risk management is the study of how to control risks and balance the possibility of gains.

Exam Probability: **Low**

37. *Answer choices:*

(see index for correct answer)

- a. Foundation IRB
- b. Standardized approach
- c. Basic indicator approach
- d. Market risk

Guidance: level 1

:: Investment ::

In finance, the benefit from an _________ is called a return. The return may consist of a gain realised from the sale of property or an _________ , unrealised capital appreciation , or _________ income such as dividends, interest, rental income etc., or a combination of capital gain and income. The return may also include currency gains or losses due to changes in foreign currency exchange rates.

Exam Probability: **High**

38. *Answer choices:*

(see index for correct answer)

- a. Investment
- b. Security market line
- c. Guaranteed investment contract
- d. Media for equity

Guidance: level 1

:: Banking ::

A _________ is a financial account maintained by a bank for a customer. A _________ can be a deposit account, a credit card account, a current account, or any other type of account offered by a financial institution, and represents the funds that a customer has entrusted to the financial institution and from which the customer can make withdrawals. Alternatively, accounts may be loan accounts in which case the customer owes money to the financial institution.

Exam Probability: **Medium**

39. *Answer choices:*

(see index for correct answer)

- a. Personal account
- b. Bank account
- c. Zombie bank
- d. Monetary base

Guidance: level 1

:: Investment ::

The __________ is a measure of an investment's rate of return. The term internal refers to the fact that the calculation excludes external factors, such as the risk-free rate, inflation, the cost of capital, or various financial risks.

Exam Probability: **High**

40. *Answer choices:*

(see index for correct answer)

- a. IFund
- b. Internal rate of return
- c. Investor lead

- d. Multi-manager investment

Guidance: level 1

:: Generally Accepted Accounting Principles ::

_________ is a small amount of discretionary funds in the form of cash used for expenditures where it is not sensible to make any disbursement by cheque, because of the inconvenience and costs of writing, signing, and then cashing the cheque.

Exam Probability: **Low**

41. *Answer choices:*

(see index for correct answer)

- a. Deferral
- b. Operating income before depreciation and amortization
- c. Goodwill
- d. Net income

Guidance: level 1

:: Basic financial concepts ::

In finance, maturity or _________ refers to the final payment date of a loan or other financial instrument, at which point the principal is due to be paid.

Exam Probability: **Medium**

42. *Answer choices:*

(see index for correct answer)

- a. Maturity date
- b. Leverage cycle
- c. Financial transaction
- d. Present value of costs

Guidance: level 1

:: ::

An _________ is the production of goods or related services within an economy. The major source of revenue of a group or company is the indicator of its relevant _________. When a large group has multiple sources of revenue generation, it is considered to be working in different industries. Manufacturing _________ became a key sector of production and labour in European and North American countries during the Industrial Revolution, upsetting previous mercantile and feudal economies. This came through many successive rapid advances in technology, such as the production of steel and coal.

Exam Probability: **High**

43. *Answer choices:*

(see index for correct answer)

- a. levels of analysis
- b. information systems assessment
- c. Industry
- d. corporate values

Guidance: level 1

:: Markets (customer bases) ::

In economics, _________ is the economic price for which a good or service is offered in the marketplace. It is of interest mainly in the study of microeconomics. Market value and _________ are equal only under conditions of market efficiency, equilibrium, and rational expectations.

Exam Probability: **High**

44. *Answer choices:*

(see index for correct answer)

- a. Perfect market
- b. Two-sided market
- c. Horizontal market

- d. Parity product

Guidance: level 1

:: Real estate valuation ::

_________ or OMV is the price at which an asset would trade in a competitive auction setting. _________ is often used interchangeably with open _________, fair value or fair _________, although these terms have distinct definitions in different standards, and may or may not differ in some circumstances.

Exam Probability: **Medium**

45. *Answer choices:*

(see index for correct answer)

- a. PropertyShark
- b. Lamudi
- c. International Right of Way Association
- d. Market value

Guidance: level 1

:: Inventory ::

_________ is the amount of inventory a company has in stock at the end of its fiscal year. It is closely related with _________ cost, which is the amount of money spent to get these goods in stock. It should be calculated at the lower of cost or market.

Exam Probability: **Medium**

46. *Answer choices:*

(see index for correct answer)

- a. Order picking
- b. Ending inventory
- c. Phantom inventory
- d. Spare part

Guidance: level 1

:: Generally Accepted Accounting Principles ::

The first published description of the process is found in Luca Pacioli`s 1494 work Summa de arithmetica, in the section titled Particularis de Computis et Scripturis. Although he did not use the term, he essentially prescribed a technique similar to a post-closing _________ .

Exam Probability: **High**

47. *Answer choices:*

(see index for correct answer)

- a. Financial position of the United States
- b. Depreciation
- c. Trial balance
- d. Paid in capital

Guidance: level 1

:: ::

A __________ is the process of presenting a topic to an audience. It is typically a demonstration, introduction, lecture, or speech meant to inform, persuade, inspire, motivate, or to build good will or to present a new idea or product. The term can also be used for a formal or ritualized introduction or offering, as with the __________ of a debutante. __________s in certain formats are also known as keynote address.

Exam Probability: **High**

48. *Answer choices:*

(see index for correct answer)

- a. levels of analysis
- b. Presentation
- c. personal values
- d. interpersonal communication

Guidance: level 1

:: ::

The __________ is a private, non-profit organization standard-setting body whose primary purpose is to establish and improve Generally Accepted Accounting Principles within the United States in the public`s interest. The Securities and Exchange Commission designated the FASB as the organization responsible for setting accounting standards for public companies in the US. The FASB replaced the American Institute of Certified Public Accountants` Accounting Principles Board on July 1, 1973.

Exam Probability: **High**

49. *Answer choices:*

(see index for correct answer)

- a. co-culture
- b. empathy
- c. hierarchical
- d. Financial Accounting Standards Board

Guidance: level 1

:: Management accounting ::

In economics, __________ s, indirect costs or overheads are business expenses that are not dependent on the level of goods or services produced by the business. They tend to be time-related, such as interest or rents being paid per month, and are often referred to as overhead costs. This is in contrast to variable costs, which are volume-related and unknown at the beginning of the accounting year. For a simple example, such as a bakery, the monthly rent for the baking facilities, and the monthly payments for the security system and basic phone line are __________ s, as they do not change according to how much bread the bakery produces and sells. On the other hand, the wage costs of the bakery are variable, as the bakery will have to hire more workers if the production of bread increases. Economists reckon __________ as a entry barrier for new entrepreneurs.

Exam Probability: **Medium**

50. *Answer choices:*

(see index for correct answer)

- a. Invested capital
- b. Management accounting
- c. Fixed cost
- d. Process costing

Guidance: level 1

:: Marketing ::

A __________ is an overall experience of a customer that distinguishes an organization or product from its rivals in the eyes of the customer. __________ s are used in business, marketing, and advertising. Name __________ s are sometimes distinguished from generic or store __________ s.

Exam Probability: **High**

51. *Answer choices:*

(see index for correct answer)

- a. Net idol
- b. Marketing communications planning framework
- c. Consumer culture theory
- d. Behance

Guidance: level 1

:: ::

__________ is the consumption and saving opportunity gained by an entity within a specified timeframe, which is generally expressed in monetary terms. For households and individuals, " __________ is the sum of all the wages, salaries, profits, interest payments, rents, and other forms of earnings received in a given period of time."

Exam Probability: **Medium**

52. *Answer choices:*

(see index for correct answer)

- a. Income
- b. personal values
- c. similarity-attraction theory
- d. surface-level diversity

Guidance: level 1

:: Inventory ::

It requires a detailed physical count, so that the company knows exactly how many of each goods brought on specific dates remained at year end inventory. When this information is found, the amount of goods are multiplied by their purchase cost at their purchase date, to get a number for the ending inventory cost.

Exam Probability: **Medium**

53. *Answer choices:*

(see index for correct answer)

- a. Stock obsolescence
- b. Decomposition
- c. Inventory optimization
- d. Cost of goods sold

Guidance: level 1

:: Retirement ::

An _________ is a series of payments made at equal intervals. Examples of annuities are regular deposits to a savings account, monthly home mortgage payments, monthly insurance payments and pension payments. Annuities can be classified by the frequency of payment dates. The payments may be made weekly, monthly, quarterly, yearly, or at any other regular interval of time.

Exam Probability: **Low**

54. *Answer choices:*

(see index for correct answer)

- a. Mortality drag
- b. Annuity
- c. Life annuity
- d. Retirement Estimator

Guidance: level 1

:: Pharmaceutical industry ::

A _________ is a document in which data collected for a clinical trial is first recorded. This data is usually later entered in the case report form. The International Conference on Harmonisation of Technical Requirements for Registration of Pharmaceuticals for Human Use guidelines define _________ s as "original documents, data, and records." _________ s contain source data, which is defined as "all information in original records and certified copies of original records of clinical findings, observations, or other activities in a clinical trial necessary for the reconstruction and evaluation of the trial."

Exam Probability: **Low**

55. *Answer choices:*

(see index for correct answer)

- a. RAJ Pharma
- b. BUKO Pharma-Kampagne
- c. Norwegian Medicines Agency
- d. Biodollar

Guidance: level 1

:: Management accounting ::

In finance, the _________ or net present worth applies to a series of cash flows occurring at different times. The present value of a cash flow depends on the interval of time between now and the cash flow. It also depends on the discount rate. NPV accounts for the time value of money. It provides a method for evaluating and comparing capital projects or financial products with cash flows spread over time, as in loans, investments, payouts from insurance contracts plus many other applications.

Exam Probability: **High**

56. *Answer choices:*

(see index for correct answer)

- a. Net present value
- b. Cost accounting
- c. Managerial risk accounting
- d. Variable Costing

Guidance: level 1

:: Accounting journals and ledgers ::

The subledger, or _________, provides details behind entries in the general ledger used in accounting. The subledger shows detail for part of the accounting records such as property and equipment, prepaid expenses, etc. The detail would include such items as date the item was purchased or expense incurred, a description of the item, the original balance, and the net book value. The total of the subledger would match the line item amount on the general ledger. This corresponding line item in the general ledger is referred to as the controlling account. The _________ balance is compared with its controlling account balance as part of the process of preparing a trial balance.

Exam Probability: **High**

57. *Answer choices:*

(see index for correct answer)

- a. Journal entry
- b. General journal
- c. Subledger
- d. Cash receipts journal

Guidance: level 1

:: Financial ratios ::

_________ is a measure of how revenue growth translates into growth in operating income. It is a measure of leverage, and of how risky, or volatile, a company's operating income is.

Exam Probability: **High**

58. *Answer choices:*

(see index for correct answer)

- a. Texas ratio
- b. Operating leverage
- c. Days payable outstanding
- d. Treynor ratio

Guidance: level 1

:: International trade ::

_________ involves the transfer of goods or services from one person or entity to another, often in exchange for money. A system or network that allows _________ is called a market.

Exam Probability: **Low**

59. *Answer choices:*

(see index for correct answer)

- a. Authorized economic operator
- b. Maquiladora
- c. Trade
- d. Umba sapphire

Guidance: level 1

Human resource management

Human resource (HR) management is the strategic approach to the effective management of organization workers so that they help the business gain a competitive advantage. It is designed to maximize employee performance in service of an employer's strategic objectives. HR is primarily concerned with the management of people within organizations, focusing on policies and on systems. HR departments are responsible for overseeing employee-benefits design, employee recruitment, training and development, performance appraisal, and rewarding (e.g., managing pay and benefit systems). HR also concerns itself with organizational change and industrial relations, that is, the balancing of organizational practices with requirements arising from collective bargaining and from governmental laws.

:: Industrial engineering ::

_________ is the formal process that sits alongside Requirements analysis and focuses on the human elements of the requirements.

Exam Probability: **Low**

1. *Answer choices:*

(see index for correct answer)

- a. PFD allowance
- b. Needs analysis
- c. Richard Muther
- d. Society of Industrial Engineering

Guidance: level 1

:: Parental leave ::

_________ , or family leave, is an employee benefit available in almost all countries. The term " _________ " may include maternity, paternity, and adoption leave; or may be used distinctively from "maternity leave" and "paternity leave" to describe separate family leave available to either parent to care for small children. In some countries and jurisdictions, "family leave" also includes leave provided to care for ill family members. Often, the minimum benefits and eligibility requirements are stipulated by law.

Exam Probability: **High**

2. *Answer choices:*

(see index for correct answer)

- a. Cleveland Board of Education v. LaFleur
- b. Maternity and Parental Leave, etc Regulations 1999
- c. Parental leave
- d. Geduldig v. Aiello

Guidance: level 1

:: Labor rights ::

A _________ is a wrong or hardship suffered, real or supposed, which forms legitimate grounds of complaint. In the past, the word meant the infliction or cause of hardship.

Exam Probability: **Low**

3. *Answer choices:*

(see index for correct answer)

- a. China Labor Watch
- b. Kate Mullany House
- c. China Labour Bulletin
- d. The Hyatt 100

Guidance: level 1

:: Labour relations ::

__________ is the practice of hiring more workers than are needed to perform a given job, or to adopt work procedures which appear pointless, complex and time-consuming merely to employ additional workers. The term "make-work" is sometimes used as a synonym for __________ .

Exam Probability: **High**

4. *Answer choices:*

(see index for correct answer)

- a. Broad left
- b. Featherbedding
- c. Employee voice
- d. Delta Board Council

Guidance: level 1

:: Human resource management ::

The __________ is a free online database that contains hundreds of occupational definitions to help students, job seekers, businesses and workforce development professionals to understand today`s world of work in the United States. It was developed under the sponsorship of the US Department of Labor/Employment and Training Administration through a grant to the North Carolina Employment Security Commission during the 1990s. John L. Holland`s vocational model, often referred to as the Holland Codes, is used in the "Interests" section of the O*NET.

Exam Probability: **High**

5. *Answer choices:*

(see index for correct answer)

- a. Senior management
- b. Focal Point Review
- c. Occupational Information Network
- d. Enterprise architecture

Guidance: level 1

:: Human resource management ::

Frederick Herzberg, an American psychologist, originally developed the concept of ` _________ ` in 1968, in an article that he published on pioneering studies at A T&T. The concept stemmed from Herzberg`s motivator-hygiene theory, which is based on the premise that job attitude is a construct of two independent factors, namely job satisfaction and job dissatisfaction. Job satisfaction encompasses intrinsic factors that arise from the work itself, including achievement and advancement; whilst job dissatisfaction stems from factors external to the actual work, including company policy and the quality of supervision.

Exam Probability: **Low**

6. *Answer choices:*

(see index for correct answer)

- a. Human relations movement
- b. Job enrichment
- c. Human resource policies
- d. Employee silence

Guidance: level 1

:: Recruitment ::

The _________ is an American nonprofit professional association established in 1956 in Bethlehem, Pennsylvania, for college career services, recruiting practitioners, and others who wish to hire the college educated.

Exam Probability: **Medium**

7. *Answer choices:*

(see index for correct answer)

- a. Vacancy led recruitment
- b. contract of employment
- c. South West African Native Labour Association
- d. Recruitment process insourcing

Guidance: level 1

:: Labor ::

_________ refers to the process of grouping activities into departments. Division of labour creates specialists who need coordination. This coordination is facilitated by grouping specialists together in departments.

Exam Probability: **Low**

8. *Answer choices:*

(see index for correct answer)

- a. Departmentalization
- b. Union label
- c. Dirty, dangerous and demeaning
- d. Hot desking

Guidance: level 1

:: Educational assessment and evaluation ::

An _________ is a component of a competence to do a certain kind of work at a certain level. Outstanding _________ can be considered "talent". An _________ may be physical or mental. _________ is inborn potential to do certain kinds of work whether developed or undeveloped. Ability is developed knowledge, understanding, learned or acquired abilities or attitude. The innate nature of _________ is in contrast to skills and achievement, which represent knowledge or ability that is gained through learning.

Exam Probability: **Medium**

9. *Answer choices:*

(see index for correct answer)

- a. Class rank
- b. Aptitude
- c. LJ Create
- d. National Testing Service

Guidance: level 1

:: Employment compensation ::

In government contracting, a _________ is defined as the hourly wage, usual benefits and overtime, paid to the majority of workers, laborers, and mechanics within a particular area. This is usually the union wage.

Exam Probability: **High**

10. *Answer choices:*

(see index for correct answer)

- a. Prevailing wage
- b. Medical Care and Sickness Benefits Convention, 1969
- c. Federal Wage System
- d. Pay Bands

Guidance: level 1

:: Employment compensation ::

_________s is a method for companies to give their management or employees a bonus if the company performs well financially. Such a method is called a `plan`. SARs resemble employee stock options in that the holder/employee benefits from an increase in stock price. They differ from options in that the holder/employee does not have to purchase anything to receive the proceeds. They are not required to pay the exercise price, but just receive the amount of the increase in cash or stock.

Exam Probability: **Low**

11. *Answer choices:*

(see index for correct answer)

- a. ADP, LLC
- b. Paid Educational Leave Convention, 1974
- c. Stock appreciation right
- d. Dearness allowance

Guidance: level 1

:: Behavior ::

_________ refers to behavior-change procedures that were employed during the 1970s and early 1980s. Based on methodological behaviorism, overt behavior was modified with presumed consequences, including artificial positive and negative reinforcement contingencies to increase desirable behavior, or administering positive and negative punishment and/or extinction to reduce problematic behavior. For the treatment of phobias, habituation and punishment were the basic principles used in flooding, a subcategory of desensitization.

Exam Probability: **High**

12. *Answer choices:*

(see index for correct answer)

- a. theory of reasoned action
- b. Behavior modification

Guidance: level 1

:: Organizational behavior ::

Greenberg introduced the concept of _________ with regard to how an employee judges the behaviour of the organization and the employee`s resulting attitude and behaviour. .

Exam Probability: **Low**

13. *Answer choices:*

(see index for correct answer)

- a. Self-policing
- b. Collaborative partnerships
- c. Achievement Motivation Inventory
- d. Organizational justice

Guidance: level 1

:: Business law ::

In professional sports, a __________ is a player who is eligible to freely sign with any club or franchise; i.e., not under contract to any specific team. The term is also used in reference to a player who is under contract at present but who is allowed to solicit offers from other teams. In some circumstances, the __________ `s options are limited by league rules.

Exam Probability: **Medium**

14. *Answer choices:*

(see index for correct answer)

- a. Contract failure
- b. Trading while insolvent
- c. Free agent
- d. Limited liability

Guidance: level 1

:: Behaviorism ::

In behavioral psychology, __________ is a consequence applied that will strengthen an organism`s future behavior whenever that behavior is preceded by a specific antecedent stimulus. This strengthening effect may be measured as a higher frequency of behavior , longer duration , greater magnitude , or shorter latency . There are two types of __________ , known as positive __________ and negative __________ ; positive is where by a reward is offered on expression of the wanted behaviour and negative is taking away an undesirable element in the persons environment whenever the desired behaviour is achieved.

Exam Probability: **High**

15. *Answer choices:*

(see index for correct answer)

- a. Systematic desensitization
- b. Reinforcement
- c. Programmed instruction
- d. social facilitation

Guidance: level 1

:: Recruitment ::

A __________ , also referred commonly as a career fair or career expo, is an event in which employers, recruiters, and schools give information to potential employees. Job seekers attend these while trying to make a good impression to potential coworkers by speaking face-to-face with one another, filling out résumés, and asking questions in attempt to get a good feel on the work needed. Likewise, online __________ s are held, giving job seekers another way to get in contact with probable employers using the internet.

Exam Probability: **Low**

16. *Answer choices:*

(see index for correct answer)

- a. Job fair

- b. Higher Education Recruitment Consortium
- c. Europass
- d. Staff Selection Commission

Guidance: level 1

:: Cognitive biases ::

In personality psychology, _________ is the degree to which people believe that they have control over the outcome of events in their lives, as opposed to external forces beyond their control. Understanding of the concept was developed by Julian B. Rotter in 1954, and has since become an aspect of personality studies. A person`s "locus" is conceptualized as internal or external .

Exam Probability: **Low**

17. *Answer choices:*

(see index for correct answer)

- a. Affect heuristic
- b. Forer effect
- c. Negativity bias
- d. Self-fulfilling prophecy

Guidance: level 1

:: ::

__________ medicine is an approach to medical practice intended to optimize decision-making by emphasizing the use of evidence from well-designed and well-conducted research. Although all medicine based on science has some degree of empirical support, EBM goes further, classifying evidence by its epistemologic strength and requiring that only the strongest types can yield strong recommendations; weaker types can yield only weak recommendations. The term was originally used to describe an approach to teaching the practice of medicine and improving decisions by individual physicians about individual patients. Use of the term rapidly expanded to include a previously described approach that emphasized the use of evidence in the design of guidelines and policies that apply to groups of patients and populations . It has subsequently spread to describe an approach to decision-making that is used at virtually every level of health care as well as other fields .

Exam Probability: **Medium**

18. *Answer choices:*

(see index for correct answer)

- a. surface-level diversity
- b. deep-level diversity
- c. Character
- d. Evidence-based

Guidance: level 1

:: Management education ::

_________ refers to simulation games that are used as an educational tool for teaching business. _________ s may be carried out for various business training such as: general management, finance, organizational behaviour, human resources, etc. Often, the term "business simulation" is used with the same meaning.

Exam Probability: **High**

19. *Answer choices:*

(see index for correct answer)

- a. Public administration
- b. Business game
- c. Doctor of Business Administration
- d. Foundry School

Guidance: level 1

:: Industrial agreements ::

_________ is a process in labour relations, where a trade union gains a new and superior entitlement from one employer and then uses that agreement as a precedent to demand the same entitlement or a superior one from other employers.

Exam Probability: **High**

20. *Answer choices:*

(see index for correct answer)

- a. Collaborative bargaining
- b. McCrone Agreement
- c. Union security agreement
- d. Ex parte H.V. McKay

Guidance: level 1

:: Validity (statistics) ::

__________ is the extent to which a test accurately measures what it is supposed to measure. In the fields of psychological testing and educational testing, "validity refers to the degree to which evidence and theory support the interpretations of test scores entailed by proposed uses of tests". Although classical models divided the concept into various "validities" , the currently dominant view is that validity is a single unitary construct.

Exam Probability: **Low**

21. *Answer choices:*

(see index for correct answer)

- a. Test validity
- b. Verification and validation
- c. Content validity
- d. Statistical conclusion

Guidance: level 1

:: Management ::

A _________ is when two or more people come together to discuss one or more topics, often in a formal or business setting, but _________ s also occur in a variety of other environments. Many various types of _________ s exist.

Exam Probability: **High**

22. *Answer choices:*

(see index for correct answer)

- a. Interim management
- b. Meeting
- c. Bed management
- d. Management entrenchment

Guidance: level 1

:: Job interview ::

An __________ is a survey conducted with an individual who is separating from an organization or relationship. Most commonly, this occurs between an employee and an organization, a student and an educational institution, or a member and an association. An organization can use the information gained from an __________ to assess what should be improved, changed, or remain intact. More so, an organization can use the results from __________ s to reduce employee, student, or member turnover and increase productivity and engagement, thus reducing the high costs associated with turnover. Some examples of the value of conducting __________ s include shortening the recruiting and hiring process, reducing absenteeism, improving innovation, sustaining performance, and reducing possible litigation if issues mentioned in the __________ are addressed. It is important for each organization to customize its own __________ in order to maintain the highest levels of survey validity and reliability.

Exam Probability: **High**

23. *Answer choices:*

(see index for correct answer)

- a. Informational interview
- b. Exit interview
- c. Mock interview
- d. Microsoft interview

Guidance: level 1

:: Life skills ::

_________ , emotional leadership , emotional quotient and _________ quotient , is the capability of individuals to recognize their own emotions and those of others, discern between different feelings and label them appropriately, use emotional information to guide thinking and behavior, and manage and/or adjust emotions to adapt to environments or achieve one`s goal.

Exam Probability: **High**

24. *Answer choices:*

(see index for correct answer)

- a. multiple intelligence
- b. coping mechanism
- c. emotion work
- d. Emotional intelligence

Guidance: level 1

:: Management ::

_________ is a technique used by some employers to rotate their employees` assigned jobs throughout their employment. Employers practice this technique for a number of reasons. It was designed to promote flexibility of employees and to keep employees interested into staying with the company/organization which employs them. There is also research that shows how _________ s help relieve the stress of employees who work in a job that requires manual labor.

Exam Probability: **Low**

25. *Answer choices:*

(see index for correct answer)

- a. Power to the edge
- b. Managing stage boundaries
- c. Job rotation
- d. Records manager

Guidance: level 1

:: Employee relations ::

The __________ can be used to bring together employment and job-related information which employees need to know. It typically has three types of content.

Exam Probability: **High**

26. *Answer choices:*

(see index for correct answer)

- a. Industry Federation of the State of Rio de Janeiro
- b. Employee morale
- c. Employee handbook
- d. Employee motivation

Guidance: level 1

:: ::

_________ is the process of collecting, analyzing and/or reporting information regarding the performance of an individual, group, organization, system or component. _________ is not a new concept, some of the earliest records of human activity relate to the counting or recording of activities.

Exam Probability: **Medium**

27. *Answer choices:*

(see index for correct answer)

- a. Character
- b. deep-level diversity
- c. surface-level diversity
- d. interpersonal communication

Guidance: level 1

:: Foreign workers ::

A __________ or guest worker is a human who works in a country other than the one of which he or she is a citizen. Some __________ s are using a guest worker program in a country with more preferred job prospects than their home country. Guest workers are often either sent or invited to work outside their home country, or have acquired a job before they left their home country, whereas migrant workers often leave their home country without having a specific job at hand.

Exam Probability: **Medium**

28. *Answer choices:*

(see index for correct answer)

- a. Migrant domestic workers
- b. Foreign workers in Saudi Arabia
- c. Kalayaan
- d. Foreign worker

Guidance: level 1

:: Types of marketing ::

In microeconomics and management, __________ is an arrangement in which the supply chain of a company is owned by that company. Usually each member of the supply chain produces a different product or service, and the products combine to satisfy a common need. It is contrasted with horizontal integration, wherein a company produces several items which are related to one another. __________ has also described management styles that bring large portions of the supply chain not only under a common ownership, but also into one corporation .

Exam Probability: **Low**

29. *Answer choices:*

(see index for correct answer)

- a. Limited edition candy
- b. Consumer Generated Advertising
- c. Community marketing
- d. Vertical integration

Guidance: level 1

:: Organizational structure ::

An _________ defines how activities such as task allocation, coordination, and supervision are directed toward the achievement of organizational aims.

Exam Probability: **Medium**

30. *Answer choices:*

(see index for correct answer)

- a. The Starfish and the Spider
- b. Followership
- c. Blessed Unrest
- d. Organizational structure

Guidance: level 1

:: Multiple choice ::

The __________ is a standardized psychometric test of adult personality and psychopathology. Psychologists and other mental health professionals use various versions of the MMPI to help develop treatment plans; assist with differential diagnosis; help answer legal questions ; screen job candidates during the personnel selection process; or as part of a therapeutic assessment procedure.

Exam Probability: **Low**

31. *Answer choices:*

(see index for correct answer)

- a. Eddy Test
- b. Millon Clinical Multiaxial Inventory
- c. Minnesota Multiphasic Personality Inventory
- d. Multiple choice

Guidance: level 1

:: Recruitment ::

_________ is a recruitment strategy that uses mobile technology to attract, engage and convert candidates. Common _________ tactics include mobile career sites, _________ by text, _________ apps and social recruiting. _________ is often cited as a growing opportunity for recruiters to connect with candidates more efficiently with "over 89% of job seekers saying their mobile device will be an important tool and resource for their job search." Traditionally, recruiters have used emails and phone calls to engage candidates, but the increase in mobile usage among job seekers has contributed to _________`s rising popularity.

Exam Probability: **Medium**

32. *Answer choices:*

(see index for correct answer)

- a. Employment discrimination against persons with criminal records in the United States
- b. Mobile recruiting
- c. Internet recruiting
- d. Witwatersrand Native Labour Association

Guidance: level 1

:: Employment ::

A flat organization has an organizational structure with few or no levels of middle management between staff and executives. An organization`s structure refers to the nature of the distribution of the units and positions within it, also to the nature of the relationships among those units and positions. Tall and flat organizations differ based on how many levels of management are present in the organization, and how much control managers are endowed with.

Exam Probability: **Low**

33. *Answer choices:*

(see index for correct answer)

- a. EuroMayDay
- b. Fly-in fly-out
- c. Service voucher
- d. Delayering

Guidance: level 1

:: Workplace ::

A __________ is a process through which feedback from an employee`s subordinates, colleagues, and supervisor, as well as a self-evaluation by the employee themselves is gathered. Such feedback can also include, when relevant, feedback from external sources who interact with the employee, such as customers and suppliers or other interested stakeholders. __________ is so named because it solicits feedback regarding an employee`s behavior from a variety of points of view . It therefore may be contrasted with "downward feedback" , or "upward feedback" delivered to supervisory or management employees by subordinates only.

Exam Probability: **Low**

34. *Answer choices:*

(see index for correct answer)

- a. Feminisation of the workplace
- b. Workplace aggression
- c. Control freak
- d. Staff turnover

Guidance: level 1

:: Employment ::

__________ is measuring the output of a particular business process or procedure, then modifying the process or procedure to increase the output, increase efficiency, or increase the effectiveness of the process or procedure. __________ can be applied to either individual performance such as an athlete or organizational performance such as a racing team or a commercial business.

Exam Probability: **Low**

35. *Answer choices:*

(see index for correct answer)

- a. Iron rice bowl
- b. Mountbatten Institute
- c. Performance improvement
- d. Per diem

Guidance: level 1

:: Labor terms ::

_________ , often called DI or disability income insurance, or income protection, is a form of insurance that insures the beneficiary`s earned income against the risk that a disability creates a barrier for a worker to complete the core functions of their work. For example, the worker may suffer from an inability to maintain composure in the case of psychological disorders or an injury, illness or condition that causes physical impairment or incapacity to work. It encompasses paid sick leave, short-term disability benefits , and long-term disability benefits . Statistics show that in the US a disabling accident occurs, on average, once every second. In fact, nearly 18.5% of Americans are currently living with a disability, and 1 out of every 4 persons in the US workforce will suffer a disabling injury before retirement.

Exam Probability: **High**

36. *Answer choices:*

(see index for correct answer)

- a. Displaced workers
- b. Civilian workers
- c. Civilian noninstitutional population
- d. Disability insurance

Guidance: level 1

:: ::

A __________ is an occupation founded upon specialized educational training, the purpose of which is to supply disinterested objective counsel and service to others, for a direct and definite compensation, wholly apart from expectation of other business gain. The term is a truncation of the term "liberal __________ ", which is, in turn, an Anglicization of the French term " __________ libérale". Originally borrowed by English users in the 19th century, it has been re-borrowed by international users from the late 20th, though the class overtones of the term do not seem to survive retranslation: "liberal __________ s" are, according to the European Union`s Directive on Recognition of __________ al Qualifications "those practiced on the basis of relevant __________ al qualifications in a personal, responsible and __________ ally independent capacity by those providing intellectual and conceptual services in the interest of the client and the public".

Exam Probability: **High**

37. *Answer choices:*

(see index for correct answer)

- a. corporate values
- b. deep-level diversity
- c. Profession
- d. surface-level diversity

Guidance: level 1

:: Evaluation methods ::

In social psychology, _________ is the process of looking at oneself in order to assess aspects that are important to one`s identity. It is one of the motives that drive self-evaluation, along with self-verification and self-enhancement. Sedikides suggests that the _________ motive will prompt people to seek information to confirm their uncertain self-concept rather than their certain self-concept and at the same time people use _________ to enhance their certainty of their own self-knowledge. However, the _________ motive could be seen as quite different from the other two self-evaluation motives. Unlike the other two motives through _________ people are interested in the accuracy of their current self view, rather than improving their self-view. This makes _________ the only self-evaluative motive that may cause a person`s self-esteem to be damaged.

Exam Probability: **High**

38. *Answer choices:*

(see index for correct answer)

- a. Self-assessment
- b. Pick chart

- c. Video ethnography
- d. Moral statistics

Guidance: level 1

:: ::

_________ is the amount of time someone works beyond normal working hours. The term is also used for the pay received for this time. Normal hours may be determined in several ways.

Exam Probability: **Low**

39. *Answer choices:*

(see index for correct answer)

- a. levels of analysis
- b. deep-level diversity
- c. Overtime
- d. co-culture

Guidance: level 1

:: Stochastic processes ::

__________ in its modern meaning is a "new idea, creative thoughts, new imaginations in form of device or method". __________ is often also viewed as the application of better solutions that meet new requirements, unarticulated needs, or existing market needs. Such __________ takes place through the provision of more-effective products, processes, services, technologies, or business models that are made available to markets, governments and society. An __________ is something original and more effective and, as a consequence, new, that "breaks into" the market or society. __________ is related to, but not the same as, invention, as __________ is more apt to involve the practical implementation of an invention to make a meaningful impact in the market or society, and not all __________s require an invention. __________ often manifests itself via the engineering process, when the problem being solved is of a technical or scientific nature. The opposite of __________ is exnovation.

Exam Probability: **Medium**

40. *Answer choices:*

(see index for correct answer)

- a. Innovation
- b. Time reversibility
- c. G/M/1 queue
- d. Ehrenfest model

Guidance: level 1

:: ::

__________ is a form of government characterized by strong central power and limited political freedoms. Individual freedoms are subordinate to the state and there is no constitutional accountability and rule of law under an authoritarian regime. Authoritarian regimes can be autocratic with power concentrated in one person or it can be more spread out between multiple officials and government institutions. Juan Linz`s influential 1964 description of _________ characterized authoritarian political systems by four qualities.

Exam Probability: **Medium**

41. *Answer choices:*

(see index for correct answer)

- a. hierarchical perspective
- b. levels of analysis
- c. imperative
- d. functional perspective

Guidance: level 1

:: ::

_________ is overt or covert, often harmful, social interaction with the intention of inflicting damage or other unpleasantness upon another individual. It may occur either reactively or without provocation. In humans, frustration due to blocked goals can cause _________. Human _________ can be classified into direct and indirect _________; whilst the former is characterized by physical or verbal behavior intended to cause harm to someone, the latter is characterized by behavior intended to harm the social relations of an individual or group.

Exam Probability: **Medium**

42. *Answer choices:*

(see index for correct answer)

- a. co-culture
- b. Character
- c. Aggression
- d. deep-level diversity

Guidance: level 1

:: Human resource management ::

_________ refers to the ability of an organization to retain its employees. _________ can be represented by a simple statistic . However, many consider _________ as relating to the efforts by which employers attempt to retain the employees in their workforce. In this sense, retention becomes the strategies rather than the outcome.

Exam Probability: **Low**

43. *Answer choices:*

(see index for correct answer)

- a. Employee retention
- b. Workforce management
- c. Action alert
- d. Employee silence

Guidance: level 1

:: Employment discrimination ::

A _________ is a metaphor used to represent an invisible barrier that keeps a given demographic from rising beyond a certain level in a hierarchy.

Exam Probability: **Low**

44. *Answer choices:*

(see index for correct answer)

- a. New South Wales selection bias
- b. Marriage bars
- c. LGBT employment discrimination in the United States
- d. United Kingdom employment equality law

Guidance: level 1

:: Management ::

In business, a _________ is the attribute that allows an organization to outperform its competitors. A _________ may include access to natural resources, such as high-grade ores or a low-cost power source, highly skilled labor, geographic location, high entry barriers, and access to new technology.

Exam Probability: **High**

45. *Answer choices:*

(see index for correct answer)

- a. Competitive advantage
- b. Crisis management
- c. Certified management consultant
- d. Meeting

Guidance: level 1

:: Production and manufacturing ::

_________ consists of organization-wide efforts to "install and make permanent climate where employees continuously improve their ability to provide on demand products and services that customers will find of particular value." "Total" emphasizes that departments in addition to production are obligated to improve their operations; "management" emphasizes that executives are obligated to actively manage quality through funding, training, staffing, and goal setting. While there is no widely agreed-upon approach, TQM efforts typically draw heavily on the previously developed tools and techniques of quality control. TQM enjoyed widespread attention during the late 1980s and early 1990s before being overshadowed by ISO 9000, Lean manufacturing, and Six Sigma.

Exam Probability: **Low**

46. *Answer choices:*

(see index for correct answer)

- a. Process control
- b. Nuffield Tools and Gauges
- c. Total Quality Management
- d. Production plan

Guidance: level 1

:: Offshoring ::

Outsourcing is an agreement in which one company hires another company to be responsible for a planned or existing activity that is or could be done internally,and sometimes involves transferring employees and assets from one firm to another.

Exam Probability: **Medium**

47. *Answer choices:*

(see index for correct answer)

- a. Body shopping
- b. Global labor arbitrage
- c. Nearshoring
- d. Software testing outsourcing

Guidance: level 1

:: ::

__________ involves the development of an action plan designed to motivate and guide a person or group toward a goal. __________ can be guided by goal-setting criteria such as SMART criteria. __________ is a major component of personal-development and management literature.

Exam Probability: **Medium**

48. *Answer choices:*

(see index for correct answer)

- a. interpersonal communication
- b. levels of analysis
- c. hierarchical perspective

- d. imperative

Guidance: level 1

:: ::

_________ is a form of development in which a person called a coach supports a learner or client in achieving a specific personal or professional goal by providing training and guidance. The learner is sometimes called a coachee. Occasionally, _________ may mean an informal relationship between two people, of whom one has more experience and expertise than the other and offers advice and guidance as the latter learns; but _________ differs from mentoring in focusing on specific tasks or objectives, as opposed to more general goals or overall development.

Exam Probability: **Low**

49. *Answer choices:*

(see index for correct answer)

- a. interpersonal communication
- b. process perspective
- c. Coaching
- d. levels of analysis

Guidance: level 1

:: Sociological theories ::

A _________ is a systematic process for determining and addressing needs, or "gaps" between current conditions and desired conditions or "wants". The discrepancy between the current condition and wanted condition must be measured to appropriately identify the need. The need can be a desire to improve current performance or to correct a deficiency.

Exam Probability: **Low**

50. *Answer choices:*

(see index for correct answer)

- a. comfort zone
- b. Needs assessment
- c. social constructionism
- d. resource mobilization

Guidance: level 1

:: Industrial agreements ::

A ________ , in labor relations, is a group of employees with a clear and identifiable community of interests who are represented by a single labor union in collective bargaining and other dealings with management. Examples would be non-management professors, law enforcement professionals, blue-collar workers, clerical and administrative employees, etc. Geographic location as well as the number of facilities included in ________ s can be at issue during representation cases.

Exam Probability: **Medium**

51. *Answer choices:*

(see index for correct answer)

- a. McCrone Agreement
- b. Collective bargaining
- c. Industrial Disputes Act 1947
- d. Industrial arbitration

Guidance: level 1

:: Psychometrics ::

In statistics and research, ________ is typically a measure based on the correlations between different items on the same test . It measures whether several items that propose to measure the same general construct produce similar scores. For example, if a respondent expressed agreement with the statements "I like to ride bicycles" and "I've enjoyed riding bicycles in the past", and disagreement with the statement "I hate bicycles", this would be indicative of good ________ of the test.

Exam Probability: **High**

52. *Answer choices:*

(see index for correct answer)

- a. Congruence coefficient
- b. Bipolar spectrum diagnostic scale
- c. Sequential probability ratio test
- d. Statistical inference

Guidance: level 1

:: Management ::

_________ or executive pay is composed of the financial compensation and other non-financial awards received by an executive from their firm for their service to the organization. It is typically a mixture of salary, bonuses, shares of or call options on the company stock, benefits, and perquisites, ideally configured to take into account government regulations, tax law, the desires of the organization and the executive, and rewards for performance.

Exam Probability: **Low**

53. *Answer choices:*

(see index for correct answer)

- a. Corporate transparency
- b. Dynamic enterprise modeling

- c. Twelve leverage points
- d. Executive compensation

Guidance: level 1

:: United Kingdom labour law ::

The _________ was a series of programs, public work projects, financial reforms, and regulations enacted by President Franklin D. Roosevelt in the United States between 1933 and 1936. It responded to needs for relief, reform, and recovery from the Great Depression. Major federal programs included the Civilian Conservation Corps , the Civil Works Administration , the Farm Security Administration , the National Industrial Recovery Act of 1933 and the Social Security Administration . They provided support for farmers, the unemployed, youth and the elderly. The _________ included new constraints and safeguards on the banking industry and efforts to re-inflate the economy after prices had fallen sharply. _________ programs included both laws passed by Congress as well as presidential executive orders during the first term of the presidency of Franklin D. Roosevelt.

Exam Probability: **Medium**

54. *Answer choices:*

(see index for correct answer)

- a. Transnational Works Council Directive
- b. Working Time Regulations 1998
- c. Paternity and Adoption Leave Regulations 2002
- d. Coal Industry Commission Act 1919

Guidance: level 1

:: Employee relations ::

__________ are tools used by organizational leadership to gain feedback on and measure employee engagement, employee morale, and performance. Usually answered anonymously, surveys are also used to gain a holistic picture of employees` feelings on such areas as working conditions, supervisory impact, and motivation that regular channels of communication may not. Surveys are considered effective in this regard provided they are well-designed, effectively administered, have validity, and evoke changes and improvements.

Exam Probability: **Medium**

55. *Answer choices:*

(see index for correct answer)

- a. Employee morale
- b. Industry Federation of the State of Rio de Janeiro
- c. employee stock ownership
- d. Employee surveys

Guidance: level 1

:: Parental leave ::

__________ is a type of employment discrimination that occurs when expectant women are fired, not hired, or otherwise discriminated against due to their pregnancy or intention to become pregnant. Common forms of __________ include not being hired due to visible pregnancy or likelihood of becoming pregnant, being fired after informing an employer of one`s pregnancy, being fired after maternity leave, and receiving a pay dock due to pregnancy. Convention on the Elimination of All Forms of Discrimination against Women prohibits dismissal on the grounds of maternity or pregnancy and ensures right to maternity leave or comparable social benefits. The Maternity Protection Convention C 183 proclaims adequate protection for pregnancy as well. Though women have some protection in the United States because of the __________ Act of 1978, it has not completely curbed the incidence of __________ . The Equal Rights Amendment could ensure more robust sex equality ensuring that women and men could both work and have children at the same time.

Exam Probability: **High**

56. *Answer choices:*

(see index for correct answer)

- a. Parental leave
- b. Motherhood penalty
- c. Pregnancy discrimination
- d. Parental leave economics

Guidance: level 1

:: Organizational theory ::

_________ is the process of creating, retaining, and transferring knowledge within an organization. An organization improves over time as it gains experience. From this experience, it is able to create knowledge. This knowledge is broad, covering any topic that could better an organization. Examples may include ways to increase production efficiency or to develop beneficial investor relations. Knowledge is created at four different units: individual, group, organizational, and inter organizational.

Exam Probability: **High**

57. *Answer choices:*

(see index for correct answer)

- a. Cooperation
- b. Contingency theory
- c. Organizational learning
- d. Formal consensus

Guidance: level 1

:: Business law ::

A _________ is an arrangement where parties, known as partners, agree to cooperate to advance their mutual interests. The partners in a _________ may be individuals, businesses, interest-based organizations, schools, governments or combinations. Organizations may partner to increase the likelihood of each achieving their mission and to amplify their reach. A _________ may result in issuing and holding equity or may be only governed by a contract.

Exam Probability: **High**

58. *Answer choices:*

(see index for correct answer)

- a. European Patent Convention
- b. Partnership
- c. Agency in English law
- d. Personal Property Security Act

Guidance: level 1

:: ::

_______ is the extraction of valuable minerals or other geological materials from the earth, usually from an ore body, lode, vein, seam, reef or placer deposit. These deposits form a mineralized package that is of economic interest to the miner.

Exam Probability: **Medium**

59. *Answer choices:*

(see index for correct answer)

- a. Sarbanes-Oxley act of 2002
- b. interpersonal communication
- c. co-culture

- d. process perspective

Guidance: level 1

Information systems

Information systems (IS) are formal, sociotechnical, organizational systems designed to collect, process, store, and distribute information. In a sociotechnical perspective Information Systems are composed by four components: technology, process, people and organizational structure.

:: Business process ::

_________ is a discipline in operations management in which people use various methods to discover, model, analyze, measure, improve, optimize, and automate business processes. BPM focuses on improving corporate performance by managing business processes. Any combination of methods used to manage a company`s business processes is BPM. Processes can be structured and repeatable or unstructured and variable. Though not required, enabling technologies are often used with BPM.

Exam Probability: **Low**

1. *Answer choices:*

(see index for correct answer)

- a. Business logic
- b. Business process reengineering
- c. Business operations
- d. Tenant screening

Guidance: level 1

:: Information systems ::

A _________ is an information system that supports business or organizational decision-making activities. DSSs serve the management, operations and planning levels of an organization and help people make decisions about problems that may be rapidly changing and not easily specified in advance—i.e. unstructured and semi-structured decision problems. _________ s can be either fully computerized or human-powered, or a combination of both.

Exam Probability: **Low**

2. *Answer choices:*

(see index for correct answer)

- a. Legal expert system
- b. Credit bureau
- c. Enterprise information access
- d. Decision support system

Guidance: level 1

:: Data collection ::

_________ is the application of data mining techniques to discover patterns from the World Wide Web. As the name proposes, this is information gathered by mining the web. It makes utilization of automated apparatuses to reveal and extricate data from servers and web2 reports, and it permits organizations to get to both organized and unstructured information from browser activities, server logs, website and link structure, page content and different sources.

Exam Probability: **Medium**

3. *Answer choices:*

(see index for correct answer)

- a. Web mining
- b. Dye tracing

- c. Synthetic Environment for Analysis and Simulations
- d. Concrete slump test

Guidance: level 1

:: Data transmission ::

In telecommunication a _________ is the means of connecting one location to another for the purpose of transmitting and receiving digital information. It can also refer to a set of electronics assemblies, consisting of a transmitter and a receiver and the interconnecting data telecommunication circuit. These are governed by a link protocol enabling digital data to be transferred from a data source to a data sink.

Exam Probability: **High**

4. *Answer choices:*

(see index for correct answer)

- a. Ultra-wideband
- b. Errored second
- c. Message format
- d. Data link

Guidance: level 1

:: Ubiquitous computing ::

A _________ , chip card, or integrated circuit card is a physical electronic authorization device, used to control access to a resource. It is typically a plastic credit card sized card with an embedded integrated circuit. Many _________ s include a pattern of metal contacts to electrically connect to the internal chip. Others are contactless, and some are both. _________ s can provide personal identification, authentication, data storage, and application processing. Applications include identification, financial, mobile phones , public transit, computer security, schools, and healthcare. _________ s may provide strong security authentication for single sign-on within organizations. Several nations have deployed _________ s throughout their populations.

Exam Probability: **Medium**

5. *Answer choices:*

(see index for correct answer)

- a. Smart card
- b. Smart environment
- c. Bluetooth low energy
- d. Tracking system

Guidance: level 1

:: ::

A _________ is a computer network that interconnects computers within a limited area such as a residence, school, laboratory, university campus or office building. By contrast, a wide area network not only covers a larger geographic distance, but also generally involves leased telecommunication circuits.

Exam Probability: **High**

6. *Answer choices:*

(see index for correct answer)

- a. cultural
- b. Local Area Network
- c. Sarbanes-Oxley act of 2002
- d. similarity-attraction theory

Guidance: level 1

:: ::

A __________ is a structure / access pattern specific to data warehouse environments, used to retrieve client-facing data. The __________ is a subset of the data warehouse and is usually oriented to a specific business line or team. Whereas data warehouses have an enterprise-wide depth, the information in __________ s pertains to a single department. In some deployments, each department or business unit is considered the owner of its __________ including all the hardware, software and data. This enables each department to isolate the use, manipulation and development of their data. In other deployments where conformed dimensions are used, this business unit ownership will not hold true for shared dimensions like customer, product, etc.

Exam Probability: **Low**

7. *Answer choices:*

(see index for correct answer)

- a. Data mart
- b. hierarchical perspective
- c. Character
- d. interpersonal communication

Guidance: level 1

:: Web security exploits ::

A __________ is a baked or cooked food that is small, flat and sweet. It usually contains flour, sugar and some type of oil or fat. It may include other ingredients such as raisins, oats, chocolate chips, nuts, etc.

Exam Probability: **Low**

8. *Answer choices:*

(see index for correct answer)

- a. Cross-site scripting
- b. Content Security Policy
- c. Evil twin
- d. Form grabbing

Guidance: level 1

:: Industrial design ::

Across the many fields concerned with _________ , including information science, computer science, human-computer interaction, communication, and industrial design, there is little agreement over the meaning of the term " _________ ", although all are related to interaction with computers and other machines with a user interface.

Exam Probability: **Medium**

9. *Answer choices:*

(see index for correct answer)

- a. World Design Capital
- b. Humanscale

- c. Britain Can Make It
- d. Interactivity

Guidance: level 1

:: ::

_________ is the fundamental facilities and systems serving a country, city, or other area, including the services and facilities necessary for its economy to function. _________ is composed of public and private physical improvements such as roads, bridges, tunnels, water supply, sewers, electrical grids, and telecommunications . In general, it has also been defined as "the physical components of interrelated systems providing commodities and services essential to enable, sustain, or enhance societal living conditions".

Exam Probability: **High**

10. *Answer choices:*

(see index for correct answer)

- a. deep-level diversity
- b. Infrastructure
- c. imperative
- d. empathy

Guidance: level 1

:: Payment systems ::

_________ s are part of a payment system issued by financial institutions, such as a bank, to a customer that enables its owner to access the funds in the customer`s designated bank accounts, or through a credit account and make payments by electronic funds transfer and access automated teller machines . Such cards are known by a variety of names including bank cards, ATM cards, MAC , client cards, key cards or cash cards.

Exam Probability: **High**

11. *Answer choices:*

(see index for correct answer)

- a. PesaDroid
- b. Payment card
- c. Letters of credit
- d. Amazon Payments

Guidance: level 1

:: E-commerce ::

The phrase _________ was originally coined in 1997 by Kevin Duffey at the launch of the Global _________ Forum, to mean "the delivery of electronic commerce capabilities directly into the consumer's hand, anywhere, via wireless technology." Many choose to think of _________ as meaning "a retail outlet in your customer's pocket."

Exam Probability: **Low**

12. *Answer choices:*

(see index for correct answer)

- a. Public eProcurement
- b. Center for the Connected Consumer
- c. IzzoNet
- d. Beamdog

Guidance: level 1

:: Computer data ::

In computer science, _________ is the ability to access an arbitrary element of a sequence in equal time or any datum from a population of addressable elements roughly as easily and efficiently as any other, no matter how many elements may be in the set. It is typically contrasted to sequential access.

Exam Probability: **High**

13. *Answer choices:*

(see index for correct answer)

- a. Text file
- b. Binary code

- c. Random access
- d. AS3

Guidance: level 1

:: Data management ::

" _________ " is a field that treats ways to analyze, systematically extract information from, or otherwise deal with data sets that are too large or complex to be dealt with by traditional data-processing application software. Data with many cases offer greater statistical power, while data with higher complexity may lead to a higher false discovery rate. _________ challenges include capturing data, data storage, data analysis, search, sharing, transfer, visualization, querying, updating, information privacy and data source. _________ was originally associated with three key concepts: volume, variety, and velocity. Other concepts later attributed with _________ are veracity and value.

Exam Probability: **Low**

14. *Answer choices:*

(see index for correct answer)

- a. Big data
- b. Cleansing and Conforming Data
- c. Microsoft Office PerformancePoint Server
- d. Tuple

Guidance: level 1

:: Business process ::

A __________ or business method is a collection of related, structured activities or tasks by people or equipment which in a specific sequence produce a service or product for a particular customer or customers. __________ es occur at all organizational levels and may or may not be visible to the customers. A __________ may often be visualized as a flowchart of a sequence of activities with interleaving decision points or as a process matrix of a sequence of activities with relevance rules based on data in the process. The benefits of using __________ es include improved customer satisfaction and improved agility for reacting to rapid market change. Process-oriented organizations break down the barriers of structural departments and try to avoid functional silos.

Exam Probability: **High**

15. *Answer choices:*

(see index for correct answer)

- a. Intention mining
- b. Process ontology
- c. Business process
- d. Change order

Guidance: level 1

:: Reputation management ::

_________ refers to the influencing and controlling of an individual`s or group`s reputation. Originally a public relations term, the growth of the internet and social media, along with _________ companies, have made search results a core part of an individual`s or group`s reputation. Online _________ , sometimes abbreviated as ORM, focuses on the management of product and service search website results. Ethical grey areas include mug shot removal sites, astroturfing customer review sites, censoring negative complaints, and using search engine optimization tactics to influence results.

Exam Probability: **High**

16. *Answer choices:*

(see index for correct answer)

- a. Reputation management
- b. The Economy of Esteem
- c. Infamy
- d. ClaimID

Guidance: level 1

:: Procurement practices ::

_________ or commercially available off-the-shelf products are packaged solutions which are then adapted to satisfy the needs of the purchasing organization, rather than the commissioning of custom-made, or bespoke, solutions. A related term, Mil-COTS, refers to COTS products for use by the U.S. military.

Exam Probability: **High**

17. *Answer choices:*

(see index for correct answer)

- a. Syndicated procurement
- b. Commercial off-the-shelf

Guidance: level 1

:: Information technology ::

_________ is the use of computers to store, retrieve, transmit, and manipulate data, or information, often in the context of a business or other enterprise. IT is considered to be a subset of information and communications technology . An _________ system is generally an information system, a communications system or, more specifically speaking, a computer system – including all hardware, software and peripheral equipment – operated by a limited group of users.

Exam Probability: **High**

18. *Answer choices:*

(see index for correct answer)

- a. CIO-plus
- b. Information technology
- c. Information and communication technologies in education

- d. Attra

Guidance: level 1

:: Computing output devices ::

An _________ is any piece of computer hardware equipment which converts information into human-readable form.

Exam Probability: **High**

19. *Answer choices:*

(see index for correct answer)

- a. Smart Display
- b. MyVu
- c. Output device
- d. GammaFax

Guidance: level 1

:: Knowledge representation ::

_________ is the system in which users apply public tags to online items, typically to make those items easier for themselves or others to find later. Over time, this can give rise to a classification system based on those tags and how often they are applied or searched for, in contrast to a taxonomic classification designed by the owners of the content and specified when it is published. This practice is also known as collaborative tagging, social classification, social indexing, and social tagging. _________ was originally "the result of personal free tagging of information [...] for one`s own retrieval", but online sharing and interaction expanded it into collaborative forms. Social tagging is the application of tags in an open online environment where the tags of other users are available to others. Collaborative tagging is tagging performed by a group of users. This type of _________ is commonly used in cooperative and collaborative projects such as research, content repositories, and social bookmarking.

Exam Probability: **High**

20. *Answer choices:*

(see index for correct answer)

- a. Digital curation
- b. Vivification
- c. Closed world assumption
- d. GermaNet

Guidance: level 1

:: Information and communication technologies for development ::

__________ is a non-profit initiative established with the goal of transforming education for children around the world; this goal was to be achieved by creating and distributing educational devices for the developing world, and by creating software and content for those devices.

Exam Probability: **Medium**

21. *Answer choices:*

(see index for correct answer)

- a. One Laptop per Child
- b. Asia-Pacific Development Information Programme
- c. Geekcorps
- d. Arid Lands Information Network

Guidance: level 1

:: Human–computer interaction ::

__________ is a database query language for relational databases. It was devised by Moshé M. Zloof at IBM Research during the mid-1970s, in parallel to the development of SQL. It is the first graphical query language, using visual tables where the user would enter commands, example elements and conditions. Many graphical front-ends for databases use the ideas from QBE today. Originally limited only for the purpose of retrieving data, QBE was later extended to allow other operations, such as inserts, deletes and updates, as well as creation of temporary tables.

Exam Probability: **High**

22. *Answer choices:*

(see index for correct answer)

- a. Steering law
- b. Multiseat desktop virtualization
- c. GOMS
- d. Law of conservation of complexity

Guidance: level 1

:: Virtual reality ::

A _________ is a computer-based simulated environment which may be populated by many users who can create a personal avatar, and simultaneously and independently explore the _________ , participate in its activities and communicate with others. These avatars can be textual, two or three-dimensional graphical representations, or live video avatars with auditory and touch sensations. In general, _________ s allow for multiple users but single player computer games, such as Skyrim, can also be considered a type of _________ .

Exam Probability: **High**

23. *Answer choices:*

(see index for correct answer)

- a. Polynomial texture mapping
- b. Stroker Serpentine
- c. Wirth Research
- d. Virtual world

Guidance: level 1

:: Data management ::

Given organizations` increasing dependency on information technology to run their operations, Business continuity planning covers the entire organization, and Disaster recovery focuses on IT.

Exam Probability: **High**

24. *Answer choices:*

(see index for correct answer)

- a. Single customer view
- b. Automated tiered storage
- c. Disaster recovery plan
- d. Document-oriented database

Guidance: level 1

:: Computer memory ::

_________ is an electronic non-volatile computer storage medium that can be electrically erased and reprogrammed.

Exam Probability: **High**

25. *Answer choices:*

(see index for correct answer)

- a. Non-uniform memory access
- b. Deterministic memory
- c. Flash memory
- d. Page address register

Guidance: level 1

:: Data security ::

In information technology, a _________ , or data _________ , or the process of backing up, refers to the copying into an archive file of computer data that is already in secondary storage—so that it may be used to restore the original after a data loss event. The verb form is "back up" , whereas the noun and adjective form is " _________ ".

Exam Probability: **Medium**

26. *Answer choices:*

(see index for correct answer)

- a. Security information management
- b. Generally Accepted Privacy Principles
- c. Computer recycling
- d. Information security management system

Guidance: level 1

:: Information systems ::

_________ , Chief Digital Information Officer or Information Technology Director, is a job title commonly given to the most senior executive in an enterprise who works for the traditional information technology and computer systems that support enterprise goals.

Exam Probability: **Low**

27. *Answer choices:*

(see index for correct answer)

- a. Chief information officer
- b. Trust management
- c. Credit bureau
- d. Business informatics

Guidance: level 1

:: Google services ::

A blog is a discussion or informational website published on the World Wide Web consisting of discrete, often informal diary-style text entries . Posts are typically displayed in reverse chronological order, so that the most recent post appears first, at the top of the web page. Until 2009, blogs were usually the work of a single individual, occasionally of a small group, and often covered a single subject or topic. In the 2010s, "multi-author blogs" emerged, featuring the writing of multiple authors and sometimes professionally edited. MABs from newspapers, other media outlets, universities, think tanks, advocacy groups, and similar institutions account for an increasing quantity of blog traffic. The rise of Twitter and other "microblogging" systems helps integrate MABs and single-author blogs into the news media. Blog can also be used as a verb, meaning to maintain or add content to a blog.

Exam Probability: **Medium**

28. *Answer choices:*

(see index for correct answer)

- a. Google Web History
- b. Google Custom Search
- c. Google Building Maker
- d. Google News Archive

Guidance: level 1

:: Information retrieval ::

_________ is the practice of making content from multiple enterprise-type sources, such as databases and intranets, searchable to a defined audience .

Exam Probability: **Medium**

29. *Answer choices:*

(see index for correct answer)

- a. European Summer School in Information Retrieval
- b. Pikimal
- c. Key Word in Context
- d. Compound term processing

Guidance: level 1

:: Network management ::

_________ is the process of administering and managing computer networks. Services provided by this discipline include fault analysis, performance management, provisioning of networks and maintaining the quality of service. Software that enables network administrators to perform their functions is called _________ software.

Exam Probability: **Medium**

30. *Answer choices:*

(see index for correct answer)

- a. Joint Inter-Domain Management
- b. Network management
- c. Common Management Information Service
- d. Private Enterprise Number

Guidance: level 1

:: ::

A __________ is an organized collection of data, generally stored and accessed electronically from a computer system. Where __________ s are more complex they are often developed using formal design and modeling techniques.

Exam Probability: **High**

31. *Answer choices:*

(see index for correct answer)

- a. Character
- b. imperative
- c. functional perspective
- d. Database

Guidance: level 1

:: ::

A _________ is the event in which two or more bodies exert forces on each other in about a relatively short time. Although the most common use of the word _________ refers to incidents in which two or more objects collide with great force, the scientific use of the term implies nothing about the magnitude of the force.

Exam Probability: **Medium**

32. *Answer choices:*

(see index for correct answer)

- a. Collision
- b. cultural
- c. interpersonal communication
- d. open system

Guidance: level 1

:: ::

A _________ or data centre is a building, dedicated space within a building, or a group of buildings used to house computer systems and associated components, such as telecommunications and storage systems.

Exam Probability: **Low**

33. *Answer choices:*

(see index for correct answer)

- a. Character
- b. Data center
- c. similarity-attraction theory
- d. open system

Guidance: level 1

:: E-commerce ::

__________ is the activity of buying or selling of products on online services or over the Internet. Electronic commerce draws on technologies such as mobile commerce, electronic funds transfer, supply chain management, Internet marketing, online transaction processing, electronic data interchange , inventory management systems, and automated data collection systems.

Exam Probability: **High**

34. *Answer choices:*

(see index for correct answer)

- a. Online auction tools
- b. Online locator service
- c. Internet Marketing Conference
- d. E-commerce

Guidance: level 1

:: Data collection ::

_________ is information that either does not have a pre-defined data model or is not organized in a pre-defined manner. Unstructured information is typically text-heavy, but may contain data such as dates, numbers, and facts as well. This results in irregularities and ambiguities that make it difficult to understand using traditional programs as compared to data stored in fielded form in databases or annotated in documents.

Exam Probability: **Medium**

35. *Answer choices:*

(see index for correct answer)

- a. Unstructured data
- b. Field recording
- c. Data farming
- d. Public survey

Guidance: level 1

:: Service-oriented (business computing) ::

__________ is a style of software design where services are provided to the other components by application components, through a communication protocol over a network. The basic principles of __________ are independent of vendors, products and technologies.A service is a discrete unit of functionality that can be accessed remotely and acted upon and updated independently, such as retrieving a credit card statement online.

Exam Probability: **High**

36. *Answer choices:*

(see index for correct answer)

- a. Service-oriented architecture implementation framework
- b. Velaro, Inc.
- c. Service-oriented architecture
- d. Adobe Campaign

Guidance: level 1

:: ::

__________ is a kind of action that occur as two or more objects have an effect upon one another. The idea of a two-way effect is essential in the concept of __________, as opposed to a one-way causal effect. A closely related term is interconnectivity, which deals with the __________ s of __________ s within systems: combinations of many simple __________ s can lead to surprising emergent phenomena. __________ has different tailored meanings in various sciences. Changes can also involve __________ .

Exam Probability: **High**

37. *Answer choices:*

(see index for correct answer)

- a. deep-level diversity
- b. levels of analysis
- c. interpersonal communication
- d. Interaction

Guidance: level 1

:: Fault tolerance ::

__________ is the property that enables a system to continue operating properly in the event of the failure of some of its components. If its operating quality decreases at all, the decrease is proportional to the severity of the failure, as compared to a naively designed system, in which even a small failure can cause total breakdown. __________ is particularly sought after in high-availability or life-critical systems. The ability of maintaining functionality when portions of a system break down is referred to as graceful degradation.

Exam Probability: **Medium**

38. *Answer choices:*

(see index for correct answer)

- a. Random fault
- b. Error-tolerant design
- c. Amplitude-shift keying
- d. Fault tolerance

Guidance: level 1

:: Google services ::

_________ is a web mapping service developed by Google. It offers satellite imagery, aerial photography, street maps, 360° panoramic views of streets , real-time traffic conditions, and route planning for traveling by foot, car, bicycle and air , or public transportation.

Exam Probability: **High**

39. *Answer choices:*

(see index for correct answer)

- a. Google Apps for Business
- b. Google Developers
- c. Google Maps
- d. Google Finance

Guidance: level 1

:: Domain name system ::

The __________ is a hierarchical and decentralized naming system for computers, services, or other resources connected to the Internet or a private network. It associates various information with domain names assigned to each of the participating entities. Most prominently, it translates more readily memorized domain names to the numerical IP addresses needed for locating and identifying computer services and devices with the underlying network protocols. By providing a worldwide, distributed directory service, the __________ has been an essential component of the functionality of the Internet since 1985.

Exam Probability: **High**

40. *Answer choices:*

(see index for correct answer)

- a. Dns Bajaj
- b. Country code top-level domain
- c. Domain Name System
- d. Subdomain

Guidance: level 1

:: Information technology management ::

_________ is the use of software to control machine tools and related ones in the manufacturing of workpieces. This is not the only definition for CAM, but it is the most common; CAM may also refer to the use of a computer to assist in all operations of a manufacturing plant, including planning, management, transportation and storage. Its primary purpose is to create a faster production process and components and tooling with more precise dimensions and material consistency, which in some cases, uses only the required amount of raw material , while simultaneously reducing energy consumption.CAM is now a system used in schools and lower educational purposes.CAM is a subsequent computer-aided process after computer-aided design and sometimes computer-aided engineering , as the model generated in CAD and verified in CAE can be input into CAM software, which then controls the machine tool. CAM is used in many schools alongside Computer-Aided Design to create objects.

Exam Probability: **Medium**

41. *Answer choices:*

(see index for correct answer)

- a. Belarc
- b. Digital asset management
- c. Cherwell Software
- d. Computer-aided manufacturing

Guidance: level 1

:: Information systems ::

In artificial intelligence, an __________ is a computer system that emulates the decision-making ability of a human expert. __________ s are designed to solve complex problems by reasoning through bodies of knowledge, represented mainly as if–then rules rather than through conventional procedural code. The first __________ s were created in the 1970s and then proliferated in the 1980s. __________ s were among the first truly successful forms of artificial intelligence software. However, some experts point out that __________ s were not part of true artificial intelligence since they lack the ability to learn autonomously from external data.An __________ is divided into two subsystems: the inference engine and the knowledge base. The knowledge base represents facts and rules. The inference engine applies the rules to the known facts to deduce new facts. Inference engines can also include explanation and debugging abilities.

Exam Probability: **Low**

42. *Answer choices:*

(see index for correct answer)

- a. VAT Information Exchange System
- b. Expert system
- c. Website Meta Language
- d. CIMACT

Guidance: level 1

:: Management ::

__________ is the identification of an organization`s assets , followed by the development, documentation, and implementation of policies and procedures for protecting these assets.

Exam Probability: **Low**

43. *Answer choices:*

(see index for correct answer)

- a. Pomodoro Technique
- b. Security management
- c. Fredmund Malik
- d. Management Week

Guidance: level 1

:: Automatic identification and data capture ::

__________ uses electromagnetic fields to automatically identify and track tags attached to objects. The tags contain electronically stored information. Passive tags collect energy from a nearby RFID reader`s interrogating radio waves. Active tags have a local power source and may operate hundreds of meters from the RFID reader. Unlike a barcode, the tag need not be within the line of sight of the reader, so it may be embedded in the tracked object. RFID is one method of automatic identification and data capture .

Exam Probability: **High**

44. *Answer choices:*

(see index for correct answer)

- a. Burst transmission
- b. Radio-frequency identification
- c. Roper Industries
- d. Watchclock

Guidance: level 1

:: Information technology management ::

The term __________ is used to refer to periods when a system is unavailable. __________ or outage duration refers to a period of time that a system fails to provide or perform its primary function. Reliability, availability, recovery, and unavailability are related concepts.The unavailability is the proportion of a time-span that a system is unavailable or offline.This is usually a result of the system failing to function because of an unplanned event, or because of routine maintenance .

Exam Probability: **High**

45. *Answer choices:*

(see index for correct answer)

- a. Ekatva
- b. User account policy
- c. E-Booking

- d. Operational-level agreement

Guidance: level 1

:: Statistical laws ::

In statistics and business, a _________ of some distributions of numbers is the portion of the distribution having a large number of occurrences far from the "head" or central part of the distribution. The distribution could involve popularities, random numbers of occurrences of events with various probabilities, etc. The term is often used loosely, with no definition or arbitrary definition, but precise definitions are possible.

Exam Probability: **High**

46. *Answer choices:*

(see index for correct answer)

- a. Safety in numbers
- b. Law of total expectation
- c. Law of total probability
- d. Long tail

Guidance: level 1

:: Database theory ::

A _________ is a digital database based on the relational model of data, as proposed by E. F. Codd in 1970.A software system used to maintain _________ s is a _________ management system . Virtually all _________ systems use SQL for querying and maintaining the database.

Exam Probability: **High**

47. *Answer choices:*

(see index for correct answer)

- a. Conjunctive query
- b. Relational database
- c. Monotonic query
- d. Chase

Guidance: level 1

:: Management ::

The _________ is a strategy performance management tool – a semi-standard structured report, that can be used by managers to keep track of the execution of activities by the staff within their control and to monitor the consequences arising from these actions.

Exam Probability: **Medium**

48. *Answer choices:*

(see index for correct answer)

- a. Product life-cycle management
- b. Business chess
- c. Balanced scorecard
- d. Performance indicator

Guidance: level 1

:: E-commerce ::

Electronic governance or e-governance is the application of information and communication technology for delivering government services, exchange of information, communication transactions, integration of various stand-alone systems and services between government-to-citizen , _________ , government-to-government , government-to-employees as well as back-office processes and interactions within the entire government framework. Through e-governance, government services are made available to citizens in a convenient, efficient, and transparent manner. The three main target groups that can be distinguished in governance concepts are government, citizens, andbusinesses/interest groups. In e-governance, there are no distinct boundaries.

Exam Probability: **Medium**

49. *Answer choices:*

(see index for correct answer)

- a. Open Market

- b. Government-to-business
- c. Notice and take down
- d. EatOye

Guidance: level 1

:: Management ::

In business, a _________ is the attribute that allows an organization to outperform its competitors. A _________ may include access to natural resources, such as high-grade ores or a low-cost power source, highly skilled labor, geographic location, high entry barriers, and access to new technology.

Exam Probability: **Medium**

50. *Answer choices:*

(see index for correct answer)

- a. Evidence-based management
- b. Community management
- c. Tacit knowledge
- d. Business economics

Guidance: level 1

:: E-commerce ::

__________ is a type of fraud that occurs on the Internet in pay-per-click online advertising. In this type of advertising, the owners of websites that post the ads are paid an amount of money determined by how many visitors to the sites click on the ads. Fraud occurs when a person, automated script or computer program imitates a legitimate user of a web browser, clicking on such an ad without having an actual interest in the target of the ad`s link. __________ is the subject of some controversy and increasing litigation due to the advertising networks being a key beneficiary of the fraud.

Exam Probability: **Low**

51. *Answer choices:*

(see index for correct answer)

- a. Live banner
- b. Online wallet
- c. Click fraud
- d. Transactional Link

Guidance: level 1

:: Security compliance ::

__________ refers to the inability to withstand the effects of a hostile environment. A window of __________ is a time frame within which defensive measures are diminished, compromised or lacking.

Exam Probability: **High**

52. *Answer choices:*

(see index for correct answer)

- a. Threat
- b. Federal Information Security Management Act of 2002
- c. Vulnerability
- d. Information assurance vulnerability alert

Guidance: level 1

:: Internet governance ::

A __________ is one of the domains at the highest level in the hierarchical Domain Name System of the Internet. The __________ names are installed in the root zone of the name space. For all domains in lower levels, it is the last part of the domain name, that is, the last label of a fully qualified domain name. For example, in the domain name www.example.com, the __________ is com. Responsibility for management of most __________ s is delegated to specific organizations by the Internet Corporation for Assigned Names and Numbers , which operates the Internet Assigned Numbers Authority , and is in charge of maintaining the DNS root zone.

Exam Probability: **Medium**

53. *Answer choices:*

(see index for correct answer)

- a. Domain name registry
- b. Top-level domain

- c. Montevideo Statement on the Future of Internet Cooperation
- d. GeoTLD

Guidance: level 1

:: Search engine optimization ::

_________ is an algorithm used by Google Search to rank web pages in their search engine results. _________ was named after Larry Page, one of the founders of Google. _________ is a way of measuring the importance of website pages. According to Google.

Exam Probability: **Medium**

54. *Answer choices:*

(see index for correct answer)

- a. Article spinning
- b. PageRank
- c. Keyword density
- d. Teknicks

Guidance: level 1

:: Data quality ::

_________ is the maintenance of, and the assurance of the accuracy and consistency of, data over its entire life-cycle, and is a critical aspect to the design, implementation and usage of any system which stores, processes, or retrieves data. The term is broad in scope and may have widely different meanings depending on the specific context even under the same general umbrella of computing. It is at times used as a proxy term for data quality, while data validation is a pre-requisite for _________ . _________ is the opposite of data corruption. The overall intent of any _________ technique is the same: ensure data is recorded exactly as intended and upon later retrieval, ensure the data is the same as it was when it was originally recorded. In short, _________ aims to prevent unintentional changes to information. _________ is not to be confused with data security, the discipline of protecting data from unauthorized parties.

Exam Probability: **High**

55. *Answer choices:*

(see index for correct answer)

- a. Data Quality Campaign
- b. Data validation
- c. Data corruption
- d. Input mask

Guidance: level 1

:: Transaction processing ::

Transaction processing is information processing in computer science that is divided into individual, indivisible operations called transactions. Each transaction must succeed or fail as a complete unit; it can never be only partially complete.

Exam Probability: **High**

56. *Answer choices:*

(see index for correct answer)

- a. Redo log
- b. Transaction processing
- c. Transaction log
- d. Transactions per second

Guidance: level 1

:: Global Positioning System ::

The __________ , originally Navstar GPS, is a satellite-based radionavigation system owned by the United States government and operated by the United States Air Force. It is a global navigation satellite system that provides geolocation and time information to a GPS receiver anywhere on or near the Earth where there is an unobstructed line of sight to four or more GPS satellites. Obstacles such as mountains and buildings block the relatively weak GPS signals.

Exam Probability: **Low**

57. *Answer choices:*

(see index for correct answer)

- a. UNAVCO
- b. Location-based game
- c. Undulation of the geoid
- d. Gpsd

Guidance: level 1

:: ::

_________ is the function of specifying access rights/privileges to resources, which is related to information security and computer security in general and to access control in particular. More formally, "to authorize" is to define an access policy. For example, human resources staff are normally authorized to access employee records and this policy is usually formalized as access control rules in a computer system. During operation, the system uses the access control rules to decide whether access requests from consumers shall be approved or disapproved . Resources include individual files or an item`s data, computer programs, computer devices and functionality provided by computer applications. Examples of consumers are computer users, computer Software and other Hardware on the computer.

Exam Probability: **Low**

58. *Answer choices:*

(see index for correct answer)

- a. process perspective
- b. Authorization
- c. functional perspective
- d. Character

Guidance: level 1

:: ::

In communications and information processing, _________ is a system of rules to convert information—such as a letter, word, sound, image, or gesture—into another form or representation, sometimes shortened or secret, for communication through a communication channel or storage in a storage medium. An early example is the invention of language, which enabled a person, through speech, to communicate what they saw, heard, felt, or thought to others. But speech limits the range of communication to the distance a voice can carry, and limits the audience to those present when the speech is uttered. The invention of writing, which converted spoken language into visual symbols, extended the range of communication across space and time.

Exam Probability: **Low**

59. *Answer choices:*

(see index for correct answer)

- a. Code
- b. Sarbanes-Oxley act of 2002
- c. interpersonal communication
- d. open system

Guidance: level 1

Marketing

Marketing is the study and management of exchange relationships. Marketing is the business process of creating relationships with and satisfying customers. With its focus on the customer, marketing is one of the premier components of business management.

Marketing is defined by the American Marketing Association as "the activity, set of institutions, and processes for creating, communicating, delivering, and exchanging offerings that have value for customers, clients, partners, and society at large."

:: Data management ::

__________ is a form of intellectual property that grants the creator of an original creative work an exclusive legal right to determine whether and under what conditions this original work may be copied and used by others, usually for a limited term of years. The exclusive rights are not absolute but limited by limitations and exceptions to __________ law, including fair use. A major limitation on __________ on ideas is that __________ protects only the original expression of ideas, and not the underlying ideas themselves.

Exam Probability: **High**

1. *Answer choices:*

(see index for correct answer)

- a. Data Reference Model
- b. Cleansing and Conforming Data
- c. Very large database
- d. Copyright

Guidance: level 1

:: Mereology ::

__________ , in the abstract, is what belongs to or with something, whether as an attribute or as a component of said thing. In the context of this article, it is one or more components , whether physical or incorporeal, of a person`s estate; or so belonging to, as in being owned by, a person or jointly a group of people or a legal entity like a corporation or even a society. Depending on the nature of the __________ , an owner of __________ has the right to consume, alter, share, redefine, rent, mortgage, pawn, sell, exchange, transfer, give away or destroy it, or to exclude others from doing these things, as well as to perhaps abandon it; whereas regardless of the nature of the __________ , the owner thereof has the right to properly use it , or at the very least exclusively keep it.

Exam Probability: **Low**

2. *Answer choices:*

(see index for correct answer)

- a. Property
- b. Mereotopology
- c. Meronomy
- d. Mereological nihilism

Guidance: level 1

:: Survey methodology ::

An _________ is a conversation where questions are asked and answers are given. In common parlance, the word " _________ " refers to a one-on-one conversation between an _________ er and an _________ ee. The _________ er asks questions to which the _________ ee responds, usually so information may be transferred from _________ ee to _________ er . Sometimes, information can be transferred in both directions. It is a communication, unlike a speech, which produces a one-way flow of information.

Exam Probability: **Medium**

3. *Answer choices:*

(see index for correct answer)

- a. Inverse probability weighting
- b. Computer-assisted survey information collection
- c. American Association for Public Opinion Research
- d. Interview

Guidance: level 1

:: ::

According to the philosopher Piyush Mathur , "Tangibility is the property that a phenomenon exhibits if it has and/or transports mass and/or energy and/or momentum".

Exam Probability: **Low**

4. *Answer choices:*

(see index for correct answer)

- a. hierarchical perspective
- b. Character
- c. open system
- d. Tangible

Guidance: level 1

:: Marketing ::

__________ is a market strategy in which a firm decides to ignore market segment differences and appeal the whole market with one offer or one strategy, which supports the idea of broadcasting a message that will reach the largest number of people possible. Traditionally __________ has focused on radio, television and newspapers as the media used to reach this broad audience. By reaching the largest audience possible, exposure to the product is maximized, and in theory this would directly correlate with a larger number of sales or buys into the product.

Exam Probability: **High**

5. *Answer choices:*

(see index for correct answer)

- a. Marketing in schools
- b. Mass marketing

- c. Pharmaceutical marketing
- d. Price war

Guidance: level 1

:: ::

__________ is the production of products for use or sale using labour and machines, tools, chemical and biological processing, or formulation. The term may refer to a range of human activity, from handicraft to high tech, but is most commonly applied to industrial design, in which raw materials are transformed into finished goods on a large scale. Such finished goods may be sold to other manufacturers for the production of other, more complex products, such as aircraft, household appliances, furniture, sports equipment or automobiles, or sold to wholesalers, who in turn sell them to retailers, who then sell them to end users and consumers.

Exam Probability: **Medium**

6. *Answer choices:*

(see index for correct answer)

- a. Manufacturing
- b. corporate values
- c. process perspective
- d. personal values

Guidance: level 1

:: Marketing ::

A _________ is an overall experience of a customer that distinguishes an organization or product from its rivals in the eyes of the customer. _________ s are used in business, marketing, and advertising. Name _________ s are sometimes distinguished from generic or store _________ s.

Exam Probability: **High**

7. *Answer choices:*

(see index for correct answer)

- a. Product sabotage
- b. Brand
- c. Interactive collateral management
- d. Product category volume

Guidance: level 1

:: Data ::

Data has two ways of being created or generated. The first is what is called `captured data`, and is found through purposeful investigation or analysis. The second is called `exhaust data`, and is gathered usually by machines or terminals as a secondary function. For example, cash registers, smartphones, and speedometers serve a main function but may collect data as a secondary task. Exhaustive data is usually too large or of little use to process and becomes `transient` or thrown away.

Exam Probability: **High**

8. *Answer choices:*

(see index for correct answer)

- a. DataSplice
- b. Data Transmission
- c. MVP tree
- d. Primary data

Guidance: level 1

:: ::

Bloomberg Businessweek is an American weekly business magazine published since 2009 by Bloomberg L.P. Businessweek, founded in 1929, aimed to provide information and interpretation about events in the business world. The magazine is headquartered in New York City. Megan Murphy served as editor from November 2016; she stepped down from the role in January 2018 and Joel Weber was appointed in her place.The magazine is published 47 times a year.

Exam Probability: **Low**

9. *Answer choices:*

(see index for correct answer)

- a. cultural
- b. imperative
- c. levels of analysis
- d. Business Week

Guidance: level 1

:: ::

_________ is an abstract concept of management of complex systems according to a set of rules and trends. In systems theory, these types of rules exist in various fields of biology and society, but the term has slightly different meanings according to context. For example.

Exam Probability: **Medium**

10. *Answer choices:*

(see index for correct answer)

- a. Character
- b. Regulation
- c. levels of analysis

- d. open system

Guidance: level 1

:: Management accounting ::

In economics, _________ s, indirect costs or overheads are business expenses that are not dependent on the level of goods or services produced by the business. They tend to be time-related, such as interest or rents being paid per month, and are often referred to as overhead costs. This is in contrast to variable costs, which are volume-related and unknown at the beginning of the accounting year. For a simple example, such as a bakery, the monthly rent for the baking facilities, and the monthly payments for the security system and basic phone line are _________ s, as they do not change according to how much bread the bakery produces and sells. On the other hand, the wage costs of the bakery are variable, as the bakery will have to hire more workers if the production of bread increases. Economists reckon _________ as a entry barrier for new entrepreneurs.

Exam Probability: **Medium**

11. *Answer choices:*

(see index for correct answer)

- a. Fixed cost
- b. Institute of Management Accountants
- c. Variable Costing
- d. Variable cost

Guidance: level 1

:: Retailing ::

A __________ is a retail establishment offering a wide range of consumer goods in different product categories known as "departments". In modern major cities, the __________ made a dramatic appearance in the middle of the 19th century, and permanently reshaped shopping habits, and the definition of service and luxury. Similar developments were under way in London , in Paris and in New York .

Exam Probability: **High**

12. *Answer choices:*

(see index for correct answer)

- a. Survival store
- b. Showrooming
- c. Shopping list
- d. Store-within-a-store

Guidance: level 1

:: Trade associations ::

A _________ , also known as an industry trade group, business association, sector association or industry body, is an organization founded and funded by businesses that operate in a specific industry. An industry _________ participates in public relations activities such as advertising, education, political donations, lobbying and publishing, but its focus is collaboration between companies. Associations may offer other services, such as producing conferences, networking or charitable events or offering classes or educational materials. Many associations are non-profit organizations governed by bylaws and directed by officers who are also members.

Exam Probability: **Low**

13. *Answer choices:*

(see index for correct answer)

- a. Property Care Association
- b. Puerto Rico Radio Broadcasters Association
- c. Trade association
- d. Swiss Insurance Association

Guidance: level 1

:: ::

_________ , or auditory perception, is the ability to perceive sounds by detecting vibrations, changes in the pressure of the surrounding medium through time, through an organ such as the ear. The academic field concerned with _________ is auditory science.

Exam Probability: **Low**

14. *Answer choices:*

(see index for correct answer)

- a. empathy
- b. Sarbanes-Oxley act of 2002
- c. Hearing
- d. Character

Guidance: level 1

:: ::

_________ is the process of gathering and measuring information on targeted variables in an established system, which then enables one to answer relevant questions and evaluate outcomes. _________ is a component of research in all fields of study including physical and social sciences, humanities, and business. While methods vary by discipline, the emphasis on ensuring accurate and honest collection remains the same. The goal for all _________ is to capture quality evidence that allows analysis to lead to the formulation of convincing and credible answers to the questions that have been posed.

Exam Probability: **High**

15. *Answer choices:*

(see index for correct answer)

- a. information systems assessment
- b. functional perspective
- c. corporate values
- d. open system

Guidance: level 1

:: Management ::

A _________ is a promise of value to be delivered, communicated, and acknowledged. It is also a belief from the customer about how value will be delivered, experienced and acquired.

Exam Probability: **High**

16. *Answer choices:*

(see index for correct answer)

- a. Evidence-based management
- b. Defensive expenditures
- c. Value proposition
- d. Perth leadership outcome model

Guidance: level 1

:: ::

_________ is change in the heritable characteristics of biological populations over successive generations. These characteristics are the expressions of genes that are passed on from parent to offspring during reproduction. Different characteristics tend to exist within any given population as a result of mutation, genetic recombination and other sources of genetic variation. _________ occurs when _________ ary processes such as natural selection and genetic drift act on this variation, resulting in certain characteristics becoming more common or rare within a population. It is this process of _________ that has given rise to biodiversity at every level of biological organisation, including the levels of species, individual organisms and molecules.

Exam Probability: **High**

17. *Answer choices:*

(see index for correct answer)

- a. information systems assessment
- b. Evolution
- c. deep-level diversity
- d. similarity-attraction theory

Guidance: level 1

:: ::

_________ is a means of protection from financial loss. It is a form of risk management, primarily used to hedge against the risk of a contingent or uncertain loss

Exam Probability: **High**

18. *Answer choices:*

(see index for correct answer)

- a. information systems assessment
- b. open system
- c. Insurance
- d. empathy

Guidance: level 1

:: Pricing ::

_________ is unwanted sound judged to be unpleasant, loud or disruptive to hearing. From a physics standpoint, _________ is indistinguishable from sound, as both are vibrations through a medium, such as air or water. The difference arises when the brain receives and perceives a sound.

Exam Probability: **Medium**

19. *Answer choices:*

(see index for correct answer)

- a. Noise
- b. Best Rate Guaranteed
- c. Value-based

- d. Hedonic index

Guidance: level 1

:: Marketing ::

A _________ is a group of customers within a business`s serviceable available market at which a business aims its marketing efforts and resources. A _________ is a subset of the total market for a product or service. The _________ typically consists of consumers who exhibit similar characteristics and are considered most likely to buy a business`s market offerings or are likely to be the most profitable segments for the business to service.

Exam Probability: **Low**

20. *Answer choices:*

(see index for correct answer)

- a. Target market
- b. Price war
- c. Pricing strategies
- d. elaboration likelihood model

Guidance: level 1

:: Marketing ::

_________ s are structured marketing strategies designed by merchants to encourage customers to continue to shop at or use the services of businesses associated with each program. These programs exist covering most types of commerce, each one having varying features and rewards-schemes.

Exam Probability: **Medium**

21. *Answer choices:*

(see index for correct answer)

- a. Product lining
- b. Marketing intelligence
- c. Pitching engine
- d. Cyberdoc

Guidance: level 1

:: Contract law ::

A _________ is a legally-binding agreement which recognises and governs the rights and duties of the parties to the agreement. A _________ is legally enforceable because it meets the requirements and approval of the law. An agreement typically involves the exchange of goods, services, money, or promises of any of those. In the event of breach of _________, the law awards the injured party access to legal remedies such as damages and cancellation.

Exam Probability: **Low**

22. *Answer choices:*

(see index for correct answer)

- a. Seaworthiness
- b. Convention on the Law Applicable to Contractual Obligations 1980
- c. Contract
- d. Efficient breach

Guidance: level 1

:: Materials ::

A _________ , also known as a feedstock, unprocessed material, or primary commodity, is a basic material that is used to produce goods, finished products, energy, or intermediate materials which are feedstock for future finished products. As feedstock, the term connotes these materials are bottleneck assets and are highly important with regard to producing other products. An example of this is crude oil, which is a _________ and a feedstock used in the production of industrial chemicals, fuels, plastics, and pharmaceutical goods; lumber is a _________ used to produce a variety of products including all types of furniture. The term " _________ " denotes materials in minimally processed or unprocessed in states; e.g., raw latex, crude oil, cotton, coal, raw biomass, iron ore, air, logs, or water i.e. "...any product of agriculture, forestry, fishing and any other mineral that is in its natural form or which has undergone the transformation required to prepare it for internationally marketing in substantial volumes."

Exam Probability: **High**

23. *Answer choices:*

(see index for correct answer)

- a. Whitetopping
- b. Intumescent
- c. Microporous material
- d. Raw material

Guidance: level 1

:: Sales ::

__________ is a business discipline which is focused on the practical application of sales techniques and the management of a firm`s sales operations. It is an important business function as net sales through the sale of products and services and resulting profit drive most commercial business. These are also typically the goals and performance indicators of __________ .

Exam Probability: **Low**

24. *Answer choices:*

(see index for correct answer)

- a. Proposal
- b. Sales management
- c. Upselling
- d. Contract of sale

Guidance: level 1

:: Marketing ::

_________ is research conducted for a problem that has not been studied more clearly, intended to establish priorities, develop operational definitions and improve the final research design. _________ helps determine the best research design, data-collection method and selection of subjects. It should draw definitive conclusions only with extreme caution. Given its fundamental nature, _________ often relies on techniques such as.

Exam Probability: **Low**

25. *Answer choices:*

(see index for correct answer)

- a. One Town One Product
- b. Exploratory research
- c. Market development
- d. Lead generation

Guidance: level 1

:: Market research ::

__________ is an organized effort to gather information about target markets or customers. It is a very important component of business strategy. The term is commonly interchanged with marketing research; however, expert practitioners may wish to draw a distinction, in that marketing research is concerned specifically about marketing processes, while __________ is concerned specifically with markets.

Exam Probability: **Low**

26. *Answer choices:*

(see index for correct answer)

- a. Technographic segmentation
- b. Vehicle Dependability Study
- c. IRI
- d. Market research

Guidance: level 1

:: Auctioneering ::

An __________ is a process of buying and selling goods or services by offering them up for bid, taking bids, and then selling the item to the highest bidder. The open ascending price __________ is arguably the most common form of __________ in use today. Participants bid openly against one another, with each subsequent bid required to be higher than the previous bid. An __________ eer may announce prices, bidders may call out their bids themselves , or bids may be submitted electronically with the highest current bid publicly displayed. In a Dutch __________ , the __________ eer begins with a high asking price for some quantity of like items; the price is lowered until a participant is willing to accept the __________ eer`s price for some quantity of the goods in the lot or until the seller`s reserve price is met. While __________ s are most associated in the public imagination with the sale of antiques, paintings, rare collectibles and expensive wines, __________ s are also used for commodities, livestock, radio spectrum and used cars. In economic theory, an __________ may refer to any mechanism or set of trading rules for exchange.

Exam Probability: **Low**

27. *Answer choices:*

(see index for correct answer)

- a. Auction
- b. Bidding fee auction
- c. Bid shading
- d. Online travel auction

Guidance: level 1

:: Competition regulators ::

The _________ is an independent agency of the United States government, established in 1914 by the _________ Act. Its principal mission is the promotion of consumer protection and the elimination and prevention of anticompetitive business practices, such as coercive monopoly. It is headquartered in the _________ Building in Washington, D.C.

Exam Probability: **Medium**

28. *Answer choices:*

(see index for correct answer)

- a. Queensland Competition Authority
- b. National Board for Prices and Incomes
- c. Federal Cartel Office
- d. United States Department of Justice Antitrust Division

Guidance: level 1

:: Business models ::

__________ es are privately owned corporations, partnerships, or sole proprietorships that have fewer employees and/or less annual revenue than a regular-sized business or corporation. Businesses are defined as "small" in terms of being able to apply for government support and qualify for preferential tax policy varies depending on the country and industry. __________ es range from fifteen employees under the Australian Fair Work Act 2009, fifty employees according to the definition used by the European Union, and fewer than five hundred employees to qualify for many U.S. __________ Administration programs. While __________ es can also be classified according to other methods, such as annual revenues, shipments, sales, assets, or by annual gross or net revenue or net profits, the number of employees is one of the most widely used measures.

Exam Probability: **High**

29. *Answer choices:*

(see index for correct answer)

- a. Subscription business model
- b. Revenue model
- c. Cooperative
- d. Business Model Canvas

Guidance: level 1

:: Communication design ::

An __________ is a series of advertisement messages that share a single idea and theme which make up an integrated marketing communication . An IMC is a platform in which a group of people can group their ideas, beliefs, and concepts into one large media base. __________ s utilize diverse media channels over a particular time frame and target identified audiences.

Exam Probability: **High**

30. *Answer choices:*

(see index for correct answer)

- a. Writer
- b. Nissa Quanstrom
- c. Advertising campaign
- d. E-Types

Guidance: level 1

:: Business models ::

A __________ , __________ company or daughter company is a company that is owned or controlled by another company, which is called the parent company, parent, or holding company. The __________ can be a company, corporation, or limited liability company. In some cases it is a government or state-owned enterprise. In some cases, particularly in the music and book publishing industries, subsidiaries are referred to as imprints.

Exam Probability: **Low**

31. *Answer choices:*

(see index for correct answer)

- a. Very small business
- b. Subsidiary
- c. Business-agile enterprise
- d. Defensive patent aggregation

Guidance: level 1

:: ::

An _______ is a systematic and independent examination of books, accounts, statutory records, documents and vouchers of an organization to ascertain how far the financial statements as well as non-financial disclosures present a true and fair view of the concern. It also attempts to ensure that the books of accounts are properly maintained by the concern as required by law. _______ ing has become such a ubiquitous phenomenon in the corporate and the public sector that academics started identifying an " _______ Society". The _______ or perceives and recognises the propositions before them for examination, obtains evidence, evaluates the same and formulates an opinion on the basis of his judgement which is communicated through their _______ ing report.

Exam Probability: **Low**

32. *Answer choices:*

(see index for correct answer)

- a. Character
- b. Audit
- c. co-culture
- d. information systems assessment

Guidance: level 1

:: ::

Consumer behaviour is the study of individuals, groups, or organizations and all the activities associated with the purchase, use and disposal of goods and services, including the consumer`s emotional, mental and behavioural responses that precede or follow these activities. Consumer behaviour emerged in the 1940s and 50s as a distinct sub-discipline in the marketing area.

Exam Probability: **High**

33. *Answer choices:*

(see index for correct answer)

- a. corporate values
- b. co-culture
- c. Consumer behavior
- d. Character

Guidance: level 1

:: Packaging ::

In work place, _________ or job _________ means good ranking with the hypothesized conception of requirements of a role. There are two types of job _________ s: contextual and task. Task _________ is related to cognitive ability while contextual _________ is dependent upon personality. Task _________ are behavioral roles that are recognized in job descriptions and by remuneration systems, they are directly related to organizational _________ , whereas, contextual _________ are value based and additional behavioral roles that are not recognized in job descriptions and covered by compensation; they are extra roles that are indirectly related to organizational _________ . Citizenship _________ like contextual _________ means a set of individual activity/contribution that supports the organizational culture.

Exam Probability: **Medium**

34. *Answer choices:*

(see index for correct answer)

- a. Dangerous Substances Directive
- b. Snap case
- c. Tetra Brik
- d. Reel

Guidance: level 1

:: Commerce ::

_________ relates to "the exchange of goods and services, especially on a large scale". It includes legal, economic, political, social, cultural and technological systems that operate in a country or in international trade.

Exam Probability: **Low**

35. *Answer choices:*

(see index for correct answer)

- a. DataCash
- b. Treasure voyages
- c. Safe harbor
- d. Linestanding

Guidance: level 1

:: ::

The _________ is an agreement signed by Canada, Mexico, and the United States, creating a trilateral trade bloc in North America. The agreement came into force on January 1, 1994, and superseded the 1988 Canada–United States Free Trade Agreement between the United States and Canada. The NAFTA trade bloc is one of the largest trade blocs in the world by gross domestic product.

Exam Probability: **High**

36. *Answer choices:*

(see index for correct answer)

- a. North American Free Trade Agreement
- b. empathy
- c. surface-level diversity
- d. hierarchical

Guidance: level 1

:: Manufacturing ::

A _________ is a building for storing goods. _________ s are used by manufacturers, importers, exporters, wholesalers, transport businesses, customs, etc. They are usually large plain buildings in industrial parks on the outskirts of cities, towns or villages.

Exam Probability: **Medium**

37. *Answer choices:*

(see index for correct answer)

- a. Discrete manufacturing
- b. Finished good
- c. Sewing
- d. Warehouse

Guidance: level 1

:: Human resource management ::

_________ encompasses values and behaviors that contribute to the unique social and psychological environment of a business. The _________ influences the way people interact, the context within which knowledge is created, the resistance they will have towards certain changes, and ultimately the way they share knowledge. _________ represents the collective values, beliefs and principles of organizational members and is a product of factors such as history, product, market, technology, strategy, type of employees, management style, and national culture; culture includes the organization's vision, values, norms, systems, symbols, language, assumptions, environment, location, beliefs and habits.

Exam Probability: **High**

38. *Answer choices:*

(see index for correct answer)

- a. Human resource management
- b. Person specification
- c. Organizational culture
- d. T-shaped skills

Guidance: level 1

:: Promotion and marketing communications ::

_________ is one of the elements of the promotional mix. . _________ uses both media and non-media marketing communications for a pre-determined, limited time to increase consumer demand, stimulate market demand or improve product availability. Examples include contests, coupons, freebies, loss leaders, point of purchase displays, premiums, prizes, product samples, and rebates.

Exam Probability: **High**

39. *Answer choices:*

(see index for correct answer)

- a. Sales promotion
- b. Slasher Sale
- c. Co-branding
- d. The One Club

Guidance: level 1

:: Product management ::

A _________ , trade mark, or trade-mark is a recognizable sign, design, or expression which identifies products or services of a particular source from those of others, although _________ s used to identify services are usually called service marks. The _________ owner can be an individual, business organization, or any legal entity. A _________ may be located on a package, a label, a voucher, or on the product itself. For the sake of corporate identity, _________ s are often displayed on company buildings. It is legally recognized as a type of intellectual property.

Exam Probability: **Low**

40. *Answer choices:*

(see index for correct answer)

- a. Trademark
- b. Product information
- c. Trademark distinctiveness
- d. Obsolescence

Guidance: level 1

:: ::

Business is the activity of making one's living or making money by producing or buying and selling products . Simply put, it is "any activity or enterprise entered into for profit. It does not mean it is a company, a corporation, partnership, or have any such formal organization, but it can range from a street peddler to General Motors."

Exam Probability: **High**

41. *Answer choices:*

(see index for correct answer)

- a. surface-level diversity
- b. Firm

- c. process perspective
- d. hierarchical perspective

Guidance: level 1

:: Marketing ::

_________ , sometimes called trigger-based or event-driven marketing, is a marketing strategy that uses two-way communication channels to allow consumers to connect with a company directly. Although this exchange can take place in person, in the last decade it has increasingly taken place almost exclusively online through email, social media, and blogs.

Exam Probability: **Low**

42. *Answer choices:*

(see index for correct answer)

- a. Product lining
- b. Marketing warfare strategies
- c. Mandatory labelling
- d. Markup

Guidance: level 1

:: Project management ::

_________ is the right to exercise power, which can be formalized by a state and exercised by way of judges, appointed executives of government, or the ecclesiastical or priestly appointed representatives of a God or other deities.

Exam Probability: **Low**

43. *Answer choices:*

(see index for correct answer)

- a. TimeTac
- b. Constructability
- c. Resource allocation
- d. Authority

Guidance: level 1

:: Advertising ::

_________ is the behavioral and cognitive process of selectively concentrating on a discrete aspect of information, whether deemed subjective or objective, while ignoring other perceivable information. It is a state of arousal. It is the taking possession by the mind in clear and vivid form of one out of what seem several simultaneous objects or trains of thought. Focalization, the concentration of consciousness, is of its essence. _________ has also been described as the allocation of limited cognitive processing resources.

Exam Probability: **High**

44. *Answer choices:*

(see index for correct answer)

- a. Yashi
- b. Attention
- c. Cidade Limpa
- d. Patent medicine

Guidance: level 1

:: Marketing analytics ::

__________ is a long-term, forward-looking approach to planning with the fundamental goal of achieving a sustainable competitive advantage. Strategic planning involves an analysis of the company`s strategic initial situation prior to the formulation, evaluation and selection of market-oriented competitive position that contributes to the company`s goals and marketing objectives.

Exam Probability: **High**

45. *Answer choices:*

(see index for correct answer)

- a. Market share analysis
- b. Advertising adstock

- c. Marketing accountability
- d. Marketing strategy

Guidance: level 1

:: Consumer behaviour ::

_________ is an activity in which a customer browses the available goods or services presented by one or more retailers with the potential intent to purchase a suitable selection of them. A typology of shopper types has been developed by scholars which identifies one group of shoppers as recreational shoppers, that is, those who enjoy _________ and view it as a leisure activity.

Exam Probability: **Low**

46. *Answer choices:*

(see index for correct answer)

- a. Double jeopardy
- b. Daniel Starch
- c. Post-consumerism
- d. Shopping

Guidance: level 1

:: Problem solving ::

In other words, _________ is a situation where a group of people meet to generate new ideas and solutions around a specific domain of interest by removing inhibitions. People are able to think more freely and they suggest as many spontaneous new ideas as possible. All the ideas are noted down and those ideas are not criticized and after _________ session the ideas are evaluated.The term was popularized by Alex Faickney Osborn in the 1953 book Applied Imagination.

Exam Probability: **Low**

47. *Answer choices:*

(see index for correct answer)

- a. Divergent thinking
- b. Convergent and divergent production
- c. Cognitive acceleration
- d. Cornelian dilemma

Guidance: level 1

:: ::

An __________ is the production of goods or related services within an economy. The major source of revenue of a group or company is the indicator of its relevant __________. When a large group has multiple sources of revenue generation, it is considered to be working in different industries. Manufacturing __________ became a key sector of production and labour in European and North American countries during the Industrial Revolution, upsetting previous mercantile and feudal economies. This came through many successive rapid advances in technology, such as the production of steel and coal.

Exam Probability: **Medium**

48. *Answer choices:*

(see index for correct answer)

- a. surface-level diversity
- b. deep-level diversity
- c. interpersonal communication
- d. open system

Guidance: level 1

:: Marketing ::

__________ is a growth strategy that identifies and develops new market segments for current products. A __________ strategy targets non-buying customers in currently targeted segments. It also targets new customers in new segments.

Exam Probability: **Low**

49. *Answer choices:*

(see index for correct answer)

- a. Notability
- b. Market development
- c. Generic brand
- d. Corporate capabilities package

Guidance: level 1

:: Advertising ::

A _________ is a document used by creative professionals and agencies to develop creative deliverables: visual design, copy, advertising, web sites, etc. The document is usually developed by the requestor and approved by the creative team of designers, writers, and project managers. In some cases, the project`s _________ may need creative director approval before work will commence.

Exam Probability: **Low**

50. *Answer choices:*

(see index for correct answer)

- a. Van lettering
- b. International Convention to Facilitate the Importation of Commercial

Samples and Advertising Material

- c. Creative brief
- d. Autosurf

Guidance: level 1

:: Goods ::

In most contexts, the concept of _________ denotes the conduct that should be preferred when posed with a choice between possible actions. _________ is generally considered to be the opposite of evil, and is of interest in the study of morality, ethics, religion and philosophy. The specific meaning and etymology of the term and its associated translations among ancient and contemporary languages show substantial variation in its inflection and meaning depending on circumstances of place, history, religious, or philosophical context.

Exam Probability: **Low**

51. *Answer choices:*

(see index for correct answer)

- a. Free good
- b. excludable
- c. Yellow goods
- d. Global public good

Guidance: level 1

:: Brand management ::

Marketing communications uses different marketing channels and tools in combination: Marketing communication channels focus on any way a business communicates a message to its desired market, or the market in general. A marketing communication tool can be anything from: advertising, personal selling, direct marketing, sponsorship, communication, and promotion to public relations.

Exam Probability: **Low**

52. *Answer choices:*

(see index for correct answer)

- a. BrandActive
- b. Promotional model
- c. Branded content
- d. Brand legacy

Guidance: level 1

:: Commercial item transport and distribution ::

Wholesaling or distributing is the sale of goods or merchandise to retailers; to industrial, commercial, institutional, or other professional business users; or to other _________ rs and related subordinated services. In general, it is the sale of goods to anyone other than a standard consumer.

Exam Probability: **High**

53. *Answer choices:*

(see index for correct answer)

- a. Ship transport
- b. Sealift
- c. Wholesale
- d. Transshipment

Guidance: level 1

:: National accounts ::

_________ is a monetary measure of the market value of all the final goods and services produced in a period of time, often annually. GDP per capita does not, however, reflect differences in the cost of living and the inflation rates of the countries; therefore using a basis of GDP per capita at purchasing power parity is arguably more useful when comparing differences in living standards between nations.

Exam Probability: **Low**

54. *Answer choices:*

(see index for correct answer)

- a. Gross domestic product
- b. Fixed capital
- c. capital formation

Guidance: level 1

:: ::

A _________ is a discussion or informational website published on the World Wide Web consisting of discrete, often informal diary-style text entries . Posts are typically displayed in reverse chronological order, so that the most recent post appears first, at the top of the web page. Until 2009, _________ s were usually the work of a single individual, occasionally of a small group, and often covered a single subject or topic. In the 2010s, "multi-author _________ s" emerged, featuring the writing of multiple authors and sometimes professionally edited. MABs from newspapers, other media outlets, universities, think tanks, advocacy groups, and similar institutions account for an increasing quantity of _________ traffic. The rise of Twitter and other "micro _________ ging" systems helps integrate MABs and single-author _________ s into the news media. _________ can also be used as a verb, meaning to maintain or add content to a _________ .

Exam Probability: **Medium**

55. *Answer choices:*

(see index for correct answer)

- a. similarity-attraction theory
- b. Blog
- c. surface-level diversity
- d. personal values

Guidance: level 1

:: Marketing ::

_________ is the process of using surveys to evaluate consumer acceptance of a new product idea prior to the introduction of a product to the market. It is important not to confuse _________ with advertising testing, brand testing and packaging testing; as is sometimes done. _________ focuses on the basic product idea, without the embellishments and puffery inherent in advertising.

Exam Probability: **Low**

56. *Answer choices:*

(see index for correct answer)

- a. Mass marketing
- b. Concept testing
- c. The International Customer Service Institute
- d. Business stature

Guidance: level 1

:: Cultural appropriation ::

__________ is a social and economic order that encourages the acquisition of goods and services in ever-increasing amounts. With the industrial revolution, but particularly in the 20th century, mass production led to an economic crisis: there was overproduction—the supply of goods would grow beyond consumer demand, and so manufacturers turned to planned obsolescence and advertising to manipulate consumer spending. In 1899, a book on __________ published by Thorstein Veblen, called The Theory of the Leisure Class, examined the widespread values and economic institutions emerging along with the widespread "leisure time" in the beginning of the 20th century. In it Veblen "views the activities and spending habits of this leisure class in terms of conspicuous and vicarious consumption and waste. Both are related to the display of status and not to functionality or usefulness."

Exam Probability: **Medium**

57. *Answer choices:*

(see index for correct answer)

- a. Consumerism
- b. Global village
- c. Racebending
- d. Yoga piracy

Guidance: level 1

:: Marketing techniques ::

The __________ or unique selling point is a marketing concept first proposed as a theory to explain a pattern in successful advertising campaigns of the early 1940s. The USP states that such campaigns made unique propositions to customers that convinced them to switch brands. The term was developed by television advertising pioneer Rosser Reeves of Ted Bates & Company. Theodore Levitt, a professor at Harvard Business School, suggested that, "Differentiation is one of the most important strategic and tactical activities in which companies must constantly engage." The term has been used to describe one`s "personal brand" in the marketplace. Today, the term is used in other fields or just casually to refer to any aspect of an object that differentiates it from similar objects.

Exam Probability: **Low**

58. *Answer choices:*

(see index for correct answer)

- a. Unique selling proposition
- b. Book signing
- c. Enterprise engagement
- d. REAN

Guidance: level 1

:: Budgets ::

A _________ is a financial plan for a defined period, often one year. It may also include planned sales volumes and revenues, resource quantities, costs and expenses, assets, liabilities and cash flows. Companies, governments, families and other organizations use it to express strategic plans of activities or events in measurable terms.

Exam Probability: **High**

59. *Answer choices:*

(see index for correct answer)

- a. Personal budget
- b. Operating budget
- c. Budget
- d. Energy budget

Guidance: level 1

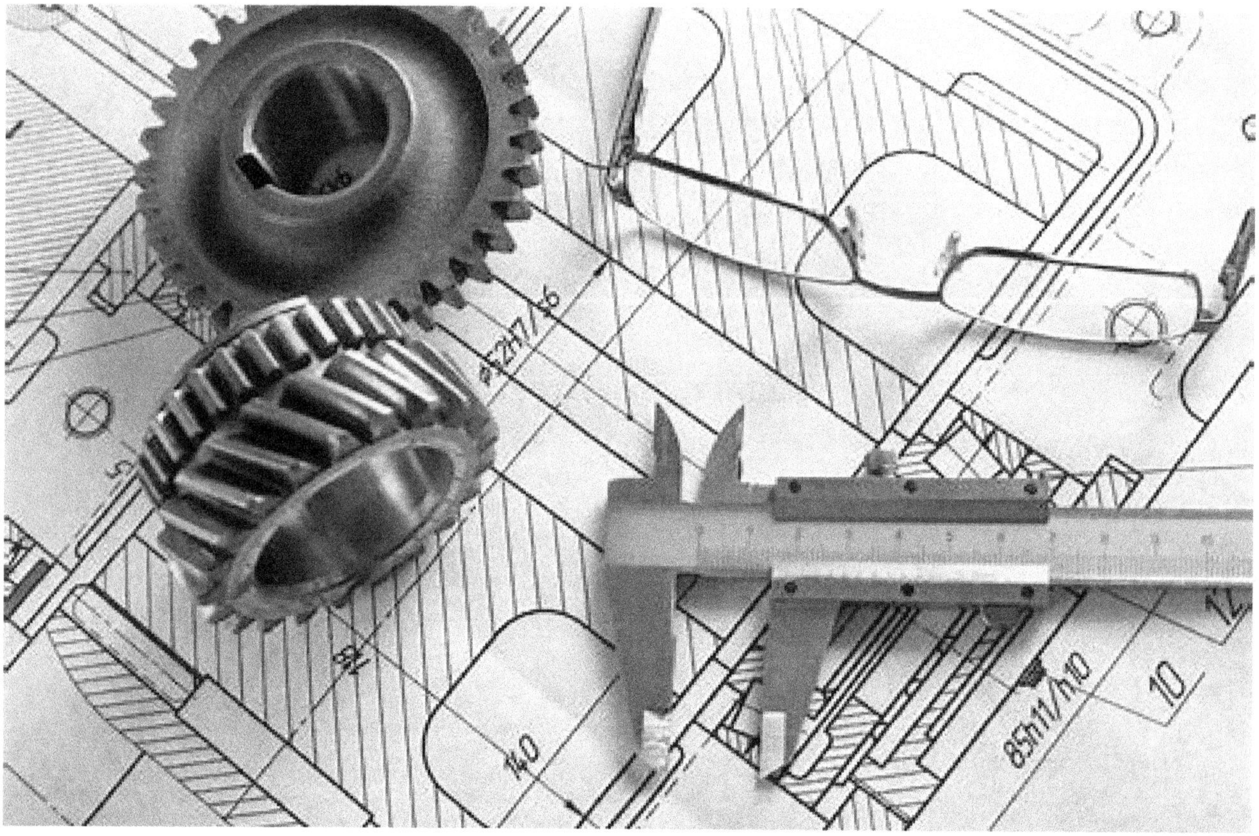

Manufacturing

Manufacturing is the production of merchandise for use or sale using labor and machines, tools, chemical and biological processing, or formulation. The term may refer to a range of human activity, from handicraft to high tech, but is most commonly applied to industrial design , in which raw materials are transformed into finished goods on a large scale. Such finished goods may be sold to other manufacturers for the production of other, more complex products, such as aircraft, household appliances, furniture, sports equipment or automobiles, or sold to wholesalers, who in turn sell them to retailers, who then sell them to end users and consumers.

:: Marketing techniques ::

A __________ is an award to be given to a person, a group of people like a sports team, or organization to recognise and reward actions or achievements. Official __________ s often involve monetary rewards as well as the fame that comes with them. Some __________ s are also associated with extravagant awarding ceremonies, such as the Academy Awards.

Exam Probability: **High**

1. *Answer choices:*

(see index for correct answer)

- a. Prize
- b. Product demonstration
- c. Demand-side platform
- d. Book signing

Guidance: level 1

:: Business process ::

A __________ or business method is a collection of related, structured activities or tasks by people or equipment which in a specific sequence produce a service or product for a particular customer or customers. __________ es occur at all organizational levels and may or may not be visible to the customers. A __________ may often be visualized as a flowchart of a sequence of activities with interleaving decision points or as a process matrix of a sequence of activities with relevance rules based on data in the process. The benefits of using __________ es include improved customer satisfaction and improved agility for reacting to rapid market change. Process-oriented organizations break down the barriers of structural departments and try to avoid functional silos.

Exam Probability: **Medium**

2. *Answer choices:*

(see index for correct answer)

- a. Extended Enterprise Modeling Language
- b. Business process
- c. Process mining
- d. Business process outsourcing to India

Guidance: level 1

:: ::

__________ refers to a business or organization attempting to acquire goods or services to accomplish its goals. Although there are several organizations that attempt to set standards in the __________ process, processes can vary greatly between organizations. Typically the word " __________ " is not used interchangeably with the word "procurement", since procurement typically includes expediting, supplier quality, and transportation and logistics in addition to __________ .

Exam Probability: **High**

3. *Answer choices:*

(see index for correct answer)

- a. hierarchical perspective
- b. information systems assessment
- c. similarity-attraction theory
- d. Purchasing

Guidance: level 1

:: Evaluation ::

__________ is a way of preventing mistakes and defects in manufactured products and avoiding problems when delivering products or services to customers; which ISO 9000 defines as "part of quality management focused on providing confidence that quality requirements will be fulfilled". This defect prevention in __________ differs subtly from defect detection and rejection in quality control and has been referred to as a shift left since it focuses on quality earlier in the process .

Exam Probability: **Medium**

4. *Answer choices:*

(see index for correct answer)

- a. American Evaluation Association
- b. Advocacy evaluation
- c. Review
- d. Academic equivalency evaluation

Guidance: level 1

:: Help desk ::

Data center management is the collection of tasks performed by those responsible for managing ongoing operation of a data center This includes Business service management and planning for the future.

Exam Probability: **Medium**

5. *Answer choices:*

(see index for correct answer)

- a. Web Help Desk
- b. Computer-aided maintenance
- c. EHelp Corporation
- d. Technical support

Guidance: level 1

:: Information systems ::

_________ is the process of creating, sharing, using and managing the knowledge and information of an organisation. It refers to a multidisciplinary approach to achieving organisational objectives by making the best use of knowledge.

Exam Probability: **Medium**

6. *Answer choices:*

(see index for correct answer)

- a. Information processor
- b. Knowledge management
- c. TOPS
- d. European Research Center for Information Systems

Guidance: level 1

:: Project management ::

__________ is the right to exercise power, which can be formalized by a state and exercised by way of judges, appointed executives of government, or the ecclesiastical or priestly appointed representatives of a God or other deities.

Exam Probability: **Low**

7. *Answer choices:*

(see index for correct answer)

- a. Authority
- b. Task
- c. Project blog
- d. Total project control

Guidance: level 1

:: Business process ::

__________ is the value to an enterprise which is derived from the techniques, procedures, and programs that implement and enhance the delivery of goods and services. __________ is one of the three components of structural capital, itself a component of intellectual capital. __________ can be seen as the value of processes to any entity, whether for profit or not-for profit, but is most commonly used in reference to for-profit entities.

Exam Probability: **Medium**

8. *Answer choices:*

(see index for correct answer)

- a. Business Process Definition Metamodel
- b. A Guide to the Business Analysis Body of Knowledge
- c. Hi-tech export
- d. Outsourced document processing

Guidance: level 1

:: ::

An _________ is a company that produces parts and equipment that may be marketed by another manufacturer. For example, Foxconn, a Taiwanese electronics contract manufacturing company, which produces a variety of parts and equipment for companies such as Apple Inc., Dell, Google, Huawei, Nintendo, etc., is the largest OEM company in the world by both scale and revenue.

Exam Probability: **High**

9. *Answer choices:*

(see index for correct answer)

- a. imperative
- b. Sarbanes-Oxley act of 2002
- c. Original equipment manufacturer
- d. corporate values

Guidance: level 1

:: Insulators ::

A _________ is a piece of soft cloth large enough either to cover or to enfold a great portion of the user's body, usually when sleeping or otherwise at rest, thereby trapping radiant bodily heat that otherwise would be lost through convection, and so keeping the body warm.

Exam Probability: **High**

10. *Answer choices:*

(see index for correct answer)

- a. Pipe insulation
- b. Dynamic insulation
- c. Sleeping bag
- d. Blanket

Guidance: level 1

:: Packaging ::

In work place, _________ or job _________ means good ranking with the hypothesized conception of requirements of a role. There are two types of job _________ s: contextual and task. Task _________ is related to cognitive ability while contextual _________ is dependent upon personality. Task _________ are behavioral roles that are recognized in job descriptions and by remuneration systems, they are directly related to organizational _________, whereas, contextual _________ are value based and additional behavioral roles that are not recognized in job descriptions and covered by compensation; they are extra roles that are indirectly related to organizational _________. Citizenship _________ like contextual _________ means a set of individual activity/contribution that supports the organizational culture.

Exam Probability: **Low**

11. *Answer choices:*

(see index for correct answer)

- a. Self-heating food packaging
- b. Performance
- c. Tamper resistance
- d. Longbox

Guidance: level 1

:: Lean manufacturing ::

_________ is a Japanese term that means "mistake-proofing" or "inadvertent error prevention". A _________ is any mechanism in any process that helps an equipment operator avoid mistakes . Its purpose is to eliminate product defects by preventing, correcting, or drawing attention to human errors as they occur. The concept was formalised, and the term adopted, by Shigeo Shingo as part of the Toyota Production System. It was originally described as baka-yoke, but as this means "fool-proofing" the name was changed to the milder _________ .

Exam Probability: **Medium**

12. *Answer choices:*

(see index for correct answer)

- a. Autonomation
- b. Poka-yoke
- c. Lean services
- d. Kanban

Guidance: level 1

:: Supply chain management ::

__________ is a core supply chain function and includes supply chain planning and supply chain execution capabilities. Specifically, __________ is the capability firms use to plan total material requirements. The material requirements are communicated to procurement and other functions for sourcing. __________ is also responsible for determining the amount of material to be deployed at each stocking location across the supply chain, establishing material replenishment plans, determining inventory levels to hold for each type of inventory , and communicating information regarding material needs throughout the extended supply chain.

Exam Probability: **Low**

13. *Answer choices:*

(see index for correct answer)

- a. Materials management
- b. Institute for Supply Management
- c. Procurement
- d. Supply chain cyber security

Guidance: level 1

:: Project management ::

__________ is a work methodology emphasizing the parallelisation of tasks , which is sometimes called simultaneous engineering or integrated product development using an integrated product team approach. It refers to an approach used in product development in which functions of design engineering, manufacturing engineering, and other functions are integrated to reduce the time required to bring a new product to market.

Exam Probability: **Low**

14. *Answer choices:*

(see index for correct answer)

- a. Product description
- b. Identifying and Managing Project Risk
- c. Case competition
- d. Concurrent engineering

Guidance: level 1

:: ::

Some scenarios associate "this kind of planning" with learning "life skills".Schedules are necessary, or at least useful, in situations where individuals need to know what time they must be at a specific location to receive a specific service, and where people need to accomplish a set of goals within a set time period.

Exam Probability: **Low**

15. *Answer choices:*

(see index for correct answer)

- a. functional perspective
- b. levels of analysis
- c. Scheduling
- d. interpersonal communication

Guidance: level 1

:: E-commerce ::

_________ is the business-to-business or business-to-consumer or business-to-government purchase and sale of supplies, work, and services through the Internet as well as other information and networking systems, such as electronic data interchange and enterprise resource planning.

Exam Probability: **Medium**

16. *Answer choices:*

(see index for correct answer)

- a. Billing and Settlement Plan
- b. E-procurement
- c. Value-added network
- d. ITransact

Guidance: level 1

:: Metals ::

A _________ is a material that, when freshly prepared, polished, or fractured, shows a lustrous appearance, and conducts electricity and heat relatively well. _________ s are typically malleable or ductile . A _________ may be a chemical element such as iron, or an alloy such as stainless steel.

Exam Probability: **Medium**

17. *Answer choices:*

(see index for correct answer)

- a. Minor metals
- b. Polymetal
- c. Metal
- d. Metal theft

Guidance: level 1

:: ::

An __________ is, most an organized examination or formal evaluation exercise. In engineering activities __________ involves the measurements, tests, and gauges applied to certain characteristics in regard to an object or activity. The results are usually compared to specified requirements and standards for determining whether the item or activity is in line with these targets, often with a Standard __________ Procedure in place to ensure consistent checking. __________ s are usually non-destructive.

Exam Probability: **High**

18. *Answer choices:*

(see index for correct answer)

- a. Inspection
- b. open system
- c. surface-level diversity
- d. deep-level diversity

Guidance: level 1

:: Chemical processes ::

_________ is the understanding and application of the fundamental principles and laws of nature that allow us to transform raw material and energy into products that are useful to society, at an industrial level. By taking advantage of the driving forces of nature such as pressure, temperature and concentration gradients, as well as the law of conservation of mass, process engineers can develop methods to synthesize and purify large quantities of desired chemical products. _________ focuses on the design, operation, control, optimization and intensification of chemical, physical, and biological processes. _________ encompasses a vast range of industries, such as agriculture, automotive, biotechnical, chemical, food, material development, mining, nuclear, petrochemical, pharmaceutical, and software development. The application of systematic computer-based methods to _________ is "process systems engineering".

Exam Probability: **High**

19. *Answer choices:*

(see index for correct answer)

- a. Process engineering
- b. OxFA process
- c. Brin process
- d. Efflorescence

Guidance: level 1

:: Packaging materials ::

__________ is a non-crystalline, amorphous solid that is often transparent and has widespread practical, technological, and decorative uses in, for example, window panes, tableware, and optoelectronics. The most familiar, and historically the oldest, types of manufactured __________ are "silicate __________es" based on the chemical compound silica , the primary constituent of sand. The term __________, in popular usage, is often used to refer only to this type of material, which is familiar from use as window __________ and in __________ bottles. Of the many silica-based __________es that exist, ordinary glazing and container __________ is formed from a specific type called soda-lime __________, composed of approximately 75% silicon dioxide , sodium oxide from sodium carbonate , calcium oxide , also called lime, and several minor additives.

Exam Probability: **High**

20. *Answer choices:*

(see index for correct answer)

- a. Inflatable air cushion
- b. Coated paper
- c. Unica
- d. Glass

Guidance: level 1

:: Quality management ::

In quality management system, a _________ is a document developed by management to express the directive of the top management with respect to quality. _________ management is a strategic item.

Exam Probability: **High**

21. *Answer choices:*

(see index for correct answer)

- a. Quality management system
- b. Quality policy
- c. QC Reporting
- d. Product quality risk in supply chain

Guidance: level 1

:: Product management ::

_________ s, also known as Shewhart charts or process-behavior charts, are a statistical process control tool used to determine if a manufacturing or business process is in a state of control.

Exam Probability: **Medium**

22. *Answer choices:*

(see index for correct answer)

- a. Discontinuation
- b. Visual brand language
- c. Product family engineering
- d. Control chart

Guidance: level 1

:: Alchemical processes ::

In chemistry, a _________ is a special type of homogeneous mixture composed of two or more substances. In such a mixture, a solute is a substance dissolved in another substance, known as a solvent. The mixing process of a _________ happens at a scale where the effects of chemical polarity are involved, resulting in interactions that are specific to solvation. The _________ assumes the phase of the solvent when the solvent is the larger fraction of the mixture, as is commonly the case. The concentration of a solute in a _________ is the mass of that solute expressed as a percentage of the mass of the whole _________. The term aqueous _________ is when one of the solvents is water.

Exam Probability: **Medium**

23. *Answer choices:*

(see index for correct answer)

- a. Congelation
- b. Unity of opposites
- c. Solution
- d. Fermentation in food processing

Guidance: level 1

:: Management ::

An _________ is a loosely coupled, self-organizing network of firms that combine their economic output to provide products and services offerings to the market. Firms in the _________ may operate independently, for example, through market mechanisms, or cooperatively through agreements and contracts. They provide value added service or product to the OEM .

Exam Probability: **High**

24. *Answer choices:*

(see index for correct answer)

- a. Extended enterprise
- b. Commercial management
- c. Association management company
- d. Operations management

Guidance: level 1

:: Information technology management ::

The term __________ is used to refer to periods when a system is unavailable. __________ or outage duration refers to a period of time that a system fails to provide or perform its primary function. Reliability, availability, recovery, and unavailability are related concepts.The unavailability is the proportion of a time-span that a system is unavailable or offline.This is usually a result of the system failing to function because of an unplanned event, or because of routine maintenance .

Exam Probability: **Medium**

25. *Answer choices:*

(see index for correct answer)

- a. Records management
- b. ESCM-CL
- c. Downtime
- d. Information technology operations

Guidance: level 1

:: Information technology management ::

__________ is a collective term for all approaches to prepare , support and help individuals, teams, and organizations in making organizational change. The most common change drivers include: technological evolution, process reviews, crisis, and consumer habit changes; pressure from new business entrants, acquisitions, mergers, and organizational restructuring. It includes methods that redirect or redefine the use of resources, business process, budget allocations, or other modes of operation that significantly change a company or organization. Organizational __________ considers the full organization and what needs to change, while __________ may be used solely to refer to how people and teams are affected by such organizational transition. It deals with many different disciplines, from behavioral and social sciences to information technology and business solutions.

Exam Probability: **Medium**

26. *Answer choices:*

(see index for correct answer)

- a. Trustworthy computing
- b. Application Portfolio Management
- c. Change management
- d. Many-to-many

Guidance: level 1

:: Chemical reactions ::

A _________ is a process that leads to the chemical transformation of one set of chemical substances to another. Classically, _________ s encompass changes that only involve the positions of electrons in the forming and breaking of chemical bonds between atoms, with no change to the nuclei , and can often be described by a chemical equation. Nuclear chemistry is a sub-discipline of chemistry that involves the _________ s of unstable and radioactive elements where both electronic and nuclear changes can occur.

Exam Probability: **Medium**

27. *Answer choices:*

(see index for correct answer)

- a. Dissociative substitution
- b. Chemical reaction
- c. Carbonylation
- d. Thermal decomposition

Guidance: level 1

:: Management accounting ::

" _________ s are the structural determinants of the cost of an activity, reflecting any linkages or interrelationships that affect it". Therefore we could assume that the _________ s determine the cost behavior within the activities, reflecting the links that these have with other activities and relationships that affect them.

Exam Probability: **Medium**

28. *Answer choices:*

(see index for correct answer)

- a. Cost driver
- b. Management accounting
- c. Direct material usage variance
- d. Profit center

Guidance: level 1

:: Materials ::

A _________ , also known as a feedstock, unprocessed material, or primary commodity, is a basic material that is used to produce goods, finished products, energy, or intermediate materials which are feedstock for future finished products. As feedstock, the term connotes these materials are bottleneck assets and are highly important with regard to producing other products. An example of this is crude oil, which is a _________ and a feedstock used in the production of industrial chemicals, fuels, plastics, and pharmaceutical goods; lumber is a _________ used to produce a variety of products including all types of furniture. The term " _________ " denotes materials in minimally processed or unprocessed in states; e.g., raw latex, crude oil, cotton, coal, raw biomass, iron ore, air, logs, or water i.e. "...any product of agriculture, forestry, fishing and any other mineral that is in its natural form or which has undergone the transformation required to prepare it for internationally marketing in substantial volumes."

Exam Probability: **Low**

29. *Answer choices:*

(see index for correct answer)

- a. Raw material
- b. Whitetopping
- c. Food contact materials
- d. Ultralight material

Guidance: level 1

:: Management ::

_________ is the practice of initiating, planning, executing, controlling, and closing the work of a team to achieve specific goals and meet specific success criteria at the specified time.

Exam Probability: **Medium**

30. *Answer choices:*

(see index for correct answer)

- a. Project management
- b. Marketing plan
- c. Bed management
- d. Business-oriented architecture

Guidance: level 1

:: Sampling (statistics) ::

__________ uses statistical sampling to determine whether to accept or reject a production lot of material. It has been a common quality control technique used in industry. It is usually done as products leaves the factory, or in some cases even within the factory. Most often a producer supplies a consumer a number of items and a decision to accept or reject the items is made by determining the number of defective items in a sample from the lot. The lot is accepted if the number of defects falls below where the acceptance number or otherwise the lot is rejected.

Exam Probability: **Low**

31. *Answer choices:*

(see index for correct answer)

- a. Sampling frame
- b. Acceptance sampling
- c. Unmatched count
- d. Selective recruitment

Guidance: level 1

:: Data management ::

__________ is an object-oriented program and library developed by CERN. It was originally designed for particle physics data analysis and contains several features specific to this field, but it is also used in other applications such as astronomy and data mining. The latest release is 6.16.00, as of 2018-11-14.

Exam Probability: **Medium**

32. *Answer choices:*

(see index for correct answer)

- a. Data aggregator
- b. ROOT
- c. CERF
- d. Junction table

Guidance: level 1

:: Help desk ::

A high-explosive anti-tank warhead is a type of shaped charge explosive that uses the Munroe effect to penetrate thick tank armor. The warhead functions by having the explosive charge collapse a metal liner inside the warhead into a high-velocity superplastic jet. This superplastic jet is capable of penetrating armor steel to a depth of seven or more times the diameter of the charge but is usually used to immobilize or destroy tanks. Due to the way they work, they do not have to be fired as fast as an armor piercing shell, allowing less recoil. Contrary to a widespread misconception , the jet does not melt its way through armor, as its effect is purely kinetic in nature. The _________ warhead has become less effective against tanks and other armored vehicles due to the use of composite armor, explosive-reactive armor, and active protection systems which destroy the _________ warhead before it hits the tank. Even though _________ rounds are less effective against the heavy armor found on 2010s main battle tanks, _________ warheads remain a threat against less-armored parts of a main battle tank and against lighter armored vehicles or unarmored vehicles and helicopters.

Exam Probability: **High**

33. *Answer choices:*

(see index for correct answer)

- a. KnowledgeBase Manager Pro
- b. Web Help Desk
- c. SysAid Technologies
- d. Computer-aided maintenance

Guidance: level 1

:: Data management ::

__________ is the ability of a physical product to remain functional, without requiring excessive maintenance or repair, when faced with the challenges of normal operation over its design lifetime. There are several measures of __________ in use, including years of life, hours of use, and number of operational cycles. In economics, goods with a long usable life are referred to as durable goods.

Exam Probability: **Medium**

34. *Answer choices:*

(see index for correct answer)

- a. Semantic integration
- b. Durability
- c. Log trigger
- d. Core Data

Guidance: level 1

:: Fault-tolerant computer systems ::

_________ decision-making is a group decision-making process in which group members develop, and agree to support a decision in the best interest of the whole group or common goal. _________ may be defined professionally as an acceptable resolution, one that can be supported, even if not the "favourite" of each individual. It has its origin in the Latin word consensus , which is from consentio meaning literally feel together. It is used to describe both the decision and the process of reaching a decision. _________ decision-making is thus concerned with the process of deliberating and finalizing a decision, and the social, economic, legal, environmental and political effects of applying this process.

Exam Probability: **High**

35. *Answer choices:*

(see index for correct answer)

- a. Consensus
- b. Uptime
- c. Computer cluster
- d. SpaceWire

Guidance: level 1

:: Asset ::

In financial accounting, an _________ is any resource owned by the business. Anything tangible or intangible that can be owned or controlled to produce value and that is held by a company to produce positive economic value is an _________. Simply stated, _________s represent value of ownership that can be converted into cash . The balance sheet of a firm records the monetary value of the _________s owned by that firm. It covers money and other valuables belonging to an individual or to a business.

Exam Probability: **Low**

36. *Answer choices:*

(see index for correct answer)

- a. Asset
- b. Current asset

Guidance: level 1

:: Project management ::

_________ is a process of setting goals, planning and/or controlling the organizing and leading the execution of any type of activity, such as.

Exam Probability: **Medium**

37. *Answer choices:*

(see index for correct answer)

- a. Team performance management
- b. Time horizon
- c. Task management
- d. Collaborative project management

Guidance: level 1

:: Business planning ::

__________ is a critical component to the successful delivery of any project, programme or activity. A stakeholder is any individual, group or organization that can affect, be affected by, or perceive itself to be affected by a programme.

Exam Probability: **High**

38. *Answer choices:*

(see index for correct answer)

- a. Business war games
- b. Exit planning
- c. Customer Demand Planning
- d. Gap analysis

Guidance: level 1

:: Quality management ::

__________ ensures that an organization, product or service is consistent. It has four main components: quality planning, quality assurance, quality control and quality improvement. __________ is focused not only on product and service quality, but also on the means to achieve it. __________, therefore, uses quality assurance and control of processes as well as products to achieve more consistent quality.What a customer wants and is willing to pay for it determines quality. It is written or unwritten commitment to a known or unknown consumer in the market . Thus, quality can be defined as fitness for intended use or, in other words, how well the product performs its intended function

Exam Probability: **Low**

39. *Answer choices:*

(see index for correct answer)

- a. Quality Management Maturity Grid
- b. PQASSO
- c. Quality management
- d. TL 9000

Guidance: level 1

:: Production and manufacturing ::

_________ is a comprehensive and rigorous industrial process by which a previously sold, leased, used, worn or non-functional product or part is returned to a 'like-new' or 'better-than-new' condition, from both a quality and performance perspective, through a controlled, reproducible and sustainable process.

Exam Probability: **Medium**

40. *Answer choices:*

(see index for correct answer)

- a. Continuous production
- b. Remanufacturing
- c. Fiberglass molding
- d. Queueing theory

Guidance: level 1

:: ::

In a supply chain, a _________ , or a seller, is an enterprise that contributes goods or services. Generally, a supply chain _________ manufactures inventory/stock items and sells them to the next link in the chain. Today, these terms refer to a supplier of any good or service.

Exam Probability: **High**

41. *Answer choices:*

(see index for correct answer)

- a. functional perspective
- b. surface-level diversity
- c. Vendor
- d. Character

Guidance: level 1

:: Process management ::

A __________ is a diagram commonly used in chemical and process engineering to indicate the general flow of plant processes and equipment. The PFD displays the relationship between major equipment of a plant facility and does not show minor details such as piping details and designations. Another commonly used term for a PFD is a flowsheet.

Exam Probability: **Low**

42. *Answer choices:*

(see index for correct answer)

- a. Process flow diagram
- b. Chemical plant cost indexes
- c. Theory of constraints
- d. Value grid

Guidance: level 1

:: Industries ::

The ________ comprises the companies that produce industrial chemicals. Central to the modern world economy, it converts raw materials into more than 70,000 different products. The plastics industry contains some overlap, as most chemical companies produce plastic as well as other chemicals.

Exam Probability: **Low**

43. *Answer choices:*

(see index for correct answer)

- a. Video game industry
- b. Chemical industry
- c. Housing industry
- d. Alcohol industry

Guidance: level 1

:: Metal forming ::

_________ is a type of motion that combines rotation and translation of that object with respect to a surface , such that, if ideal conditions exist, the two are in contact with each other without sliding.

Exam Probability: **Medium**

44. *Answer choices:*

(see index for correct answer)

- a. Heading
- b. Ironing
- c. Goldbeating
- d. Lankford coefficient

Guidance: level 1

:: Costs ::

_________ is the process used by companies to reduce their costs and increase their profits. Depending on a company's services or product, the strategies can vary. Every decision in the product development process affects cost.

Exam Probability: **High**

45. *Answer choices:*

(see index for correct answer)

- a. Direct labor cost
- b. Explicit cost
- c. Opportunity cost of capital
- d. Incremental cost-effectiveness ratio

Guidance: level 1

:: Waste ::

_________ are unwanted or unusable materials. _________ is any substance which is discarded after primary use, or is worthless, defective and of no use. A by-product by contrast is a joint product of relatively minor economic value. A _________ product may become a by-product, joint product or resource through an invention that raises a _________ product`s value above zero.

Exam Probability: **High**

46. *Answer choices:*

(see index for correct answer)

- a. Uncontrolled waste
- b. Toxic waste
- c. Ship graveyard
- d. Coal slurry

Guidance: level 1

:: Production and manufacturing ::

__________ is the process of determining the production capacity needed by an organization to meet changing demands for its products. In the context of __________ , design capacity is the maximum amount of work that an organization is capable of completing in a given period. Effective capacity is the maximum amount of work that an organization is capable of completing in a given period due to constraints such as quality problems, delays, material handling, etc.

Exam Probability: **High**

47. *Answer choices:*

(see index for correct answer)

- a. Countercurrent exchange
- b. Managed services
- c. Critical to quality
- d. Profibus

Guidance: level 1

:: Outsourcing ::

A _________ is a document that solicits proposal, often made through a bidding process, by an agency or company interested in procurement of a commodity, service, or valuable asset, to potential suppliers to submit business proposals. It is submitted early in the procurement cycle, either at the preliminary study, or procurement stage.

Exam Probability: **Low**

48. *Answer choices:*

(see index for correct answer)

- a. LEO
- b. Oregon Bridge Delivery Partners
- c. Request for proposal
- d. Chris Ducker

Guidance: level 1

:: Lean manufacturing ::

_________ is a scheduling system for lean manufacturing and just-in-time manufacturing . Taiichi Ohno, an industrial engineer at Toyota, developed _________ to improve manufacturing efficiency. _________ is one method to achieve JIT. The system takes its name from the cards that track production within a factory. For many in the automotive sector, _________ is known as the "Toyota nameplate system" and as such the term is not used by some other automakers.

Exam Probability: **Low**

49. *Answer choices:*

(see index for correct answer)

- a. CONWIP
- b. Kanban
- c. Mura
- d. Heijunka box

Guidance: level 1

:: Project management ::

A _________ is a team whose members usually belong to different groups, functions and are assigned to activities for the same project. A team can be divided into sub-teams according to need. Usually _________ s are only used for a defined period of time. They are disbanded after the project is deemed complete. Due to the nature of the specific formation and disbandment, _________ s are usually in organizations.

Exam Probability: **Medium**

50. *Answer choices:*

(see index for correct answer)

- a. Project team
- b. Cost database

- c. Lean project management
- d. Burn down chart

Guidance: level 1

:: Management ::

__________ is a method of quality control which employs statistical methods to monitor and control a process. This helps to ensure that the process operates efficiently, producing more specification-conforming products with less waste . SPC can be applied to any process where the "conforming product" output can be measured. Key tools used in SPC include run charts, control charts, a focus on continuous improvement, and the design of experiments. An example of a process where SPC is applied is manufacturing lines.

Exam Probability: **High**

51. *Answer choices:*

(see index for correct answer)

- a. DMSMS
- b. Discovery-driven planning
- c. Kata
- d. Line manager

Guidance: level 1

:: Unit operations ::

_________ is a discipline of thermal engineering that concerns the generation, use, conversion, and exchange of thermal energy between physical systems. _________ is classified into various mechanisms, such as thermal conduction, thermal convection, thermal radiation, and transfer of energy by phase changes. Engineers also consider the transfer of mass of differing chemical species, either cold or hot, to achieve _________. While these mechanisms have distinct characteristics, they often occur simultaneously in the same system.

Exam Probability: **Medium**

52. *Answer choices:*

(see index for correct answer)

- a. Unit Operations of Chemical Engineering
- b. Heat transfer
- c. Unit operation
- d. Clearing factor

Guidance: level 1

:: Sensitivity analysis ::

_________ is the study of how the uncertainty in the output of a mathematical model or system can be divided and allocated to different sources of uncertainty in its inputs. A related practice is uncertainty analysis, which has a greater focus on uncertainty quantification and propagation of uncertainty; ideally, uncertainty and _________ should be run in tandem.

Exam Probability: **High**

53. *Answer choices:*

(see index for correct answer)

- a. Variance-based sensitivity analysis
- b. Sensitivity analysis
- c. Fourier amplitude sensitivity testing
- d. Elementary effects method

Guidance: level 1

:: Gas technologies ::

A _________ is a rotary mechanical device that extracts energy from a fluid flow and converts it into useful work. The work produced by a _________ can be used for generating electrical power when combined with a generator. A _________ is a turbomachine with at least one moving part called a rotor assembly, which is a shaft or drum with blades attached. Moving fluid acts on the blades so that they move and impart rotational energy to the rotor. Early _________ examples are windmills and waterwheels.

Exam Probability: **Low**

54. *Answer choices:*

(see index for correct answer)

- a. Vapor recovery
- b. Turbine
- c. Glovebox
- d. Nitrogen generator

Guidance: level 1

:: ::

A _________ or till is a mechanical or electronic device for registering and calculating transactions at a point of sale. It is usually attached to a drawer for storing cash and other valuables. A modern _________ is usually attached to a printer that can print out receipts for record-keeping purposes.

Exam Probability: **High**

55. *Answer choices:*

(see index for correct answer)

- a. hierarchical perspective
- b. functional perspective
- c. levels of analysis

- d. process perspective

Guidance: level 1

:: Materials science ::

An __________ is a polymer with viscoelasticity and very weak intermolecular forces, and generally low Young`s modulus and high failure strain compared with other materials. The term, a portmanteau of elastic polymer, is often used interchangeably with rubber, although the latter is preferred when referring to vulcanisates. Each of the monomers which link to form the polymer is usually a compound of several elements among carbon, hydrogen, oxygen and silicon. __________ s are amorphous polymers maintained above their glass transition temperature, so that considerable molecular reconformation, without breaking of covalent bonds, is feasible. At ambient temperatures, such rubbers are thus relatively soft and deformable. Their primary uses are for seals, adhesives and molded flexible parts. Application areas for different types of rubber are manifold and cover segments as diverse as tires, soles for shoes, and damping and insulating elements. The importance of these rubbers can be judged from the fact that global revenues are forecast to rise to US$56 billion in 2020.

Exam Probability: **Low**

56. *Answer choices:*

(see index for correct answer)

- a. Microstructure
- b. Dynamical mean field theory
- c. Elastomer

- d. Hume-Rothery rules

Guidance: level 1

:: Management ::

A _________ is an idea of the future or desired result that a person or a group of people envisions, plans and commits to achieve. People endeavor to reach _________ s within a finite time by setting deadlines.

Exam Probability: **Medium**

57. *Answer choices:*

(see index for correct answer)

- a. Financial planning
- b. Corticon
- c. Peer pressure
- d. Goal

Guidance: level 1

:: Production and manufacturing ::

__________ is a theory of management that analyzes and synthesizes workflows. Its main objective is improving economic efficiency, especially labor productivity. It was one of the earliest attempts to apply science to the engineering of processes and to management. __________ is sometimes known as Taylorism after its founder, Frederick Winslow Taylor.

Exam Probability: **Medium**

58. *Answer choices:*

(see index for correct answer)

- a. Scientific management
- b. Countercurrent exchange
- c. Direct Clustering Algorithm
- d. Highly accelerated stress audit

Guidance: level 1

:: Distribution, retailing, and wholesaling ::

The __________ is a distribution channel phenomenon in which forecasts yield supply chain inefficiencies. It refers to increasing swings in inventory in response to shifts in customer demand as one moves further up the supply chain. The concept first appeared in Jay Forrester`s Industrial Dynamics and thus it is also known as the Forrester effect. The __________ was named for the way the amplitude of a whip increases down its length. The further from the originating signal, the greater the distortion of the wave pattern. In a similar manner, forecast accuracy decreases as one moves upstream along the supply chain. For example, many consumer goods have fairly consistent consumption at retail but this signal becomes more chaotic and unpredictable as the focus moves away from consumer purchasing behavior.

Exam Probability: **Low**

59. *Answer choices:*

(see index for correct answer)

- a. Bridgewater House, Manchester
- b. Bullwhip effect
- c. Wholesale list
- d. Sacrificial leg

Guidance: level 1

Commerce

Commerce relates to "the exchange of goods and services, especially on a large scale." It includes legal, economic, political, social, cultural and technological systems that operate in any country or internationally.

:: Management ::

__________ is the process of thinking about the activities required to achieve a desired goal. It is the first and foremost activity to achieve desired results. It involves the creation and maintenance of a plan, such as psychological aspects that require conceptual skills. There are even a couple of tests to measure someone's capability of __________ well. As such, __________ is a fundamental property of intelligent behavior. An important further meaning, often just called " __________ " is the legal context of permitted building developments.

Exam Probability: **High**

1. *Answer choices:*

(see index for correct answer)

- a. Inside job
- b. Nonconformity
- c. Pomodoro Technique
- d. Line management

Guidance: level 1

:: Dot-com bubble ::

_________ was an online grocery business that filed bankruptcy in 2001 after 3 years of operation and was later folded into Amazon.com. It was headquartered in Foster City, California, United States. It delivered products to customers` homes within a 30-minute window of their choosing. At its peak, it offered service in ten US markets: the San Francisco Bay Area; Dallas; Sacramento; San Diego; Los Angeles; Orange County, California; Chicago; Seattle; Portland, Oregon; and Atlanta, Georgia. The company had hoped to expand to 26 cities by 2001.

Exam Probability: **Low**

2. *Answer choices:*

(see index for correct answer)

- a. Freei
- b. The Industry Standard
- c. AllAdvantage
- d. Webvan

Guidance: level 1

:: ::

The ________ is a political and economic union of 28 member states that are located primarily in Europe. It has an area of 4,475,757 km2 and an estimated population of about 513 million. The EU has developed an internal single market through a standardised system of laws that apply in all member states in those matters, and only those matters, where members have agreed to act as one. EU policies aim to ensure the free movement of people, goods, services and capital within the internal market, enact legislation in justice and home affairs and maintain common policies on trade, agriculture, fisheries and regional development. For travel within the Schengen Area, passport controls have been abolished. A monetary union was established in 1999 and came into full force in 2002 and is composed of 19 EU member states which use the euro currency.

Exam Probability: **Low**

3. *Answer choices:*

(see index for correct answer)

- a. open system
- b. process perspective
- c. co-culture
- d. similarity-attraction theory

Guidance: level 1

:: ::

In a supply chain, a _________ , or a seller, is an enterprise that contributes goods or services. Generally, a supply chain _________ manufactures inventory/stock items and sells them to the next link in the chain. Today, these terms refer to a supplier of any good or service.

Exam Probability: **Medium**

4. *Answer choices:*

(see index for correct answer)

- a. Character
- b. co-culture
- c. Sarbanes-Oxley act of 2002
- d. personal values

Guidance: level 1

:: ::

_________ s are formal, sociotechnical, organizational systems designed to collect, process, store, and distribute information. In a sociotechnical perspective, _________ s are composed by four components: task, people, structure , and technology.

Exam Probability: **Medium**

5. *Answer choices:*

(see index for correct answer)

- a. Sarbanes-Oxley act of 2002
- b. corporate values
- c. Information system
- d. open system

Guidance: level 1

:: Customs duties ::

A ________ is a tax on imports or exports between sovereign states. It is a form of regulation of foreign trade and a policy that taxes foreign products to encourage or safeguard domestic industry. ________s are the simplest and oldest instrument of trade policy. Traditionally, states have used them as a source of income. Now, they are among the most widely used instruments of protection, along with import and export quotas.

Exam Probability: **Low**

6. *Answer choices:*

(see index for correct answer)

- a. Tariffication
- b. Customs area
- c. Customs racketeering
- d. You Are on Indian Land

Guidance: level 1

:: Income ::

__________ is a ratio between the net profit and cost of investment resulting from an investment of some resources. A high ROI means the investment`s gains favorably to its cost. As a performance measure, ROI is used to evaluate the efficiency of an investment or to compare the efficiencies of several different investments. In purely economic terms, it is one way of relating profits to capital invested. __________ is a performance measure used by businesses to identify the efficiency of an investment or number of different investments.

Exam Probability: **High**

7. *Answer choices:*

(see index for correct answer)

- a. Property investment calculator
- b. bottom line
- c. Return on investment
- d. Income Per User

Guidance: level 1

:: Real property law ::

A __________ is the grant of authority or rights, stating that the granter formally recognizes the prerogative of the recipient to exercise the rights specified. It is implicit that the granter retains superiority , and that the recipient admits a limited status within the relationship, and it is within that sense that __________ s were historically granted, and that sense is retained in modern usage of the term.

Exam Probability: **Low**

8. *Answer choices:*

(see index for correct answer)

- a. Defeasible estate
- b. Palestinian land laws
- c. Life estate
- d. Abstractor of title

Guidance: level 1

:: E-commerce ::

E-commerce is the activity of buying or selling of products on online services or over the Internet. __________ draws on technologies such as mobile commerce, electronic funds transfer, supply chain management, Internet marketing, online transaction processing, electronic data interchange , inventory management systems, and automated data collection systems.

Exam Probability: **Low**

9. *Answer choices:*

(see index for correct answer)

- a. Digital currency
- b. Electronic commerce
- c. Mobilpenge
- d. Marketplace Fairness Act

Guidance: level 1

:: Industrial automation ::

__________ is the technology by which a process or procedure is performed with minimal human assistance. __________ or automatic control is the use of various control systems for operating equipment such as machinery, processes in factories, boilers and heat treating ovens, switching on telephone networks, steering and stabilization of ships, aircraft and other applications and vehicles with minimal or reduced human intervention.

Exam Probability: **Medium**

10. *Answer choices:*

(see index for correct answer)

- a. Automation
- b. PLCopen
- c. Sequential function chart
- d. Automated mining

Guidance: level 1

:: Commerce ::

_________ , also known as duty _________ is defined by the United States Customs and Border Protection as the refund of certain duties, internal and revenue taxes and certain fees collected upon the importation of goods. Such refunds are only allowed upon the exportation or destruction of goods under U.S. Customs and Border Protection supervision. Duty _________ is an export promotions program sanctioned by the World Trade Organization and allows the refund of certain duties taxes and fees paid upon importation which was established in 1789 in order to promote U.S. innovation and manufacturing across the global market.

Exam Probability: **High**

11. *Answer choices:*

(see index for correct answer)

- a. Drawback
- b. Economic entity
- c. Bunker adjustment factor
- d. Fast track

Guidance: level 1

:: Confidence tricks ::

_________ is the fraudulent attempt to obtain sensitive information such as usernames, passwords and credit card details by disguising oneself as a trustworthy entity in an electronic communication. Typically carried out by email spoofing or instant messaging, it often directs users to enter personal information at a fake website which matches the look and feel of the legitimate site.

Exam Probability: **Medium**

12. *Answer choices:*

(see index for correct answer)

- a. Phishing
- b. Gem scam
- c. Children of Lieutenant Schmidt
- d. First International Bank of Grenada

Guidance: level 1

:: ::

_________ is getting a diploma or academic degree or the ceremony that is sometimes associated with it, in which students become graduates. The date of _________ is often called _________ day. The _________ ceremony itself is also called commencement, convocation or invocation.

Exam Probability: **Low**

13. *Answer choices:*

(see index for correct answer)

- a. Character
- b. surface-level diversity
- c. co-culture
- d. Graduation

Guidance: level 1

:: Marketing ::

_________ or stock is the goods and materials that a business holds for the ultimate goal of resale .

Exam Probability: **Medium**

14. *Answer choices:*

(see index for correct answer)

- a. Drug coupon
- b. Postmodern branding
- c. John Neeson
- d. Distributed presence

Guidance: level 1

:: Project management ::

Contemporary business and science treat as a _________ any undertaking, carried out individually or collaboratively and possibly involving research or design, that is carefully planned to achieve a particular aim.

Exam Probability: **Low**

15. *Answer choices:*

(see index for correct answer)

- a. Critical path drag
- b. Project initiation document
- c. Test and evaluation master plan
- d. Project

Guidance: level 1

:: International trade ::

An _________ is a good brought into a jurisdiction, especially across a national border, from an external source. The party bringing in the good is called an _________ er. An _________ in the receiving country is an export from the sending country. _________ ation and exportation are the defining financial transactions of international trade.

Exam Probability: **Medium**

16. *Answer choices:*

(see index for correct answer)

- a. Seoul Development Consensus
- b. Cartaz
- c. Spice trade
- d. Import

Guidance: level 1

:: Theories ::

A _________ union is a type of multinational political union where negotiated power is delegated to an authority by governments of member states.

Exam Probability: **Medium**

17. *Answer choices:*

(see index for correct answer)

- a. Supranational
- b. Taylorism

Guidance: level 1

:: Management ::

_________ is the identification, evaluation, and prioritization of risks followed by coordinated and economical application of resources to minimize, monitor, and control the probability or impact of unfortunate events or to maximize the realization of opportunities.

Exam Probability: **Medium**

18. *Answer choices:*

(see index for correct answer)

- a. Operations research
- b. Business-oriented architecture
- c. Industry or market research
- d. Risk management

Guidance: level 1

:: Service industries ::

_________ is travel for pleasure or business; also the theory and practice of touring, the business of attracting, accommodating, and entertaining tourists, and the business of operating tours. _________ may be international, or within the traveller`s country. The World _________ Organization defines _________ more generally, in terms which go "beyond the common perception of _________ as being limited to holiday activity only", as people "traveling to and staying in places outside their usual environment for not more than one consecutive year for leisure and not less than 24 hours, business and other purposes".

Exam Probability: **High**

19. *Answer choices:*

(see index for correct answer)

- a. Financial services
- b. Tourism
- c. Independent Financial Adviser
- d. Language industry

Guidance: level 1

:: Commercial item transport and distribution ::

A __________ , forwarder, or forwarding agent, also known as a non-vessel operating common carrier , is a person or company that organizes shipments for individuals or corporations to get goods from the manufacturer or producer to a market, customer or final point of distribution. Forwarders contract with a carrier or often multiple carriers to move the goods. A forwarder does not move the goods but acts as an expert in the logistics network. These carriers can use a variety of shipping modes, including ships, airplanes, trucks, and railroads, and often do utilize multiple modes for a single shipment. For example, the __________ may arrange to have cargo moved from a plant to an airport by truck, flown to the destination city, then moved from the airport to a customer`s building by another truck.

Exam Probability: **Low**

20. *Answer choices:*

(see index for correct answer)

- a. Containerized housing unit
- b. Mid-stream operation
- c. Unit load
- d. Container crane

Guidance: level 1

:: Packaging ::

In work place, _________ or job _________ means good ranking with the hypothesized conception of requirements of a role. There are two types of job _________ s: contextual and task. Task _________ is related to cognitive ability while contextual _________ is dependent upon personality. Task _________ are behavioral roles that are recognized in job descriptions and by remuneration systems, they are directly related to organizational _________ , whereas, contextual _________ are value based and additional behavioral roles that are not recognized in job descriptions and covered by compensation; they are extra roles that are indirectly related to organizational _________ . Citizenship _________ like contextual _________ means a set of individual activity/contribution that supports the organizational culture.

Exam Probability: **High**

21. *Answer choices:*

(see index for correct answer)

- a. Security printing
- b. Paper sack
- c. Video game packaging
- d. Performance

Guidance: level 1

:: Supply chain management ::

__________ is the process of finding and agreeing to terms, and acquiring goods, services, or works from an external source, often via a tendering or competitive bidding process. __________ is used to ensure the buyer receives goods, services, or works at the best possible price when aspects such as quality, quantity, time, and location are compared. Corporations and public bodies often define processes intended to promote fair and open competition for their business while minimizing risks such as exposure to fraud and collusion.

Exam Probability: **Medium**

22. *Answer choices:*

(see index for correct answer)

- a. Demand Solutions
- b. Supply chain cyber security
- c. Procurement
- d. Channel coordination

Guidance: level 1

:: ::

A __________ consists of one people who live in the same dwelling and share meals. It may also consist of a single family or another group of people. A dwelling is considered to contain multiple __________ s if meals or living spaces are not shared. The __________ is the basic unit of analysis in many social, microeconomic and government models, and is important to economics and inheritance.

Exam Probability: **High**

23. *Answer choices:*

(see index for correct answer)

- a. personal values
- b. functional perspective
- c. interpersonal communication
- d. Household

Guidance: level 1

:: Dot-com bubble ::

__________ is an internet portal launched in 1995 that provides a variety of content including news and weather, a metasearch engine, a web-based email, instant messaging, stock quotes, and a customizable user homepage. It is currently operated by IAC Applications of IAC, and __________ Networks. In the U.S., the main __________ site has long been a personal start page called My __________. __________ also operates an e-mail service, although it is no longer open for new customers.

Exam Probability: **Low**

24. *Answer choices:*

(see index for correct answer)

- a. Freei

- b. Excite
- c. Dot-com bubble
- d. The Industry Standard

Guidance: level 1

:: Securities (finance) ::

A _________ is a container that is traditionally constructed from stiff fibers, and can be made from a range of materials, including wood splints, runners, and cane. While most _________ s are made from plant materials, other materials such as horsehair, baleen, or metal wire can be used. _________ s are generally woven by hand. Some _________ s are fitted with a lid, while others are left open on top.

Exam Probability: **Low**

25. *Answer choices:*

(see index for correct answer)

- a. Spot price
- b. Hague Securities Convention
- c. Equipment trust certificate
- d. Principal at risk notes

Guidance: level 1

:: Marketing analytics ::

_________ is a long-term, forward-looking approach to planning with the fundamental goal of achieving a sustainable competitive advantage. Strategic planning involves an analysis of the company's strategic initial situation prior to the formulation, evaluation and selection of market-oriented competitive position that contributes to the company's goals and marketing objectives.

Exam Probability: **Low**

26. *Answer choices:*

(see index for correct answer)

- a. marketing dashboard
- b. Market share analysis
- c. Marketing accountability
- d. Marketing strategy

Guidance: level 1

:: Auctioneering ::

A __________ is a type of sealed-bid auction. Bidders submit written bids without knowing the bid of the other people in the auction. The highest bidder wins but the price paid is the second-highest bid. This type of auction is strategically similar to an English auction and gives bidders an incentive to bid their true value. The auction was first described academically by Columbia University professor William Vickrey in 1961 though it had been used by stamp collectors since 1893. In 1797 Johann Wolfgang von Goethe sold a manuscript using a sealed-bid, second-price auction.

Exam Probability: **Medium**

27. *Answer choices:*

(see index for correct answer)

- a. Auction chant
- b. Vehicle impoundment
- c. Vickrey auction
- d. Estate sale

Guidance: level 1

:: Decision theory ::

Within economics the concept of _________ is used to model worth or value, but its usage has evolved significantly over time. The term was introduced initially as a measure of pleasure or satisfaction within the theory of utilitarianism by moral philosophers such as Jeremy Bentham and John Stuart Mill. But the term has been adapted and reapplied within neoclassical economics, which dominates modern economic theory, as a _________ function that represents a consumer`s preference ordering over a choice set. As such, it is devoid of its original interpretation as a measurement of the pleasure or satisfaction obtained by the consumer from that choice.

Exam Probability: **High**

28. *Answer choices:*

(see index for correct answer)

- a. Psychological pricing
- b. Shared decision-making
- c. Utility
- d. Superiority and inferiority ranking method

Guidance: level 1

:: ::

_________ characterises the behaviour of a system or model whose components interact in multiple ways and follow local rules, meaning there is no reasonable higher instruction to define the various possible interactions.

Exam Probability: **Medium**

29. *Answer choices:*

(see index for correct answer)

- a. hierarchical perspective
- b. process perspective
- c. Sarbanes-Oxley act of 2002
- d. Complexity

Guidance: level 1

:: Marketing by medium ::

_________ , also called online marketing or Internet advertising or web advertising, is a form of marketing and advertising which uses the Internet to deliver promotional marketing messages to consumers. Many consumers find _________ disruptive and have increasingly turned to ad blocking for a variety of reasons. When software is used to do the purchasing, it is known as programmatic advertising.

Exam Probability: **Medium**

30. *Answer choices:*

(see index for correct answer)

- a. Digital marketing
- b. New media marketing

- c. Growth hacking
- d. Brand infiltration

Guidance: level 1

:: Mereology ::

_________ , in the abstract, is what belongs to or with something, whether as an attribute or as a component of said thing. In the context of this article, it is one or more components , whether physical or incorporeal, of a person's estate; or so belonging to, as in being owned by, a person or jointly a group of people or a legal entity like a corporation or even a society. Depending on the nature of the _________ , an owner of _________ has the right to consume, alter, share, redefine, rent, mortgage, pawn, sell, exchange, transfer, give away or destroy it, or to exclude others from doing these things, as well as to perhaps abandon it; whereas regardless of the nature of the _________ , the owner thereof has the right to properly use it , or at the very least exclusively keep it.

Exam Probability: **High**

31. *Answer choices:*

(see index for correct answer)

- a. Mereotopology
- b. Property
- c. Mereological essentialism
- d. Gunk

Guidance: level 1

:: Management occupations ::

_________ ship is the process of designing, launching and running a new business, which is often initially a small business. The people who create these businesses are called _________ s.

Exam Probability: **High**

32. *Answer choices:*

(see index for correct answer)

- a. Legislator
- b. Ceco
- c. Functional manager
- d. Entrepreneur

Guidance: level 1

:: Export and import control ::

" __________ " means the Government Service which is responsible for the administration of __________ law and the collection of duties and taxes and which also has the responsibility for the application of other laws and regulations relating to the importation, exportation, movement or storage of goods.

Exam Probability: **Medium**

33. *Answer choices:*

(see index for correct answer)

- a. Import parity price
- b. GOST R Conformity Declaration
- c. Plant Protection and Quarantine
- d. Export parity price

Guidance: level 1

:: Commerce ::

__________ relates to "the exchange of goods and services, especially on a large scale". It includes legal, economic, political, social, cultural and technological systems that operate in a country or in international trade.

Exam Probability: **Medium**

34. *Answer choices:*

(see index for correct answer)

- a. Straw purchase
- b. Deal transaction
- c. Commerce
- d. Church sale

Guidance: level 1

:: Business law ::

A __________ is a contractual arrangement calling for the lessee to pay the lessor for use of an asset. Property, buildings and vehicles are common assets that are __________ d. Industrial or business equipment is also __________ d.

Exam Probability: **High**

35. *Answer choices:*

(see index for correct answer)

- a. Wrongful trading
- b. Lease
- c. De facto corporation and corporation by estoppel
- d. OHADA

Guidance: level 1

:: Production economics ::

In economics long run is a theoretical concept where all markets are in equilibrium, and all prices and quantities have fully adjusted and are in equilibrium. The long run contrasts with the _________ where there are some constraints and markets are not fully in equilibrium.

Exam Probability: **High**

36. *Answer choices:*

(see index for correct answer)

- a. Short run
- b. Marginal product of labor
- c. Hicks-neutral technical change
- d. Foundations of Economic Analysis

Guidance: level 1

:: Game theory ::

To _________ is to make a deal between different parties where each party gives up part of their demand. In arguments, _________ is a concept of finding agreement through communication, through a mutual acceptance of terms—often involving variations from an original goal or desires.

Exam Probability: **High**

37. *Answer choices:*

(see index for correct answer)

- a. Replicator equation
- b. Markov perfect equilibrium
- c. Compromise
- d. Blotto games

Guidance: level 1

:: Marketing techniques ::

__________ is the activity of dividing a broad consumer or business market, normally consisting of existing and potential customers, into sub-groups of consumers based on some type of shared characteristics. In dividing or segmenting markets, researchers typically look for common characteristics such as shared needs, common interests, similar lifestyles or even similar demographic profiles. The overall aim of segmentation is to identify high yield segments – that is, those segments that are likely to be the most profitable or that have growth potential – so that these can be selected for special attention .

Exam Probability: **Low**

38. *Answer choices:*

(see index for correct answer)

- a. Market segmentation
- b. Intermarket segmentation

- c. Drip marketing
- d. Product placement

Guidance: level 1

:: ::

__________ , in general use, is a devotion and faithfulness to a nation, cause, philosophy, country, group, or person. Philosophers disagree on what can be an object of __________ , as some argue that __________ is strictly interpersonal and only another human being can be the object of __________ . The definition of __________ in law and political science is the fidelity of an individual to a nation, either one`s nation of birth, or one`s declared home nation by oath .

Exam Probability: **Low**

39. *Answer choices:*

(see index for correct answer)

- a. Loyalty
- b. personal values
- c. surface-level diversity
- d. hierarchical perspective

Guidance: level 1

:: ::

_________ is the study and management of exchange relationships. _________ is the business process of creating relationships with and satisfying customers. With its focus on the customer, _________ is one of the premier components of business management.

Exam Probability: **Low**

40. *Answer choices:*

(see index for correct answer)

- a. functional perspective
- b. co-culture
- c. cultural
- d. empathy

Guidance: level 1

:: Behavior modification ::

In psychotherapy and mental health, _________ has a positive sense of empowering individuals, or a negative sense of encouraging dysfunctional behavior.

Exam Probability: **Medium**

41. *Answer choices:*

(see index for correct answer)

- a. behavioural change
- b. Thought stopping

Guidance: level 1

:: Auctioneering ::

An __________ is a process of buying and selling goods or services by offering them up for bid, taking bids, and then selling the item to the highest bidder. The open ascending price __________ is arguably the most common form of __________ in use today. Participants bid openly against one another, with each subsequent bid required to be higher than the previous bid. An __________ eer may announce prices, bidders may call out their bids themselves , or bids may be submitted electronically with the highest current bid publicly displayed. In a Dutch __________ , the __________ eer begins with a high asking price for some quantity of like items; the price is lowered until a participant is willing to accept the __________ eer`s price for some quantity of the goods in the lot or until the seller`s reserve price is met. While __________ s are most associated in the public imagination with the sale of antiques, paintings, rare collectibles and expensive wines, __________ s are also used for commodities, livestock, radio spectrum and used cars. In economic theory, an __________ may refer to any mechanism or set of trading rules for exchange.

Exam Probability: **High**

42. *Answer choices:*

(see index for correct answer)

- a. Auction catalog
- b. Demsetz auction
- c. Online trading community
- d. Proxy bid

Guidance: level 1

:: ::

__________ is a process whereby a person assumes the parenting of another, usually a child, from that person`s biological or legal parent or parents. Legal __________ s permanently transfers all rights and responsibilities, along with filiation, from the biological parent or parents.

Exam Probability: **Low**

43. *Answer choices:*

(see index for correct answer)

- a. co-culture
- b. information systems assessment
- c. functional perspective
- d. levels of analysis

Guidance: level 1

:: ::

__________ are electronic transfer of money from one bank account to another, either within a single financial institution or across multiple institutions, via computer-based systems, without the direct intervention of bank staff.

Exam Probability: **High**

44. *Answer choices:*

(see index for correct answer)

- a. Electronic funds transfer
- b. cultural
- c. hierarchical
- d. corporate values

Guidance: level 1

:: ::

Employment is a relationship between two parties, usually based on a contract where work is paid for, where one party, which may be a corporation, for profit, not-for-profit organization, co-operative or other entity is the employer and the other is the employee. Employees work in return for payment, which may be in the form of an hourly wage, by piecework or an annual salary, depending on the type of work an employee does or which sector she or he is working in. Employees in some fields or sectors may receive gratuities, bonus payment or stock options. In some types of employment, employees may receive benefits in addition to payment. Benefits can include health insurance, housing, disability insurance or use of a gym. Employment is typically governed by employment laws, regulations or legal contracts.

Exam Probability: **High**

45. *Answer choices:*

(see index for correct answer)

- a. personal values
- b. imperative
- c. Personnel
- d. open system

Guidance: level 1

:: ::

According to the philosopher Piyush Mathur , "Tangibility is the property that a phenomenon exhibits if it has and/or transports mass and/or energy and/or momentum".

Exam Probability: **Medium**

46. *Answer choices:*

(see index for correct answer)

- a. hierarchical perspective
- b. Sarbanes-Oxley act of 2002
- c. surface-level diversity
- d. Tangible

Guidance: level 1

:: ::

An _________ is a contingent motivator. Traditional _________ s are extrinsic motivators which reward actions to yield a desired outcome. The effectiveness of traditional _________ s has changed as the needs of Western society have evolved. While the traditional _________ model is effective when there is a defined procedure and goal for a task, Western society started to require a higher volume of critical thinkers, so the traditional model became less effective. Institutions are now following a trend in implementing strategies that rely on intrinsic motivations rather than the extrinsic motivations that the traditional _________ s foster.

Exam Probability: **High**

47. *Answer choices:*

(see index for correct answer)

- a. hierarchical perspective
- b. surface-level diversity
- c. personal values
- d. Incentive

Guidance: level 1

:: ::

__________ is the production of products for use or sale using labour and machines, tools, chemical and biological processing, or formulation. The term may refer to a range of human activity, from handicraft to high tech, but is most commonly applied to industrial design, in which raw materials are transformed into finished goods on a large scale. Such finished goods may be sold to other manufacturers for the production of other, more complex products, such as aircraft, household appliances, furniture, sports equipment or automobiles, or sold to wholesalers, who in turn sell them to retailers, who then sell them to end users and consumers.

Exam Probability: **High**

48. *Answer choices:*

(see index for correct answer)

- a. imperative
- b. Manufacturing
- c. process perspective
- d. co-culture

Guidance: level 1

:: ::

_________ Corporation is an American multinational technology company with headquarters in Redmond, Washington. It develops, manufactures, licenses, supports and sells computer software, consumer electronics, personal computers, and related services. Its best known software products are the _________ Windows line of operating systems, the _________ Office suite, and the Internet Explorer and Edge Web browsers. Its flagship hardware products are the Xbox video game consoles and the _________ Surface lineup of touchscreen personal computers. As of 2016, it is the world`s largest software maker by revenue, and one of the world`s most valuable companies. The word " _________ " is a portmanteau of "microcomputer" and "software". _________ is ranked No. 30 in the 2018 Fortune 500 rankings of the largest United States corporations by total revenue.

Exam Probability: **Medium**

49. *Answer choices:*

(see index for correct answer)

- a. co-culture
- b. imperative
- c. Microsoft
- d. process perspective

Guidance: level 1

:: Insolvency ::

_________ is a legal process through which people or other entities who cannot repay debts to creditors may seek relief from some or all of their debts. In most jurisdictions, _________ is imposed by a court order, often initiated by the debtor.

Exam Probability: **High**

50. *Answer choices:*

(see index for correct answer)

- a. Conservatorship
- b. Preferential creditor
- c. Bankruptcy
- d. Official Committee of Equity Security Holders

Guidance: level 1

:: Management ::

In business, a _________ is the attribute that allows an organization to outperform its competitors. A _________ may include access to natural resources, such as high-grade ores or a low-cost power source, highly skilled labor, geographic location, high entry barriers, and access to new technology.

Exam Probability: **Low**

51. *Answer choices:*

(see index for correct answer)

- a. Community-based management
- b. Private defense agency
- c. Organizational conflict
- d. Competitive advantage

Guidance: level 1

:: ::

Senior management, executive management, upper management, or a _________ is generally a team of individuals at the highest level of management of an organization who have the day-to-day tasks of managing that organization — sometimes a company or a corporation.

Exam Probability: **Medium**

52. *Answer choices:*

(see index for correct answer)

- a. functional perspective
- b. Management team
- c. levels of analysis
- d. empathy

Guidance: level 1

:: ::

_________ is the exchange of capital, goods, and services across international borders or territories.

Exam Probability: **High**

53. *Answer choices:*

(see index for correct answer)

- a. surface-level diversity
- b. International trade
- c. corporate values
- d. Character

Guidance: level 1

:: Stock market ::

_________ is freedom from, or resilience against, potential harm caused by others. Beneficiaries of _________ may be of persons and social groups, objects and institutions, ecosystems or any other entity or phenomenon vulnerable to unwanted change by its environment.

Exam Probability: **Low**

54. *Answer choices:*

(see index for correct answer)

- a. Shadow stock
- b. Security
- c. Stop price
- d. Stock exchange

Guidance: level 1

:: Project management ::

_________ is the right to exercise power, which can be formalized by a state and exercised by way of judges, appointed executives of government, or the ecclesiastical or priestly appointed representatives of a God or other deities.

Exam Probability: **Low**

55. *Answer choices:*

(see index for correct answer)

- a. Cost estimate
- b. Responsibility assignment matrix
- c. Concurrent engineering

- d. Integrated product team

Guidance: level 1

:: Goods ::

In most contexts, the concept of _________ denotes the conduct that should be preferred when posed with a choice between possible actions. _________ is generally considered to be the opposite of evil, and is of interest in the study of morality, ethics, religion and philosophy. The specific meaning and etymology of the term and its associated translations among ancient and contemporary languages show substantial variation in its inflection and meaning depending on circumstances of place, history, religious, or philosophical context.

Exam Probability: **High**

56. *Answer choices:*

(see index for correct answer)

- a. Ersatz good
- b. Merit good
- c. Case
- d. Intermediate good

Guidance: level 1

:: ::

_________ s and acquisitions are transactions in which the ownership of companies, other business organizations, or their operating units are transferred or consolidated with other entities. As an aspect of strategic management, M&A can allow enterprises to grow or downsize, and change the nature of their business or competitive position.

Exam Probability: **Medium**

57. *Answer choices:*

(see index for correct answer)

- a. information systems assessment
- b. imperative
- c. deep-level diversity
- d. Merger

Guidance: level 1

:: Supply chain management ::

A _________ is a type of auction in which the traditional roles of buyer and seller are reversed. Thus, there is one buyer and many potential sellers. In an ordinary auction , buyers compete to obtain goods or services by offering increasingly higher prices. In contrast, in a _________ , the sellers compete to obtain business from the buyer and prices will typically decrease as the sellers underbid each other.

Exam Probability: **Medium**

58. *Answer choices:*

(see index for correct answer)

- a. ICON-SCM
- b. Logistics Bureau
- c. Reverse auction
- d. Helveta

Guidance: level 1

:: Marketing ::

__________ is a concept introduced in a book of the same name in 1999 by marketing expert Seth Godin. __________ is a non-traditional marketing technique that advertises goods and services when advance consent is given.

Exam Probability: **Low**

59. *Answer choices:*

(see index for correct answer)

- a. Configurator
- b. Consumer culture theory
- c. Meta marketing
- d. Permission marketing

Guidance: level 1

Business ethics

Business ethics (also known as corporate ethics) is a form of applied ethics or professional ethics, that examines ethical principles and moral or ethical problems that can arise in a business environment. It applies to all aspects of business conduct and is relevant to the conduct of individuals and entire organizations. These ethics originate from individuals, organizational statements or from the legal system. These norms, values, ethical, and unethical practices are what is used to guide business. They help those businesses maintain a better connection with their stakeholders.

:: ::

_________ ism is a form of government characterized by strong central power and limited political freedoms. Individual freedoms are subordinate to the state and there is no constitutional accountability and rule of law under an _________ regime. _________ regimes can be autocratic with power concentrated in one person or it can be more spread out between multiple officials and government institutions. Juan Linz`s influential 1964 description of _________ ism characterized _________ political systems by four qualities.

Exam Probability: **High**

1. *Answer choices:*

(see index for correct answer)

- a. open system
- b. Sarbanes-Oxley act of 2002
- c. Authoritarian
- d. levels of analysis

Guidance: level 1

:: Corporate scandals ::

Exxon Mobil Corporation, doing business as _________, is an American multinational oil and gas corporation headquartered in Irving, Texas. It is the largest direct descendant of John D. Rockefeller`s Standard Oil Company, and was formed on November 30, 1999 by the merger of Exxon and Mobil. _________ `s primary brands are Exxon, Mobil, Esso, and _________ Chemical.

Exam Probability: **High**

2. *Answer choices:*

(see index for correct answer)

- a. Lerner Newspapers
- b. Aluminium price-fixing conspiracy
- c. ExxonMobil
- d. Avon Products

Guidance: level 1

:: Human resource management ::

_________ is the ethics of an organization, and it is how an organization responds to an internal or external stimulus. _________ is interdependent with the organizational culture. Although it is akin to both organizational behavior and industrial and organizational psychology as well as business ethics on the micro and macro levels, _________ is neither OB or I/O psychology, nor is it solely business ethics . _________ express the values of an organization to its employees and/or other entities irrespective of governmental and/or regulatory laws.

Exam Probability: **Low**

3. *Answer choices:*

(see index for correct answer)

- a. Job enrichment
- b. Organizational ethics
- c. Talent management system
- d. Employee relationship management

Guidance: level 1

:: Television terminology ::

A __________ organization , also known as a non-business entity, not-for-profit organization, or __________ institution, is dedicated to furthering a particular social cause or advocating for a shared point of view. In economic terms, it is an organization that uses its surplus of the revenues to further achieve its ultimate objective, rather than distributing its income to the organization`s shareholders, leaders, or members. __________ s are tax exempt or charitable, meaning they do not pay income tax on the money that they receive for their organization. They can operate in religious, scientific, research, or educational settings.

Exam Probability: **Medium**

4. *Answer choices:*

(see index for correct answer)

- a. not-for-profit
- b. distance learning
- c. Nonprofit
- d. Satellite television

Guidance: level 1

:: Social responsibility ::

The United Nations Global Compact is a non-binding United Nations pact to encourage businesses worldwide to adopt sustainable and socially responsible policies, and to report on their implementation. The _________ is a principle-based framework for businesses, stating ten principles in the areas of human rights, labor, the environment and anti-corruption. Under the Global Compact, companies are brought together with UN agencies, labor groups and civil society. Cities can join the Global Compact through the Cities Programme.

Exam Probability: **High**

5. *Answer choices:*

(see index for correct answer)

- a. Clann Credo
- b. UN Global Compact
- c. Socially responsible marketing
- d. Mallen Baker

Guidance: level 1

:: ::

_________ , O.S.A. was a German professor of theology, composer, priest, monk, and a seminal figure in the Protestant Reformation.

Exam Probability: **Medium**

6. *Answer choices:*

(see index for correct answer)

- a. Martin Luther
- b. personal values
- c. Character
- d. hierarchical

Guidance: level 1

:: Management ::

_________ or executive pay is composed of the financial compensation and other non-financial awards received by an executive from their firm for their service to the organization. It is typically a mixture of salary, bonuses, shares of or call options on the company stock, benefits, and perquisites, ideally configured to take into account government regulations, tax law, the desires of the organization and the executive, and rewards for performance.

Exam Probability: **Medium**

7. *Answer choices:*

(see index for correct answer)

- a. Executive compensation
- b. Project management
- c. Project team builder
- d. Power structure

Guidance: level 1

:: ::

A _________ is a problem offering two possibilities, neither of which is unambiguously acceptable or preferable. The possibilities are termed the horns of the _________ , a clichéd usage, but distinguishing the _________ from other kinds of predicament as a matter of usage.

Exam Probability: **Low**

8. *Answer choices:*

(see index for correct answer)

- a. functional perspective
- b. corporate values
- c. Dilemma
- d. personal values

Guidance: level 1

:: Advertising techniques ::

The _________ is a story from the Trojan War about the subterfuge that the Greeks used to enter the independent city of Troy and win the war. In the canonical version, after a fruitless 10-year siege, the Greeks constructed a huge wooden horse, and hid a select force of men inside including Odysseus. The Greeks pretended to sail away, and the Trojans pulled the horse into their city as a victory trophy. That night the Greek force crept out of the horse and opened the gates for the rest of the Greek army, which had sailed back under cover of night. The Greeks entered and destroyed the city of Troy, ending the war.

Exam Probability: **Medium**

9. *Answer choices:*

(see index for correct answer)

- a. Below the line
- b. Trojan horse
- c. Surrogate advertising
- d. Incomplete comparison

Guidance: level 1

:: United Kingdom labour law ::

The _________ was a series of programs, public work projects, financial reforms, and regulations enacted by President Franklin D. Roosevelt in the United States between 1933 and 1936. It responded to needs for relief, reform, and recovery from the Great Depression. Major federal programs included the Civilian Conservation Corps , the Civil Works Administration , the Farm Security Administration , the National Industrial Recovery Act of 1933 and the Social Security Administration . They provided support for farmers, the unemployed, youth and the elderly. The _________ included new constraints and safeguards on the banking industry and efforts to re-inflate the economy after prices had fallen sharply. _________ programs included both laws passed by Congress as well as presidential executive orders during the first term of the presidency of Franklin D. Roosevelt.

Exam Probability: **Low**

10. *Answer choices:*

(see index for correct answer)

- a. New Deal
- b. Employment Act 2008
- c. Employment Protection Act 1975
- d. Coal Industry Commission Act 1919

Guidance: level 1

:: ::

Cannabis, also known as _________ among other names, is a psychoactive drug from the Cannabis plant used for medical or recreational purposes. The main psychoactive part of cannabis is tetrahydrocannabinol , one of 483 known compounds in the plant, including at least 65 other cannabinoids. Cannabis can be used by smoking, vaporizing, within food, or as an extract.

Exam Probability: **Low**

11. *Answer choices:*

(see index for correct answer)

- a. Marijuana
- b. Sarbanes-Oxley act of 2002
- c. personal values
- d. information systems assessment

Guidance: level 1

:: Marketing ::

_________ is the marketing of products that are presumed to be environmentally safe. It incorporates a broad range of activities, including product modification, changes to the production process, sustainable packaging, as well as modifying advertising. Yet defining _________ is not a simple task where several meanings intersect and contradict each other; an example of this will be the existence of varying social, environmental and retail definitions attached to this term. Other similar terms used are environmental marketing and ecological marketing.

Exam Probability: **Medium**

12. *Answer choices:*

(see index for correct answer)

- a. Profit chart
- b. Movie packaging
- c. Customer interaction tracker
- d. Medical science liaison

Guidance: level 1

:: Anti-Revisionism ::

__________ , officially the German Democratic Republic , was a country that existed from 1949 to 1990, when the eastern portion of Germany was part of the Eastern Bloc during the Cold War. It described itself as a socialist "workers` and peasants` state", and the territory was administered and occupied by Soviet forces at the end of World War II — the Soviet Occupation Zone of the Potsdam Agreement, bounded on the east by the Oder–Neisse line. The Soviet zone surrounded West Berlin but did not include it; as a result, West Berlin remained outside the jurisdiction of the GDR.

Exam Probability: **Medium**

13. *Answer choices:*

(see index for correct answer)

- a. Anti-Revisionism
- b. Ho Chi Minh Thought
- c. Hoxhaism
- d. East Germany

Guidance: level 1

:: Labour law ::

An _________ is special or specified circumstances that partially or fully exempt a person or organization from performance of a legal obligation so as to avoid an unreasonable or disproportionate burden or obstacle.

Exam Probability: **Medium**

14. *Answer choices:*

(see index for correct answer)

- a. Undue hardship
- b. Occupational exposure limit
- c. International labour law
- d. International Association of Labour Law Journals

Guidance: level 1

:: ::

The American Recovery and Reinvestment Act of 2009 , nicknamed the _________ , was a stimulus package enacted by the 111th U.S. Congress and signed into law by President Barack Obama in February 2009. Developed in response to the Great Recession, the ARRA`s primary objective was to save existing jobs and create new ones as soon as possible. Other objectives were to provide temporary relief programs for those most affected by the recession and invest in infrastructure, education, health, and renewable energy.

Exam Probability: **High**

15. *Answer choices:*

(see index for correct answer)

- a. hierarchical
- b. functional perspective
- c. personal values
- d. Recovery Act

Guidance: level 1

:: ::

Competition law is a law that promotes or seeks to maintain market competition by regulating anti-competitive conduct by companies. Competition law is implemented through public and private enforcement. Competition law is known as " _________ law" in the United States for historical reasons, and as "anti-monopoly law" in China and Russia. In previous years it has been known as trade practices law in the United Kingdom and Australia. In the European Union, it is referred to as both _________ and competition law.

Exam Probability: **High**

16. *Answer choices:*

(see index for correct answer)

- a. process perspective
- b. hierarchical perspective
- c. Antitrust
- d. Sarbanes-Oxley act of 2002

Guidance: level 1

:: ::

The Ethics & Compliance Initiative was formed in 2015 and consists of three nonprofit organizations: the Ethics Research Center, the Ethics & Compliance Association, and the Ethics & Compliance Certification Institute. Based in Arlington, Virginia, United States, ECI is devoted to the advancement of high ethical standards and practices in public and private institutions, and provides research about ethical standards, workplace integrity, and compliance practices and processes.

Exam Probability: **Medium**

17. *Answer choices:*

(see index for correct answer)

- a. Ethics Resource Center

- b. personal values
- c. process perspective
- d. similarity-attraction theory

Guidance: level 1

:: Minimum wage ::

The _________ are working people whose incomes fall below a given poverty line due to lack of work hours and/or low wages.Largely because they are earning such low wages, the _________ face numerous obstacles that make it difficult for many of them to find and keep a job, save up money, and maintain a sense of self-worth.

Exam Probability: **Low**

18. *Answer choices:*

(see index for correct answer)

- a. Minimum wage in Taiwan
- b. Minimum wage in the United States
- c. National Anti-Sweating League
- d. Working poor

Guidance: level 1

:: ::

__________ is a non-governmental environmental organization with offices in over 39 countries and an international coordinating body in Amsterdam, the Netherlands. __________ was founded in 1971 by Irving Stowe, and Dorothy Stowe, Canadian and US ex-pat environmental activists. __________ states its goal is to "ensure the ability of the Earth to nurture life in all its diversity" and focuses its campaigning on worldwide issues such as climate change, deforestation, overfishing, commercial whaling, genetic engineering, and anti-nuclear issues. It uses direct action, lobbying, research, and ecotage to achieve its goals. The global organization does not accept funding from governments, corporations, or political parties, relying on three million individual supporters and foundation grants. __________ has a general consultative status with the United Nations Economic and Social Council and is a founding member of the INGO Accountability Charter, an international non-governmental organization that intends to foster accountability and transparency of non-governmental organizations.

Exam Probability: **Medium**

19. *Answer choices:*

(see index for correct answer)

- a. Greenpeace
- b. open system
- c. process perspective
- d. interpersonal communication

Guidance: level 1

:: Separation of investment and commercial banking ::

The _________ refers to § 619 of the Dodd–Frank Wall Street Reform and Consumer Protection Act . The rule was originally proposed by American economist and former United States Federal Reserve Chairman Paul Volcker to restrict United States banks from making certain kinds of speculative investments that do not benefit their customers. Volcker argued that such speculative activity played a key role in the financial crisis of 2007–2008. The rule is often referred to as a ban on proprietary trading by commercial banks, whereby deposits are used to trade on the bank`s own accounts, although a number of exceptions to this ban were included in the Dodd-Frank law.

Exam Probability: **High**

20. *Answer choices:*

(see index for correct answer)

- a. Commercial bank
- b. Volcker Rule
- c. Bancassurance
- d. GLBA

Guidance: level 1

:: ::

_________ in the United States is a federal and state program that helps with medical costs for some people with limited income and resources. _________ also offers benefits not normally covered by Medicare, including nursing home care and personal care services. The Health Insurance Association of America describes _________ as "a government insurance program for persons of all ages whose income and resources are insufficient to pay for health care." _________ is the largest source of funding for medical and health-related services for people with low income in the United States, providing free health insurance to 74 million low-income and disabled people as of 2017. It is a means-tested program that is jointly funded by the state and federal governments and managed by the states, with each state currently having broad leeway to determine who is eligible for its implementation of the program. States are not required to participate in the program, although all have since 1982. _________ recipients must be U.S. citizens or qualified non-citizens, and may include low-income adults, their children, and people with certain disabilities. Poverty alone does not necessarily qualify someone for _________ .

Exam Probability: **High**

21. *Answer choices:*

(see index for correct answer)

- a. Character
- b. interpersonal communication
- c. Medicaid
- d. process perspective

Guidance: level 1

:: Electronic feedback ::

_________ occurs when outputs of a system are routed back as inputs as part of a chain of cause-and-effect that forms a circuit or loop. The system can then be said to feed back into itself. The notion of cause-and-effect has to be handled carefully when applied to _________ systems.

Exam Probability: **Medium**

22. *Answer choices:*

(see index for correct answer)

- a. feedback loop
- b. Positive feedback

Guidance: level 1

:: Competition regulators ::

The _________ is an independent agency of the United States government, established in 1914 by the _________ Act. Its principal mission is the promotion of consumer protection and the elimination and prevention of anticompetitive business practices, such as coercive monopoly. It is headquartered in the _________ Building in Washington, D.C.

Exam Probability: **High**

23. *Answer choices:*

(see index for correct answer)

- a. Federal Trade Commission
- b. United States Department of Justice Antitrust Division
- c. Competition Commission of India
- d. Competition Authority

Guidance: level 1

:: Real estate ::

__________ s serve several societal needs – primarily as shelter from weather, security, living space, privacy, to store belongings, and to comfortably live and work. A __________ as a shelter represents a physical division of the human habitat and the outside .

Exam Probability: **High**

24. *Answer choices:*

(see index for correct answer)

- a. Building
- b. Land monopoly
- c. Property condition assessment
- d. Cadastre

Guidance: level 1

:: Labor rights ::

The __________ is the concept that people have a human __________, or engage in productive employment, and may not be prevented from doing so. The __________ is enshrined in the Universal Declaration of Human Rights and recognized in international human rights law through its inclusion in the International Covenant on Economic, Social and Cultural Rights, where the __________ emphasizes economic, social and cultural development.

Exam Probability: **Low**

25. *Answer choices:*

(see index for correct answer)

- a. Kate Mullany House
- b. Grievance
- c. Kim Bobo
- d. Swift raids

Guidance: level 1

:: United States law ::

The ABA _________, created by the American Bar Association , are a set of rules that prescribe baseline standards of legal ethics and professional responsibility for lawyers in the United States. They were promulgated by the ABA House of Delegates upon the recommendation of the Kutak Commission in 1983. The rules are merely recommendations, or models, and are not themselves binding. However, having a common set of Model Rules facilitates a common discourse on legal ethics, and simplifies professional responsibility training as well as the day-to-day application of such rules. As of 2015, 49 states and four territories have adopted the rules in whole or in part, of which the most recent to do so was the Commonwealth of the Northern Mariana Islands in March 2015. California is the only state that has not adopted the ABA Model Rules, while Puerto Rico is the only U.S. jurisdiction outside of confederation has not adopted them but instead has its own Código de Ética Profesional.

Exam Probability: **Low**

26. *Answer choices:*

(see index for correct answer)

- a. Pro se
- b. judgment notwithstanding the verdict

Guidance: level 1

:: Business ethics ::

_________ is an area of applied ethics which deals with the moral principles behind the operation and regulation of marketing. Some areas of _________ overlap with media ethics.

Exam Probability: **Low**

27. *Answer choices:*

(see index for correct answer)

- a. Fair value
- b. Burson-Marsteller
- c. Black Company
- d. MBA Oath

Guidance: level 1

:: Financial regulatory authorities of the United States ::

The _________ is an agency of the United States government responsible for consumer protection in the financial sector. CFPB`s jurisdiction includes banks, credit unions, securities firms, payday lenders, mortgage-servicing operations, foreclosure relief services, debt collectors and other financial companies operating in the United States.

Exam Probability: **Low**

28. *Answer choices:*

(see index for correct answer)

- a. Internal Revenue Service
- b. National Futures Association

- c. Municipal Securities Rulemaking Board
- d. National Credit Union Administration

Guidance: level 1

:: Monopoly (economics) ::

The _________ of 1890 was a United States antitrust law that regulates competition among enterprises, which was passed by Congress under the presidency of Benjamin Harrison.

Exam Probability: **Medium**

29. *Answer choices:*

(see index for correct answer)

- a. Intellectual property
- b. Sherman Antitrust Act
- c. Competition Commission
- d. Government monopoly

Guidance: level 1

:: ::

The _________ to Fight AIDS, Tuberculosis and Malaria is an international financing organization that aims to "attract, leverage and invest additional resources to end the epidemics of HIV/AIDS, tuberculosis and malaria to support attainment of the Sustainable Development Goals established by the United Nations." A public-private partnership, the organization maintains its secretariat in Geneva, Switzerland. The organization began operations in January 2002. Microsoft founder Bill Gates was one of the first private foundations among many bilateral donors to provide seed money for the partnership.

Exam Probability: **Medium**

30. *Answer choices:*

(see index for correct answer)

- a. Sarbanes-Oxley act of 2002
- b. Global Fund
- c. hierarchical
- d. levels of analysis

Guidance: level 1

:: United States federal trade legislation ::

The _________ of 1914 established the Federal Trade Commission. The Act, signed into law by Woodrow Wilson in 1914, outlaws unfair methods of competition and outlaws unfair acts or practices that affect commerce.

Exam Probability: **High**

31. *Answer choices:*

(see index for correct answer)

- a. Export Administration Act of 1979
- b. Iran Nonproliferation Act of 2000
- c. Magnitsky Act
- d. Federal Trade Commission Act

Guidance: level 1

:: ::

The _________ , founded in 1912, is a private, nonprofit organization whose self-described mission is to focus on advancing marketplace trust, consisting of 106 independently incorporated local BBB organizations in the United States and Canada, coordinated under the Council of _________ s in Arlington, Virginia.

Exam Probability: **Low**

32. *Answer choices:*

(see index for correct answer)

- a. Character
- b. Better Business Bureau

- c. levels of analysis
- d. interpersonal communication

Guidance: level 1

:: Anti-competitive behaviour ::

_________ is a secret cooperation or deceitful agreement in order to deceive others, although not necessarily illegal, as a conspiracy. A secret agreement between two or more parties to limit open competition by deceiving, misleading, or defrauding others of their legal rights, or to obtain an objective forbidden by law typically by defrauding or gaining an unfair market advantage is an example of _________ . It is an agreement among firms or individuals to divide a market, set prices, limit production or limit opportunities.It can involve "unions, wage fixing, kickbacks, or misrepresenting the independence of the relationship between the colluding parties". In legal terms, all acts effected by _________ are considered void.

Exam Probability: **High**

33. *Answer choices:*

(see index for correct answer)

- a. Anti-siphoning law
- b. Copyright misuse
- c. SK Hynix
- d. Collusion

Guidance: level 1

:: Offshoring ::

A __________ is the temporary suspension or permanent termination of employment of an employee or, more commonly, a group of employees for business reasons, such as personnel management or downsizing an organization. Originally, __________ referred exclusively to a temporary interruption in work, or employment but this has evolved to a permanent elimination of a position in both British and US English, requiring the addition of "temporary" to specify the original meaning of the word. A __________ is not to be confused with wrongful termination. Laid off workers or displaced workers are workers who have lost or left their jobs because their employer has closed or moved, there was insufficient work for them to do, or their position or shift was abolished . Downsizing in a company is defined to involve the reduction of employees in a workforce. Downsizing in companies became a popular practice in the 1980s and early 1990s as it was seen as a way to deliver better shareholder value as it helps to reduce the costs of employers . Indeed, recent research on downsizing in the U.S., UK, and Japan suggests that downsizing is being regarded by management as one of the preferred routes to help declining organizations, cutting unnecessary costs, and improve organizational performance. Usually a __________ occurs as a cost cutting measure.

Exam Probability: **High**

34. *Answer choices:*

(see index for correct answer)

- a. Layoff
- b. Programmers Guild
- c. Offshore company

- d. TeleTech

Guidance: level 1

:: Ethical banking ::

A __________ or community development finance institution - abbreviated in both cases to CDFI - is a financial institution that provides credit and financial services to underserved markets and populations, primarily in the USA but also in the UK. A CDFI may be a community development bank, a community development credit union , a community development loan fund , a community development venture capital fund , a microenterprise development loan fund, or a community development corporation.

Exam Probability: **Medium**

35. *Answer choices:*

(see index for correct answer)

- a. Citizens Bank of Canada
- b. Community development financial institution
- c. Institute for Social Banking
- d. Triodos Bank

Guidance: level 1

:: ::

_________ refers to a business initiative to increase the access between a company and their current and potential customers through the use of the Internet. The Internet allows the company to market themselves and attract new customers to their website where they can provide product information and better customer service. Customers can place orders electronically, therefore reducing expensive long distant phone calls and postage costs of placing orders, while saving time on behalf of the customer and company.

Exam Probability: **Medium**

36. *Answer choices:*

(see index for correct answer)

- a. interpersonal communication
- b. open system
- c. levels of analysis
- d. Global reach

Guidance: level 1

:: Dutch inventions ::

The Fairtrade certification initiative was created to form a new method for economic trade. This method takes an ethical standpoint, and considers the producers first.

Exam Probability: **Low**

37. *Answer choices:*

(see index for correct answer)

- a. Fair Trade Certified
- b. Fairtrade

Guidance: level 1

:: ::

_________ Ltd. is the world`s 2nd largest offshore drilling contractor and is based in Vernier, Switzerland. The company has offices in 20 countries, including Switzerland, Canada, United States, Norway, Scotland, India, Brazil, Singapore, Indonesia and Malaysia.

Exam Probability: **High**

38. *Answer choices:*

(see index for correct answer)

- a. Transocean
- b. hierarchical perspective
- c. Character
- d. surface-level diversity

Guidance: level 1

:: Reputation management ::

_________ or image of a social entity is an opinion about that entity, typically as a result of social evaluation on a set of criteria.

Exam Probability: **High**

39. *Answer choices:*

(see index for correct answer)

- a. Advogato
- b. 123people
- c. Reputation
- d. BrandYourself

Guidance: level 1

:: Supply chain management terms ::

In business and finance, _________ is a system of organizations, people, activities, information, and resources involved inmoving a product or service from supplier to customer. _________ activities involve the transformation of natural resources, raw materials, and components into a finished product that is delivered to the end customer. In sophisticated _________ systems, used products may re-enter the _________ at any point where residual value is recyclable. _________s link value chains.

Exam Probability: **Low**

40. *Answer choices:*

(see index for correct answer)

- a. Most valuable customers
- b. Direct shipment
- c. Supply Chain
- d. Widget

Guidance: level 1

:: Socialism ::

_________ is a label used to define the first currents of modern socialist thought as exemplified by the work of Henri de Saint-Simon, Charles Fourier, Étienne Cabet and Robert Owen.

Exam Probability: **High**

41. *Answer choices:*

(see index for correct answer)

- a. International Socialist Commission
- b. Class conflict
- c. Market abolitionism
- d. Kim Se-jin

Guidance: level 1

:: Globalization-related theories ::

_________ is an economic system based on the private ownership of the means of production and their operation for profit. Characteristics central to _________ include private property, capital accumulation, wage labor, voluntary exchange, a price system, and competitive markets. In a capitalist market economy, decision-making and investment are determined by every owner of wealth, property or production ability in financial and capital markets, whereas prices and the distribution of goods and services are mainly determined by competition in goods and services markets.

Exam Probability: **High**

42. *Answer choices:*

(see index for correct answer)

- a. postmodernism
- b. post-industrial
- c. Capitalism

Guidance: level 1

:: ::

The Catholic Church, also known as the Roman Catholic Church, is the largest Christian church, with approximately 1.3 billion baptised Catholics worldwide as of 2017. As the world`s oldest continuously functioning international institution, it has played a prominent role in the history and development of Western civilisation. The church is headed by the Bishop of Rome, known as the pope. Its central administration, the Holy See, is in the Vatican City, an enclave within the city of Rome in Italy.

Exam Probability: **Low**

43. *Answer choices:*

(see index for correct answer)

- a. Character
- b. Catholicism
- c. open system
- d. similarity-attraction theory

Guidance: level 1

:: ::

An __________ is the release of a liquid petroleum hydrocarbon into the environment, especially the marine ecosystem, due to human activity, and is a form of pollution. The term is usually given to marine __________s, where oil is released into the ocean or coastal waters, but spills may also occur on land. __________s may be due to releases of crude oil from tankers, offshore platforms, drilling rigs and wells, as well as spills of refined petroleum products and their by-products, heavier fuels used by large ships such as bunker fuel, or the spill of any oily refuse or waste oil.

Exam Probability: **High**

44. *Answer choices:*

(see index for correct answer)

- a. Sarbanes-Oxley act of 2002
- b. personal values
- c. process perspective
- d. empathy

Guidance: level 1

:: ::

A __________ is an astronomical body orbiting a star or stellar remnant that is massive enough to be rounded by its own gravity, is not massive enough to cause thermonuclear fusion, and has cleared its neighbouring region of __________esimals.

Exam Probability: **High**

45. *Answer choices:*

(see index for correct answer)

- a. Sarbanes-Oxley act of 2002
- b. functional perspective
- c. Character
- d. Planet

Guidance: level 1

:: Nepotism ::

_________ is the granting of favour to relatives in various fields, including business, politics, entertainment, sports, religion and other activities. The term originated with the assignment of nephews to important positions by Catholic popes and bishops. Trading parliamentary employment for favors is a modern-day example of _________ . Criticism of _________ , however, can be found in ancient Indian texts such as the Kural literature.

Exam Probability: **Low**

46. *Answer choices:*

(see index for correct answer)

- a. Wasta
- b. Nepotism

- c. Crachach
- d. Monklandsgate

Guidance: level 1

:: Writs ::

In common law, a writ of _________ is a writ whereby a private individual who assists a prosecution can receive all or part of any penalty imposed. Its name is an abbreviation of the Latin phrase _________ pro domino rege quam pro se ipso in hac parte sequitur, meaning "[he] who sues in this matter for the king as well as for himself."

Exam Probability: **Low**

47. *Answer choices:*

(see index for correct answer)

- a. Writ of execution
- b. Qui tam

Guidance: level 1

:: Management ::

__________ is the identification, evaluation, and prioritization of risks followed by coordinated and economical application of resources to minimize, monitor, and control the probability or impact of unfortunate events or to maximize the realization of opportunities.

Exam Probability: **High**

48. *Answer choices:*

(see index for correct answer)

- a. Innovation leadership
- b. Fall guy
- c. Crisis plan
- d. Director

Guidance: level 1

:: Professional ethics ::

In the mental health field, a __________ is a situation where multiple roles exist between a therapist, or other mental health practitioner, and a client. __________ s are also referred to as multiple relationships, and these two terms are used interchangeably in the research literature. The American Psychological Association Ethical Principles of Psychologists and Code of Conduct is a resource that outlines ethical standards and principles to which practitioners are expected to adhere. Standard 3.05 of the APA ethics code outlines the definition of multiple relationships. Dual or multiple relationships occur when.

Exam Probability: **Medium**

49. *Answer choices:*

(see index for correct answer)

- a. ethical code
- b. Continuous professional development
- c. Dual relationship

Guidance: level 1

:: Auditing ::

_________ is a general term that can reflect various types of evaluations intended to identify environmental compliance and management system implementation gaps, along with related corrective actions. In this way they perform an analogous function to financial audits. There are generally two different types of _________ s: compliance audits and management systems audits. Compliance audits tend to be the primary type in the US or within US-based multinationals.

Exam Probability: **High**

50. *Answer choices:*

(see index for correct answer)

- a. Sales tax audit
- b. Quality audit

- c. Management audit
- d. Environmental audit

Guidance: level 1

:: Leadership ::

__________ is a theory of leadership where a leader works with teams to identify needed change, creating a vision to guide the change through inspiration, and executing the change in tandem with committed members of a group; it is an integral part of the Full Range Leadership Model. __________ serves to enhance the motivation, morale, and job performance of followers through a variety of mechanisms; these include connecting the follower`s sense of identity and self to a project and to the collective identity of the organization; being a role model for followers in order to inspire them and to raise their interest in the project; challenging followers to take greater ownership for their work, and understanding the strengths and weaknesses of followers, allowing the leader to align followers with tasks that enhance their performance.

Exam Probability: **Medium**

51. *Answer choices:*

(see index for correct answer)

- a. Outstanding leadership theory
- b. Love leadership
- c. BTS Group
- d. Transformational leadership

Guidance: level 1

:: ::

_________ or accountancy is the measurement, processing, and communication of financial information about economic entities such as businesses and corporations. The modern field was established by the Italian mathematician Luca Pacioli in 1494. _________ , which has been called the "language of business", measures the results of an organization`s economic activities and conveys this information to a variety of users, including investors, creditors, management, and regulators. Practitioners of _________ are known as accountants. The terms " _________ " and "financial reporting" are often used as synonyms.

Exam Probability: **High**

52. *Answer choices:*

(see index for correct answer)

- a. empathy
- b. Accounting
- c. hierarchical perspective
- d. deep-level diversity

Guidance: level 1

:: Data management ::

_________ is a form of intellectual property that grants the creator of an original creative work an exclusive legal right to determine whether and under what conditions this original work may be copied and used by others, usually for a limited term of years. The exclusive rights are not absolute but limited by limitations and exceptions to _________ law, including fair use. A major limitation on _________ on ideas is that _________ protects only the original expression of ideas, and not the underlying ideas themselves.

Exam Probability: **High**

53. *Answer choices:*

(see index for correct answer)

- a. Database schema
- b. Cleansing and Conforming Data
- c. Data frame
- d. Copyright

Guidance: level 1

:: Agricultural labor ::

The _________ of America, or more commonly just _________ , is a labor union for farmworkers in the United States. It originated from the merger of two workers` rights organizations, the Agricultural Workers Organizing Committee led by organizer Larry Itliong, and the National Farm Workers Association led by César Chávez and Dolores Huerta. They became allied and transformed from workers` rights organizations into a union as a result of a series of strikes in 1965, when the mostly Filipino farmworkers of the AWOC in Delano, California initiated a grape strike, and the NFWA went on strike in support. As a result of the commonality in goals and methods, the NFWA and the AWOC formed the _________ Organizing Committee on August 22, 1966.This organization was accepted into the AFL-CIO in 1972 and changed its name to the _________ Union.

Exam Probability: **Medium**

54. *Answer choices:*

(see index for correct answer)

- a. Obshchina
- b. Rural tenancy
- c. United Farm Workers
- d. Harvest excursion

Guidance: level 1

:: ::

The __________ of 1906 was the first of a series of significant consumer protection laws which was enacted by Congress in the 20th century and led to the creation of the Food and Drug Administration. Its main purpose was to ban foreign and interstate traffic in adulterated or mislabeled food and drug products, and it directed the U.S. Bureau of Chemistry to inspect products and refer offenders to prosecutors. It required that active ingredients be placed on the label of a drug's packaging and that drugs could not fall below purity levels established by the United States Pharmacopeia or the National Formulary. The Jungle by Upton Sinclair with its graphic and revolting descriptions of unsanitary conditions and unscrupulous practices rampant in the meatpacking industry, was an inspirational piece that kept the public's attention on the important issue of unhygienic meat processing plants that later led to food inspection legislation. Sinclair quipped, "I aimed at the public's heart and by accident I hit it in the stomach," as outraged readers demanded and got the pure food law.

Exam Probability: **High**

55. *Answer choices:*

(see index for correct answer)

- a. functional perspective
- b. Pure Food and Drug Act
- c. cultural
- d. process perspective

Guidance: level 1

:: ::

Bernard Lawrence __________ is an American former market maker, investment advisor, financier, fraudster, and convicted felon, who is currently serving a federal prison sentence for offenses related to a massive Ponzi scheme. He is the former non-executive chairman of the NASDAQ stock market, the confessed operator of the largest Ponzi scheme in world history, and the largest financial fraud in U.S. history. Prosecutors estimated the fraud to be worth $64.8 billion based on the amounts in the accounts of __________`s 4,800 clients as of November 30, 2008.

Exam Probability: **Medium**

56. *Answer choices:*

(see index for correct answer)

- a. process perspective
- b. functional perspective
- c. cultural
- d. Madoff

Guidance: level 1

:: Auditing ::

__________ refers to the independence of the internal auditor or of the external auditor from parties that may have a financial interest in the business being audited. Independence requires integrity and an objective approach to the audit process. The concept requires the auditor to carry out his or her work freely and in an objective manner.

Exam Probability: **Low**

57. *Answer choices:*

(see index for correct answer)

- a. Mitigating control
- b. Auditor independence
- c. Professional Evaluation and Certification Board
- d. Utility bill audit

Guidance: level 1

:: Corporate scandals ::

_________ was a bank based in the Caribbean, which operated from 1986 to 2009 when it went into receivership. It was an affiliate of the Stanford Financial Group and failed when the its parent was seized by United States authorities in early 2009 as part of the investigation into Allen Stanford.

Exam Probability: **Medium**

58. *Answer choices:*

(see index for correct answer)

- a. Great Phenol Plot
- b. ExxonMobil
- c. Madoff investment scandal

- d. Stanford International Bank

Guidance: level 1

:: ::

The ________ is an American stock exchange located at 11 Wall Street, Lower Manhattan, New York City, New York. It is by far the world`s largest stock exchange by market capitalization of its listed companies at US$30.1 trillion as of February 2018. The average daily trading value was approximately US$169 billion in 2013. The NYSE trading floor is located at 11 Wall Street and is composed of 21 rooms used for the facilitation of trading. A fifth trading room, located at 30 Broad Street, was closed in February 2007. The main building and the 11 Wall Street building were designated National Historic Landmarks in 1978.

Exam Probability: **Low**

59. *Answer choices:*

(see index for correct answer)

- a. similarity-attraction theory
- b. New York Stock Exchange
- c. imperative
- d. process perspective

Guidance: level 1

Accounting

Accounting or accountancy is the measurement, processing, and communication of financial information about economic entities such as businesses and corporations. The modern field was established by the Italian mathematician Luca Pacioli in 1494. Accounting, which has been called the "language of business", measures the results of an organization's economic activities and conveys this information to a variety of users, including investors, creditors, management, and regulators.

:: Management accounting ::

_________ is a method of identifying and evaluating activities that a business performs, using activity-based costing to carry out a value chain analysis or a re-engineering initiative to improve strategic and operational decisions in an organization.

Exam Probability: **High**

1. *Answer choices:*

(see index for correct answer)

- a. Activity-based management
- b. Bridge life-cycle cost analysis
- c. Customer profitability
- d. Direct material price variance

Guidance: level 1

:: Marketing ::

_________ or stock is the goods and materials that a business holds for the ultimate goal of resale .

Exam Probability: **Low**

2. *Answer choices:*

(see index for correct answer)

- a. Enterprise marketing management
- b. Inventory
- c. Sales contest
- d. Consumer culture theory

Guidance: level 1

:: Management accounting ::

The _________ is a professional membership organization headquartered in Montvale, New Jersey, United States, operating in four global regions: The Americas, Asia/Pacific, Europe, and Middle East/India.

Exam Probability: **Low**

3. *Answer choices:*

(see index for correct answer)

- a. Institute of Management Accountants
- b. Chartered Institute of Management Accountants
- c. Cost driver
- d. Management accounting

Guidance: level 1

:: Expense ::

_________ relates to the cost of borrowing money. It is the price that a lender charges a borrower for the use of the lender`s money. On the income statement, _________ can represent the cost of borrowing money from banks, bond investors, and other sources. _________ is different from operating expense and CAPEX, for it relates to the capital structure of a company, and it is usually tax-deductible.

Exam Probability: **Low**

4. *Answer choices:*

(see index for correct answer)

- a. Corporate travel
- b. Tax expense
- c. Accretion expense
- d. Momentem

Guidance: level 1

:: Accounting systems ::

In bookkeeping, a _________ statement is a process that explains the difference on a specified date between the bank balance shown in an organization`s bank statement, as supplied by the bank and the corresponding amount shown in the organization`s own accounting records.

Exam Probability: **Medium**

5. *Answer choices:*

(see index for correct answer)

- a. Accounting reform
- b. Purchase ledger
- c. Dome Publishing
- d. Counting house

Guidance: level 1

:: Finance ::

_________ , in finance and accounting, means stated value or face value. From this come the expressions at par , over par and under par .

Exam Probability: **High**

6. *Answer choices:*

(see index for correct answer)

- a. Financial audit
- b. NOPAT
- c. Receivership
- d. Par value

Guidance: level 1

:: ::

A __________ is a tax paid to a governing body for the sales of certain goods and services. Usually laws allow the seller to collect funds for the tax from the consumer at the point of purchase. When a tax on goods or services is paid to a governing body directly by a consumer, it is usually called a use tax. Often laws provide for the exemption of certain goods or services from sales and use tax.

Exam Probability: **High**

7. *Answer choices:*

(see index for correct answer)

- a. process perspective
- b. corporate values
- c. Character
- d. interpersonal communication

Guidance: level 1

:: ::

An __________ is a contingent motivator. Traditional __________ s are extrinsic motivators which reward actions to yield a desired outcome. The effectiveness of traditional __________ s has changed as the needs of Western society have evolved. While the traditional __________ model is effective when there is a defined procedure and goal for a task, Western society started to require a higher volume of critical thinkers, so the traditional model became less effective. Institutions are now following a trend in implementing strategies that rely on intrinsic motivations rather than the extrinsic motivations that the traditional __________ s foster.

Exam Probability: **High**

8. *Answer choices:*

(see index for correct answer)

- a. Sarbanes-Oxley act of 2002
- b. cultural
- c. hierarchical
- d. Incentive

Guidance: level 1

:: Inventory ::

__________ is the amount of inventory a company has in stock at the end of its fiscal year. It is closely related with __________ cost, which is the amount of money spent to get these goods in stock. It should be calculated at the lower of cost or market.

Exam Probability: **Low**

9. *Answer choices:*

(see index for correct answer)

- a. Stock keeping unit
- b. Ending inventory
- c. Inventory control problem
- d. Perpetual inventory

Guidance: level 1

:: ::

Generally speaking, a _________ begins on the New Year's Day of the given calendar system and ends on the day before the following New Year's Day, and thus consists of a whole number of days. A year can also be measured by starting on any other named day of the calendar, and ending on the day before this named day in the following year. This may be termed a "year's time", but not a " _________ ". To reconcile the _________ with the astronomical cycle certain years contain extra days .

Exam Probability: **High**

10. *Answer choices:*

(see index for correct answer)

- a. cultural

- b. imperative
- c. Calendar year
- d. open system

Guidance: level 1

:: United States federal income tax ::

Under United States tax law, the __________ is a dollar amount that non-itemizers may subtract from their income before income tax is applied. Taxpayers may choose either itemized deductions or the __________, but usually choose whichever results in the lesser amount of tax payable. The __________ is available to US citizens and aliens who are resident for tax purposes and who are individuals, married persons, and heads of household. The __________ is based on filing status and typically increases each year. It is not available to nonresident aliens residing in the United States . Additional amounts are available for persons who are blind and/or are at least 65 years of age.

Exam Probability: **Medium**

11. *Answer choices:*

(see index for correct answer)

- a. Standard deduction
- b. Dealer equity option
- c. Philippines Charitable Giving Assistance Act
- d. Rabbi trust

Guidance: level 1

:: Finance ::

A __________ , publicly-traded company, publicly-held company, publicly-listed company, or public limited company is a corporation whose ownership is dispersed among the general public in many shares of stock which are freely traded on a stock exchange or in over-the-counter markets. In some jurisdictions, public companies over a certain size must be listed on an exchange. A __________ can be listed or unlisted .

Exam Probability: **Low**

12. *Answer choices:*

(see index for correct answer)

- a. Revaluation of fixed assets
- b. Natural borrowing limit
- c. Public company
- d. Merchant cash advance

Guidance: level 1

:: International Financial Reporting Standards ::

_________, usually called IFRS, are standards issued by the IFRS Foundation and the International Accounting Standards Board to provide a common global language for business affairs so that company accounts are understandable and comparable across international boundaries. They are a consequence of growing international shareholding and trade and are particularly important for companies that have dealings in several countries. They are progressively replacing the many different national accounting standards. They are the rules to be followed by accountants to maintain books of accounts which are comparable, understandable, reliable and relevant as per the users internal or external. IFRS, with the exception of IAS 29 Financial Reporting in Hyperinflationary Economies and IFRIC 7 Applying the Restatement Approach under IAS 29, are authorized in terms of the historical cost paradigm. IAS 29 and IFRIC 7 are authorized in terms of the units of constant purchasing power paradigm.IAS 2 is related to inventories in this standard we talk about the stock its production process etcIFRS began as an attempt to harmonize accounting across the European Union but the value of harmonization quickly made the concept attractive around the world. However, it has been debated whether or not de facto harmonization has occurred. Standards that were issued by IASC are still within use today and go by the name International Accounting Standards , while standards issued by IASB are called IFRS. IAS were issued between 1973 and 2001 by the Board of the International Accounting Standards Committee . On 1 April 2001, the new International Accounting Standards Board took over from the IASC the responsibility for setting International Accounting Standards. During its first meeting the new Board adopted existing IAS and Standing Interpretations Committee standards . The IASB has continued to develop standards calling the new standards " _________ ".

Exam Probability: **Low**

13. *Answer choices:*

(see index for correct answer)

- a. Convergence of accounting standards
- b. International Financial Reporting Standards
- c. International Public Sector Accounting Standards

- d. IAS 39

Guidance: level 1

:: ::

In production, research, retail, and accounting, a _________ is the value of money that has been used up to produce something or deliver a service, and hence is not available for use anymore. In business, the _________ may be one of acquisition, in which case the amount of money expended to acquire it is counted as _________ . In this case, money is the input that is gone in order to acquire the thing. This acquisition _________ may be the sum of the _________ of production as incurred by the original producer, and further _________ s of transaction as incurred by the acquirer over and above the price paid to the producer. Usually, the price also includes a mark-up for profit over the _________ of production.

Exam Probability: **Medium**

14. *Answer choices:*

(see index for correct answer)

- a. functional perspective
- b. Cost
- c. personal values
- d. imperative

Guidance: level 1

:: E-commerce ::

__________ is an e-commerce payment system used in the Netherlands, based on online banking. Introduced in 2005, this payment method allows customers to buy on the Internet using direct online transfers from their bank account.

Exam Probability: **Medium**

15. *Answer choices:*

(see index for correct answer)

- a. BuildDirect
- b. IDEAL
- c. Public key certificate
- d. AsiaPay

Guidance: level 1

:: Accounting in the United States ::

Founded in 1887, the _________ is the national professional organization of Certified Public Accountants in the United States, with more than 418,000 members in 143 countries in business and industry, public practice, government, education, student affiliates and international associates. It sets ethical standards for the profession and U.S. auditing standards for audits of private companies, non-profit organizations, federal, state and local governments. It also develops and grades the Uniform CPA Examination. The AICPA maintains offices in New York City; Washington, DC; Durham, NC; and Ewing, NJ. The AICPA celebrated the 125th anniversary of its founding in 2012.

Exam Probability: **High**

16. *Answer choices:*

(see index for correct answer)

- a. Positive assurance
- b. Revolving fund
- c. Variable interest entity
- d. Institute of Internal Auditors

Guidance: level 1

:: Income taxes ::

An _________ is a tax imposed on individuals or entities that varies with respective income or profits . _________ generally is computed as the product of a tax rate times taxable income. Taxation rates may vary by type or characteristics of the taxpayer.

Exam Probability: **Low**

17. *Answer choices:*

(see index for correct answer)

- a. Income tax
- b. Rouanet Law
- c. Income tax in Singapore
- d. Personal allowance

Guidance: level 1

:: ::

__________ is the field of accounting concerned with the summary, analysis and reporting of financial transactions related to a business. This involves the preparation of financial statements available for public use. Stockholders, suppliers, banks, employees, government agencies, business owners, and other stakeholders are examples of people interested in receiving such information for decision making purposes.

Exam Probability: **Medium**

18. *Answer choices:*

(see index for correct answer)

- a. Character
- b. similarity-attraction theory

- c. Financial accounting
- d. corporate values

Guidance: level 1

:: Financial ratios ::

The ________ is a financial ratio indicating the relative proportion of shareholders` equity and debt used to finance a company`s assets. Closely related to leveraging, the ratio is also known as risk, gearing or leverage. The two components are often taken from the firm`s balance sheet or statement of financial position , but the ratio may also be calculated using market values for both, if the company`s debt and equity are publicly traded, or using a combination of book value for debt and market value for equity financially.

Exam Probability: **Medium**

19. *Answer choices:*

(see index for correct answer)

- a. Like for like
- b. Earnings yield
- c. Debt-to-equity ratio
- d. Greeks

Guidance: level 1

:: Financial ratios ::

_________ is a measure of how revenue growth translates into growth in operating income. It is a measure of leverage, and of how risky, or volatile, a company`s operating income is.

Exam Probability: **High**

20. *Answer choices:*

(see index for correct answer)

- a. PE ratio
- b. WHIS ratio
- c. Operating margin
- d. Savings ratio

Guidance: level 1

:: Taxation ::

_________ refers to instances where a taxpayer can delay paying taxes to some future period. In theory, the net taxes paid should be the same. Taxes can sometimes be deferred indefinitely, or may be taxed at a lower rate in the future, particularly for deferral of income taxes.

Exam Probability: **Low**

21. *Answer choices:*

(see index for correct answer)

- a. Steuerberater
- b. Tax wedge
- c. Tax deferral
- d. Intra-European Organisation of Tax Administrations

Guidance: level 1

:: Asset ::

In accounting, a __________ is any asset which can reasonably be expected to be sold, consumed, or exhausted through the normal operations of a business within the current fiscal year or operating cycle . Typical __________ s include cash, cash equivalents, short-term investments , accounts receivable, stock inventory, supplies, and the portion of prepaid liabilities which will be paid within a year.In simple words, assets which are held for a short period are known as __________ s. Such assets are expected to be realised in cash or consumed during the normal operating cycle of the business.

Exam Probability: **High**

22. *Answer choices:*

(see index for correct answer)

- a. Current asset
- b. Asset

Guidance: level 1

:: Financial ratios ::

The _________ or dividend-price ratio of a share is the dividend per share, divided by the price per share. It is also a company's total annual dividend payments divided by its market capitalization, assuming the number of shares is constant. It is often expressed as a percentage.

Exam Probability: **Medium**

23. *Answer choices:*

(see index for correct answer)

- a. Capital recovery factor
- b. interest margin
- c. Dividend yield
- d. Debt-to-capital ratio

Guidance: level 1

:: Financial ratios ::

The _________ shows the percentage of how profitable a company's assets are in generating revenue.

Exam Probability: **Low**

24. *Answer choices:*

(see index for correct answer)

- a. Return on assets
- b. Fixed-asset turnover
- c. Sustainable growth rate
- d. Short interest ratio

Guidance: level 1

:: Real property law ::

A _________ or millage rate is an ad valorem tax on the value of a property, usually levied on real estate. The tax is levied by the governing authority of the jurisdiction in which the property is located. This can be a national government, a federated state, a county or geographical region or a municipality. Multiple jurisdictions may tax the same property. This tax can be contrasted to a rent tax which is based on rental income or imputed rent, and a land value tax, which is a levy on the value of land, excluding the value of buildings and other improvements.

Exam Probability: **High**

25. *Answer choices:*

(see index for correct answer)

- a. Chalking the door
- b. Escheat
- c. Property tax
- d. Abstractor of title

Guidance: level 1

:: Generally Accepted Accounting Principles ::

_________ , also referred to as the bottom line, net income, or net earnings is a measure of the profitability of a venture after accounting for all costs and taxes. It is the actual profit, and includes the operating expenses that are excluded from gross profit.

Exam Probability: **Medium**

26. *Answer choices:*

(see index for correct answer)

- a. Cost pool
- b. Consolidation
- c. Treasury stock
- d. Net profit

Guidance: level 1

:: Accounting in the United States ::

The __________ is a private-sector, nonprofit corporation created by the Sarbanes–Oxley Act of 2002 to oversee the audits of public companies and other issuers in order to protect the interests of investors and further the public interest in the preparation of informative, accurate and independent audit reports. The PCAOB also oversees the audits of broker-dealers, including compliance reports filed pursuant to federal securities laws, to promote investor protection. All PCAOB rules and standards must be approved by the U.S. Securities and Exchange Commission .

Exam Probability: **Medium**

27. *Answer choices:*

(see index for correct answer)

- a. International Qualification Examination
- b. Accounting Research Bulletins
- c. Public Company Accounting Oversight Board
- d. Comprehensive Performance Assessment

Guidance: level 1

:: Accounting systems ::

In accounting, the controlling account is an account in the general ledger for which a corresponding subsidiary ledger has been created. The subsidiary ledger allows for tracking transactions within the controlling account in more detail. Individual transactions are posted both to the controlling account and the corresponding subsidiary ledger, and the totals for both are compared when preparing a trial balance to ensure accuracy.

Exam Probability: **Medium**

28. *Answer choices:*

(see index for correct answer)

- a. Accounting practice
- b. Control account
- c. Unified ledger accounting
- d. Waste book

Guidance: level 1

:: ::

_________ is the consumption and saving opportunity gained by an entity within a specified timeframe, which is generally expressed in monetary terms. For households and individuals, " _________ is the sum of all the wages, salaries, profits, interest payments, rents, and other forms of earnings received in a given period of time."

Exam Probability: **Low**

29. *Answer choices:*

(see index for correct answer)

- a. imperative
- b. functional perspective
- c. similarity-attraction theory
- d. Income

Guidance: level 1

:: Management accounting ::

__________ s are costs that change as the quantity of the good or service that a business produces changes. __________ s are the sum of marginal costs over all units produced. They can also be considered normal costs. Fixed costs and __________ s make up the two components of total cost. Direct costs are costs that can easily be associated with a particular cost object. However, not all __________ s are direct costs. For example, variable manufacturing overhead costs are __________ s that are indirect costs, not direct costs. __________ s are sometimes called unit-level costs as they vary with the number of units produced.

Exam Probability: **Low**

30. *Answer choices:*

(see index for correct answer)

- a. Responsibility center
- b. Cash and cash equivalents

- c. Overhead
- d. Fixed cost

Guidance: level 1

:: Business law ::

The expression " __________ " is somewhat confusing as it has a different meaning based on the context that is under consideration.From a product characteristic stand point, this type of a lease, as distinguished from a finance lease, is one where the lessor takes residual risk. As such, the lease is non full payout. From an accounting stand point, this type of lease results in off balance sheet financing.

Exam Probability: **Low**

31. *Answer choices:*

(see index for correct answer)

- a. Business license
- b. Operating lease
- c. Single business enterprise
- d. Business method patent

Guidance: level 1

:: International trade ::

In finance, an _________ is the rate at which one currency will be exchanged for another. It is also regarded as the value of one country's currency in relation to another currency. For example, an interbank _________ of 114 Japanese yen to the United States dollar means that ¥114 will be exchanged for each US$1 or that US$1 will be exchanged for each ¥114. In this case it is said that the price of a dollar in relation to yen is ¥114, or equivalently that the price of a yen in relation to dollars is $1/114.

Exam Probability: **High**

32. *Answer choices:*

(see index for correct answer)

- a. Denied trade screening
- b. Exchange rate
- c. Comparative advantage
- d. Harmonized System

Guidance: level 1

:: Actuarial science ::

The _________ is the greater benefit of receiving money now rather than an identical sum later. It is founded on time preference.

Exam Probability: **Low**

33. *Answer choices:*

(see index for correct answer)

- a. Computational finance
- b. 100-year flood
- c. Mathematical statistics
- d. RiskMetrics

Guidance: level 1

:: Accounting software ::

_________ is a freely available and global framework for exchanging business information. _________ allows the expression of semantic meaning commonly required in business reporting. The language is XML-based and uses the XML syntax and related XML technologies such as XML Schema, XLink, XPath, and Namespaces. One use of _________ is to define and exchange financial information, such as a financial statement. The _________ Specification is developed and published by _________ International, Inc. .

Exam Probability: **Low**

34. *Answer choices:*

(see index for correct answer)

- a. Cheqbook
- b. XBRL
- c. Unit4

- d. DHPOS

Guidance: level 1

:: Fundamental analysis ::

_________ is the monetary value of earnings per outstanding share of common stock for a company.

Exam Probability: **Medium**

35. *Answer choices:*

(see index for correct answer)

- a. Restricted stock
- b. Fundamental analysis
- c. Public float
- d. Terminal value

Guidance: level 1

:: ::

_________ is a costing method that identifies activities in an organization and assigns the cost of each activity to all products and services according to the actual consumption by each. This model assigns more indirect costs into direct costs compared to conventional costing.

Exam Probability: **High**

36. *Answer choices:*

(see index for correct answer)

- a. empathy
- b. Sarbanes-Oxley act of 2002
- c. Character
- d. co-culture

Guidance: level 1

:: ::

An _________ is an asset that lacks physical substance. It is defined in opposition to physical assets such as machinery and buildings. An _________ is usually very hard to evaluate. Patents, copyrights, franchises, goodwill, trademarks, and trade names. The general interpretation also includes software and other intangible computer based assets are all examples of _________ s. _________ s generally—though not necessarily—suffer from typical market failures of non-rivalry and non-excludability.

Exam Probability: **High**

37. *Answer choices:*

(see index for correct answer)

- a. personal values
- b. functional perspective
- c. hierarchical perspective
- d. open system

Guidance: level 1

:: Budgets ::

A __________ is a financial plan for a defined period, often one year. It may also include planned sales volumes and revenues, resource quantities, costs and expenses, assets, liabilities and cash flows. Companies, governments, families and other organizations use it to express strategic plans of activities or events in measurable terms.

Exam Probability: **Medium**

38. *Answer choices:*

(see index for correct answer)

- a. Black budget
- b. Budget
- c. Budgeted cost of work scheduled
- d. Performance-based budgeting

Guidance: level 1

:: Basic financial concepts ::

In finance, maturity or _________ refers to the final payment date of a loan or other financial instrument, at which point the principal is due to be paid.

Exam Probability: **Medium**

39. *Answer choices:*

(see index for correct answer)

- a. balloon payment
- b. Maturity date
- c. Deflation
- d. Short interest

Guidance: level 1

:: Fraud ::

In law, _________ is intentional deception to secure unfair or unlawful gain, or to deprive a victim of a legal right. _________ can violate civil law , a criminal law , or it may cause no loss of money, property or legal right but still be an element of another civil or criminal wrong. The purpose of _________ may be monetary gain or other benefits, for example by obtaining a passport, travel document, or driver`s license, or mortgage _________ , where the perpetrator may attempt to qualify for a mortgage by way of false statements.

Exam Probability: **High**

40. *Answer choices:*

(see index for correct answer)

- a. Telemarketing fraud
- b. Identity theft
- c. Fraud
- d. Adoption fraud

Guidance: level 1

:: United States Generally Accepted Accounting Principles ::

A _________ is a set of U.S. government financial statements comprising the financial report of a state, municipal or other governmental entity that complies with the accounting requirements promulgated by the Governmental Accounting Standards Board . GASB provides standards for the content of a CAFR in its annually updated publication Codification of Governmental Accounting and Financial Reporting Standards. The U.S. Federal Government adheres to standards determined by the Federal Accounting Standards Advisory Board .

Exam Probability: **Low**

41. *Answer choices:*

(see index for correct answer)

- a. Permanent fund
- b. Available for sale
- c. Comprehensive annual financial report
- d. Working Group on Financial Markets

Guidance: level 1

:: ::

The U.S. _________ is an independent agency of the United States federal government. The SEC holds primary responsibility for enforcing the federal securities laws, proposing securities rules, and regulating the securities industry, the nation's stock and options exchanges, and other activities and organizations, including the electronic securities markets in the United States.

Exam Probability: **Medium**

42. *Answer choices:*

(see index for correct answer)

- a. open system
- b. process perspective
- c. Securities and Exchange Commission
- d. functional perspective

Guidance: level 1

:: Generally Accepted Accounting Principles ::

The term _________ is most often used to describe a practice or document that is provided as a courtesy or satisfies minimum requirements, conforms to a norm or doctrine, tends to be performed perfunctorily or is considered a formality.

Exam Probability: **High**

43. *Answer choices:*

(see index for correct answer)

- a. Long-term liabilities
- b. Reserve
- c. Treasury stock

- d. Standard Business Reporting

Guidance: level 1

:: Business law ::

A __________ is an arrangement where parties, known as partners, agree to cooperate to advance their mutual interests. The partners in a __________ may be individuals, businesses, interest-based organizations, schools, governments or combinations. Organizations may partner to increase the likelihood of each achieving their mission and to amplify their reach. A __________ may result in issuing and holding equity or may be only governed by a contract.

Exam Probability: **High**

44. *Answer choices:*

(see index for correct answer)

- a. License
- b. Process agent
- c. Extraordinary resolution
- d. Partnership

Guidance: level 1

:: Financial economics ::

A __________ is defined to include property of any kind held by an assessee, whether connected with their business or profession or not connected with their business or profession. It includes all kinds of property, movable or immovable, tangible or intangible, fixed or circulating. Thus, land and building, plant and machinery, motorcar, furniture, jewellery, route permits, goodwill, tenancy rights, patents, trademarks, shares, debentures, securities, units, mutual funds, zero-coupon bonds etc. are __________ s.

Exam Probability: **Low**

45. *Answer choices:*

(see index for correct answer)

- a. Asset specificity
- b. Capital asset
- c. Holding value
- d. Forward rate

Guidance: level 1

:: Accounting terminology ::

__________ are liabilities that reflect expenses that have not yet been paid or logged under accounts payable during an accounting period; in other words, a company`s obligation to pay for goods and services that have been provided for which invoices have not yet been received. Examples would include accrued wages payable, accrued sales tax payable, and accrued rent payable.

Exam Probability: **Low**

46. *Answer choices:*

(see index for correct answer)

- a. Fair value accounting
- b. Checkoff
- c. Statement of financial position
- d. Accrued liabilities

Guidance: level 1

:: Investment ::

In economics, _________ is spending which increases the availability of fixed capital goods or means of production and goods inventories. It is the total spending on newly produced physical capital and on inventories —that is, gross investment—minus replacement investment, which simply replaces depreciated capital goods. It is productive capital formation plus net additions to the stock of housing and the stock of inventories.

Exam Probability: **Low**

47. *Answer choices:*

(see index for correct answer)

- a. Investor profile
- b. Market timing

- c. The Investment Answer
- d. Net asset value

Guidance: level 1

:: Legal terms ::

A __________ is a gathering of people who have been invited by a host for the purposes of socializing, conversation, recreation, or as part of a festival or other commemoration of a special occasion. A __________ will typically feature food and beverages, and often music and dancing or other forms of entertainment. In many Western countries, parties for teens and adults are associated with drinking alcohol such as beer, wine, or distilled spirits.

Exam Probability: **High**

48. *Answer choices:*

(see index for correct answer)

- a. Appearance of impropriety
- b. Party
- c. Felony
- d. Prejudice

Guidance: level 1

:: Business law ::

A ________ is a form of partnership similar to a general partnership except that while a general partnership must have at least two general partners , a ________ must have at least one GP and at least one limited partner.

Exam Probability: **Low**

49. *Answer choices:*

(see index for correct answer)

- a. Hundi
- b. Limited partnership
- c. Output contract
- d. OHADA

Guidance: level 1

:: Generally Accepted Accounting Principles ::

Financial statements prepared and presented by a company typically follow an external standard that specifically guides their preparation. These standards vary across the globe and are typically overseen by some combination of the private accounting profession in that specific nation and the various government regulators. Variations across countries may be considerable, making cross-country evaluation of financial data challenging.

Exam Probability: **Low**

50. *Answer choices:*

(see index for correct answer)

- a. French generally accepted accounting principles
- b. Write-off
- c. Paid in capital
- d. Generally Accepted Accounting Principles

Guidance: level 1

:: Budgets ::

__________ is a method of budgeting in which all expenses must be justified and approved for each new period. Developed by Peter Pyhrr in the 1970s, __________ starts from a "zero base" at the beginning of every budget period, analyzing needs and costs of every function within an organization and allocating funds accordingly, regardless of how much money has previously been budgeted to any given line item.

Exam Probability: **Medium**

51. *Answer choices:*

(see index for correct answer)

- a. Budget set
- b. Personal budget
- c. Performance-based budgeting
- d. Zero-based budgeting

Guidance: level 1

:: Asset ::

In financial accounting, an _________ is any resource owned by the business. Anything tangible or intangible that can be owned or controlled to produce value and that is held by a company to produce positive economic value is an _________ . Simply stated, _________ s represent value of ownership that can be converted into cash . The balance sheet of a firm records the monetary value of the _________ s owned by that firm. It covers money and other valuables belonging to an individual or to a business.

Exam Probability: **High**

52. *Answer choices:*

(see index for correct answer)

- a. Asset
- b. Fixed asset

Guidance: level 1

:: ::

An inheritance or _________ is a tax paid by a person who inherits money or property or a levy on the estate of a person who has died.

Exam Probability: **Low**

53. *Answer choices:*

(see index for correct answer)

- a. personal values
- b. information systems assessment
- c. Character
- d. process perspective

Guidance: level 1

:: Legal terms ::

_________ or _________ interest, in law, is anything that functions contrary to a party`s interest. This word should not be confused with averse.

Exam Probability: **High**

54. *Answer choices:*

(see index for correct answer)

- a. Integration clause
- b. Legal transplant
- c. Adverse
- d. Consent decree

Guidance: level 1

:: Management accounting ::

__________ , or dollar contribution per unit, is the selling price per unit minus the variable cost per unit. "Contribution" represents the portion of sales revenue that is not consumed by variable costs and so contributes to the coverage of fixed costs. This concept is one of the key building blocks of break-even analysis.

Exam Probability: **Medium**

55. *Answer choices:*

(see index for correct answer)

- a. Semi-variable cost
- b. Dual overhead rate
- c. Double counting
- d. Relevant cost

Guidance: level 1

:: ::

A _________ is an individual or institution that legally owns one or more shares of stock in a public or private corporation. _________ s may be referred to as members of a corporation. Legally, a person is not a _________ in a corporation until their name and other details are entered in the corporation`s register of _________ s or members.

Exam Probability: **Medium**

56. *Answer choices:*

(see index for correct answer)

- a. similarity-attraction theory
- b. hierarchical
- c. Character
- d. Shareholder

Guidance: level 1

:: Data security ::

_________ is the concept of having more than one person required to complete a task. In business the separation by sharing of more than one individual in one single task is an internal control intended to prevent fraud and error. The concept is alternatively called segregation of duties or, in the political realm, separation of powers. In democracies, the separation of legislation from administration serves a similar purpose. The concept is addressed in technical systems and in information technology equivalently and generally addressed as redundancy.

Exam Probability: **Low**

57. *Answer choices:*

(see index for correct answer)

- a. Security information and event management
- b. Separation of duties
- c. Federation Against Software Theft
- d. Administrative share

Guidance: level 1

:: Financial ratios ::

_________ or interest coverage ratio is a measure of a company's ability to honor its debt payments. It may be calculated as either EBIT or EBITDA divided by the total interest payable.

Exam Probability: **Low**

58. *Answer choices:*

(see index for correct answer)

- a. Earnings yield
- b. Average collection period
- c. Debt-to-GDP ratio
- d. Cash flow return on investment

Guidance: level 1

:: Generally Accepted Accounting Principles ::

In business and accounting, _________ is an entity`s income minus cost of goods sold, expenses and taxes for an accounting period. It is computed as the residual of all revenues and gains over all expenses and losses for the period, and has also been defined as the net increase in shareholders` equity that results from a company`s operations. In the context of the presentation of financial statements, the IFRS Foundation defines _________ as synonymous with profit and loss. The difference between revenue and the cost of making a product or providing a service, before deducting overheads, payroll, taxation, and interest payments. This is different from operating income .

Exam Probability: **High**

59. *Answer choices:*

(see index for correct answer)

- a. Net income
- b. deferred revenue
- c. Earnings before interest, taxes and depreciation
- d. Goodwill

Guidance: level 1

INDEX: Correct Answers

Foundations of Business

1. c: Competitive advantage

2. c: Inventory

3. : Need

4. d: Arthur Andersen

5. : Good

6. c: Resource management

7. : Perception

8. : Import

9. d: Analysis

10. d: Bribery

11. b: Debt

12. : Variable cost

13. : Shareholders

14. : Alliance

15. b: Competitor

16. a: Bias

17. b: Balanced scorecard

18. b: Error

19. : Utility

20. c: Market value

21. d: Patent

22. d: Recession

23. c: Balance sheet

24. d: Common stock

25. : Question

26. d: Quality management

27. d: Marketing

28. : Efficiency

29. d: Credit card

30. : Reputation

31. c: Exercise

32. b: Restructuring

33. : Logistics

34. c: Technology

35. d: Duty

36. d: Consumer Protection

37. d: Fixed cost

38. a: Economies of scale

39. b: Fraud

40. d: Purchasing

41. d: Organizational culture

42. d: Sharing

43. d: Diagram

44. : Internal control

45. : Size

46. c: Review

47. c: Information systems

48. b: Raw material

49. c: Accounts receivable

50. b: Revenue

51. c: Image

52. c: Market research

53. c: Information technology

54. d: Present value

55. : Income statement

56. : Direct investment

57. a: Economic growth

58. d: Office

59. : Integrity

Management

1. c: Mediation

2. : Leadership

3. d: Sales

4. d: Recruitment

5. a: Intranet

6. c: Statistic

7. a: Knowledge management

8. c: Centralization

9. d: Contingency theory

10. a: Executive officer

11. c: Job design

12. b: Situational leadership

13. c: Project management

14. c: Labor relations

15. a: Management system

16. d: Industrial Revolution

17. c: Governance

18. : Goal

19. a: Organization chart

20. b: Theory X

21. b: Delegation

22. a: Patent

23. a: Tariff

24. a: Social loafing

25. : Expert

26. : Inventory

27. a: Telecommuting

28. c: Motivation

29. d: Quality assurance

30. : Inspection

31. d: Dilemma

32. : Chief executive

33. : Protection

34. d: Job enrichment

35. c: Questionnaire

36. b: Business plan

37. : Resource allocation

38. b: Individualism

39. c: Transactional leadership

40. a: Transformational leadership

41. c: Stereotype

42. a: Trade agreement

43. b: Project manager

44. d: Operations management

45. a: Corporate governance

46. : Information

47. a: Cooperative

48. a: Project team

49. b: Warehouse

50. : Collaboration

51. d: Resource

52. a: Kaizen

53. a: Leadership development

54. b: Change management

55. c: Standard deviation

56. : Environmental protection

57. a: Autonomy

58. b: Free trade

59. d: Enron

Business law

1. a: De jure

2. a: Probate

3. b: Management

4. : Revenue

5. a: Trustee

6. a: Substantive law

7. d: Supreme Court

8. : Lease

9. : Consumer credit

10. b: Criminal procedure

11. a: Incentive

12. d: Corruption

13. a: Free trade

14. c: Affirmative action

15. a: Social responsibility

16. b: First Amendment

17. a: Plaintiff

18. b: Limited liability

19. a: Contract Clause

20. d: Voidable contract

21. a: Presentment

22. b: Garnishment

23. : Injunction

24. : Foreign Corrupt Practices Act

25. a: Limited partnership

26. d: Advertising

27. c: Voidable

28. : Subrogation

29. a: Sherman Antitrust

30. : Statute

31. a: Statute of limitations

32. d: Consideration

33. b: Expense

34. c: Uniform Commercial Code

35. : Sexual harassment

36. a: Hearing

37. d: Utility

38. a: Assignee

39. d: Proximate cause

40. a: Wire fraud

41. : Contract law

42. c: Restraint of trade

43. : Offeree

44. : S corporation

45. d: Bill of lading

46. a: Service mark

47. c: Committee

48. b: Implied warranty

49. b: Prohibition

50. : Disparagement

51. b: Acceleration clause

52. a: Statutory Law

53. : Consumer protection

54. : Standing

55. : Brand

56. c: Complaint

57. : Opening statement

58. b: Advertisement

59. : Indictment

Finance

1. : Income statement

2. a: Manufacturing

3. : Exchange rate

4. b: Accounting

5. : Finished good

6. b: Futures contract

7. d: Raw material

8. b: Inflation

9. b: Policy

10. d: Bond market

11. a: Yield curve

12. a: Total cost

13. d: Stock exchange

14. : Debt

15. d: Risk assessment

16. b: Debt-to-equity ratio

17. : Ledger

18. d: Social security

19. d: Citigroup

20. c: Stock price

21. c: Managerial accounting

22. d: Break-even

23. d: Issuer

24. : Capital stock

25. : Coupon

26. a: Expected return

27. a: Gross profit

28. a: Par value

29. a: Dividend yield

30. a: Earnings per share

31. b: Incentive

32. b: Debenture

33. d: Financial management

34. : Sinking fund

35. d: Mutual fund

36. : Rate risk

37. d: Market risk

38. a: Investment

39. b: Bank account

40. b: Internal rate of return

41. : Petty cash

42. a: Maturity date

43. c: Industry

44. : Market price

45. d: Market value

46. b: Ending inventory

47. c: Trial balance

48. b: Presentation

49. d: Financial Accounting Standards Board

50. c: Fixed cost

51. : Brand

52. a: Income

53. : Specific identification

54. b: Annuity

55. : Source document

56. a: Net present value

57. : Subsidiary ledger

58. b: Operating leverage

59. c: Trade

Human resource management

1. b: Needs analysis

2. c: Parental leave

3. : Grievance

4. b: Featherbedding

5. c: Occupational Information Network

6. b: Job enrichment

7. : National Association of Colleges and Employers

8. a: Departmentalization

9. b: Aptitude

10. a: Prevailing wage

11. c: Stock appreciation right

12. b: Behavior modification

13. d: Organizational justice

14. c: Free agent

15. b: Reinforcement

16. a: Job fair

17. : Locus of control

18. d: Evidence-based

19. b: Business game

20. : Pattern bargaining

21. a: Test validity

22. b: Meeting

23. b: Exit interview

24. d: Emotional intelligence

25. c: Job rotation

26. c: Employee handbook

27. : Performance measurement

28. d: Foreign worker

29. d: Vertical integration

30. d: Organizational structure

31. c: Minnesota Multiphasic Personality Inventory

32. b: Mobile recruiting

33. d: Delayering

34. : 360-degree feedback

35. c: Performance improvement

36. d: Disability insurance

37. c: Profession

38. a: Self-assessment

39. c: Overtime

40. a: Innovation

41. : Authoritarianism

42. c: Aggression

43. a: Employee retention

44. : Glass ceiling

45. a: Competitive advantage

46. c: Total Quality Management

47. c: Nearshoring

48. : Goal setting

49. c: Coaching

50. b: Needs assessment

51. : Bargaining unit

52. : Internal consistency

53. d: Executive compensation

54. : New Deal

55. d: Employee surveys

56. c: Pregnancy discrimination

57. c: Organizational learning

58. b: Partnership

59. : Mining

Information systems

1. : Business process management

2. d: Decision support system

3. a: Web mining

4. d: Data link

5. a: Smart card

6. b: Local Area Network

7. a: Data mart

8. : Cookie

9. d: Interactivity

10. b: Infrastructure

11. b: Payment card

12. : Mobile commerce

13. c: Random access

14. a: Big data

15. c: Business process

16. a: Reputation management

17. b: Commercial off-the-shelf

18. b: Information technology

19. c: Output device

20. : Folksonomy

21. a: One Laptop per Child

22. : Query by Example

23. d: Virtual world

24. c: Disaster recovery plan

25. c: Flash memory

26. : Backup

27. a: Chief information officer

28. : Blogger

29. : Enterprise search

30. b: Network management

31. d: Database

32. a: Collision

33. b: Data center

34. d: E-commerce

35. a: Unstructured data

36. c: Service-oriented architecture

37. d: Interaction

38. d: Fault tolerance

39. c: Google Maps

40. c: Domain Name System

41. d: Computer-aided manufacturing

42. b: Expert system

43. b: Security management

44. b: Radio-frequency identification

45. : Downtime

46. d: Long tail

47. b: Relational database

48. c: Balanced scorecard

49. b: Government-to-business

50. : Competitive advantage

51. c: Click fraud

52. c: Vulnerability

53. b: Top-level domain

54. b: PageRank

55. : Data integrity

56. b: Transaction processing

57. : Global Positioning System

58. b: Authorization

59. a: Code

Marketing

1. d: Copyright

2. a: Property

3. d: Interview

4. d: Tangible

5. b: Mass marketing

6. a: Manufacturing

7. b: Brand

8. d: Primary data

9. d: Business Week

10. b: Regulation

11. a: Fixed cost

12. : Department store

13. c: Trade association

14. c: Hearing

15. : Data collection

16. c: Value proposition

17. b: Evolution

18. c: Insurance

19. a: Noise

20. a: Target market

21. : Loyalty program

22. c: Contract

23. d: Raw material

24. b: Sales management

25. b: Exploratory research

26. d: Market research

27. a: Auction

28. : Federal Trade Commission

29. : Small business

30. c: Advertising campaign

31. b: Subsidiary

32. b: Audit

33. c: Consumer behavior

34. : Performance

35. : Commerce

36. a: North American Free Trade Agreement

37. d: Warehouse

38. c: Organizational culture

39. a: Sales promotion

40. a: Trademark

41. b: Firm

42. : Interactive marketing

43. d: Authority

44. b: Attention

45. d: Marketing strategy

46. d: Shopping

47. : Brainstorming

48. : Industry

49. b: Market development

50. c: Creative brief

51. : Good

52. : Integrated marketing

53. c: Wholesale

54. a: Gross domestic product

55. b: Blog

56. b: Concept testing

57. a: Consumerism

58. a: Unique selling proposition

59. c: Budget

Manufacturing

1. a: Prize

2. b: Business process

3. d: Purchasing

4. : Quality assurance

5. d: Technical support

6. b: Knowledge management

7. a: Authority

8. : Process capital

9. c: Original equipment manufacturer

10. d: Blanket

11. b: Performance

12. b: Poka-yoke

13. a: Materials management

14. d: Concurrent engineering

15. c: Scheduling

16. b: E-procurement

17. c: Metal

18. a: Inspection

19. a: Process engineering

20. d: Glass

21. b: Quality policy

22. d: Control chart

23. c: Solution

24. a: Extended enterprise

25. c: Downtime

26. c: Change management

27. b: Chemical reaction

28. a: Cost driver

29. a: Raw material

30. a: Project management

31. b: Acceptance sampling

32. b: ROOT

33. : HEAT

34. b: Durability

35. a: Consensus

36. a: Asset

37. : Management process

38. : Stakeholder management

39. c: Quality management

40. b: Remanufacturing

41. c: Vendor

42. a: Process flow diagram

43. b: Chemical industry

44. : Rolling

45. : Cost reduction

46. : Waste

47. : Capacity planning

48. c: Request for proposal

49. b: Kanban

50. a: Project team

51. : Statistical process control

52. b: Heat transfer

53. b: Sensitivity analysis

54. b: Turbine

55. : Cash register

56. c: Elastomer

57. d: Goal

58. a: Scientific management

59. b: Bullwhip effect

Commerce

1. : Planning

2. d: Webvan

3. : European Union

4. : Vendor

5. c: Information system

6. : Tariff

7. c: Return on investment

8. : Charter

9. b: Electronic commerce

10. a: Automation

11. a: Drawback

12. a: Phishing

13. d: Graduation

14. : Inventory

15. d: Project

16. d: Import

17. a: Supranational

18. d: Risk management

19. b: Tourism

20. : Freight forwarder

21. d: Performance

22. c: Procurement

23. d: Household

24. b: Excite

25. : Basket

26. d: Marketing strategy

27. c: Vickrey auction

28. c: Utility

29. d: Complexity

30. : Online advertising

31. b: Property

32. d: Entrepreneur

33. : Customs

34. c: Commerce

35. b: Lease

36. a: Short run

37. c: Compromise

38. a: Market segmentation

39. a: Loyalty

40. : Marketing

41. c: Enabling

42. : Auction

43. : Adoption

44. a: Electronic funds transfer

45. c: Personnel

46. d: Tangible

47. d: Incentive

48. b: Manufacturing

49. c: Microsoft

50. c: Bankruptcy

51. d: Competitive advantage

52. b: Management team

53. b: International trade

54. b: Security

55. : Authority

56. : Good

57. d: Merger

58. c: Reverse auction

59. d: Permission marketing

Business ethics

1. c: Authoritarian

2. c: ExxonMobil

3. b: Organizational ethics

4. c: Nonprofit

5. b: UN Global Compact

6. a: Martin Luther

7. a: Executive compensation

8. c: Dilemma

9. b: Trojan horse

10. a: New Deal

11. a: Marijuana

12. : Green marketing

13. d: East Germany

14. a: Undue hardship

15. d: Recovery Act

16. c: Antitrust

17. a: Ethics Resource Center

18. d: Working poor

19. a: Greenpeace

20. b: Volcker Rule

21. c: Medicaid

22. c: Feedback

23. a: Federal Trade Commission

24. a: Building

25. : Right to work

26. c: Model Rules of Professional Conduct

27. : Marketing ethics

28. : Consumer Financial Protection Bureau

29. b: Sherman Antitrust Act

30. b: Global Fund

31. d: Federal Trade Commission Act

32. b: Better Business Bureau

33. d: Collusion

34. a: Layoff

35. b: Community development financial institution

36. d: Global reach

37. a: Fair Trade Certified

38. a: Transocean

39. c: Reputation

40. c: Supply Chain

41. : Utopian socialism

42. c: Capitalism

43. b: Catholicism

44. : Oil spill

45. d: Planet

46. b: Nepotism

47. b: Qui tam

48. : Risk management

49. c: Dual relationship

50. d: Environmental audit

51. d: Transformational leadership

52. b: Accounting

53. d: Copyright

54. c: United Farm Workers

55. b: Pure Food and Drug Act

56. d: Madoff

57. b: Auditor independence

58. d: Stanford International Bank

59. b: New York Stock Exchange

Accounting

1. a: Activity-based management

2. b: Inventory

3. a: Institute of Management Accountants

4. : Interest expense

5. : Bank reconciliation

6. d: Par value

7. : Sales tax

8. d: Incentive

9. b: Ending inventory

10. c: Calendar year

11. a: Standard deduction

12. c: Public company

13. b: International Financial Reporting Standards

14. b: Cost

15. b: IDEAL

16. : American Institute of Certified Public Accountants

17. a: Income tax

18. c: Financial accounting

19. c: Debt-to-equity ratio

20. : Operating leverage

21. c: Tax deferral

22. a: Current asset

23. c: Dividend yield

24. a: Return on assets

25. c: Property tax

26. d: Net profit

27. c: Public Company Accounting Oversight Board

28. b: Control account

29. d: Income

30. : Variable cost

31. b: Operating lease

32. b: Exchange rate

33. : Time value of money

34. b: XBRL

35. : Earnings per share

36. : Activity-based costing

37. : Intangible asset

38. b: Budget

39. b: Maturity date

40. c: Fraud

41. c: Comprehensive annual financial report

42. c: Securities and Exchange Commission

43. : Pro forma

44. d: Partnership

45. b: Capital asset

46. d: Accrued liabilities

47. : Net investment

48. b: Party

49. b: Limited partnership

50. d: Generally Accepted Accounting Principles

51. d: Zero-based budgeting

52. a: Asset

53. : Estate tax

54. c: Adverse

55. : Contribution margin

56. d: Shareholder

57. b: Separation of duties

58. : Times interest earned

59. a: Net income

CPSIA information can be obtained
at www.ICGtesting.com
Printed in the USA
LVHW011545301019
635718LV00004B/354/P